Since 1952 WAYNE R. ROOD has been professor of religious education at Pacific School of Religion, Berkeley, California. He holds degrees from Salem College (B.A. and B.S.), Alfred University (B.D.), Hartford Seminary Foundation (M.R.E.), and Pacific School of Religion (Th.D.).

Dr. Rood writes for such religious publications as *The Christian Century, Encounter,* and *Religion in Life* and is a frequent speaker on college and university campuses. He is also the author of *The Art of Teaching Christianity,* published

D1366822

UNDERSTANDING
CHRISTIAN
EDUCATION

UNDERSTANDING CHRISTIAN EDUCATION

by
Wayne R. Rood

Abingdon Press

Nashville
New York

Illustrations by Diana Blank

Selections from *What Is Christian Education?* and
A Social Theory of Religious Education, by George Albert
Coe, are used by permission of Charles Scribner's Sons.

Quotations from *Education into Religion*, by A. Victor
Murray, by permission of Harper & Row.

SET UP, PRINTED, AND BOUND BY THE
PARTHENON PRESS, AT NASHVILLE,
TENNESSEE, UNITED STATES OF AMERICA

CONTENTS

Situation

This is a time of blast-off. Some would say, in every department of human life. Technological change appears to increase its pace and extend its reach geo-metrically. Thus it can be estimated that more changes will take place in the life of man in the last third of the twentieth century than have occurred since he fifteenth century. If that guess be even approximately true, for the first time in history the existing generation cannot assume that the next generation will live in a culture substantially like their own.

In order to face a future that is genuinely new, one thing a Christian does is look to the past. To the secular mind, this seems an odd thing to do. A world that is all foreground is much to be preferred, a world in which things are what they appear to be, where what really matters is *Now,* and what is really im-portant is *Here.*

History matters to the Christian, *not only because he exists in time, but also* because God meets men there. He looks to the Bible, convinced that in its pages is an ancient sacred, history still at work. From a vast store of the experiences of a people peculiarly sensitive to the divine address, certain episodes and ma-terials have been worked over and tied together for the purpose of presenting a record of the relationship between God and men. The relationship still func-tions. Man's life is real because he experiences it to be—and meaningful because God participates in it.

History matters to the Christian because once a genuinely new thing did erupt in the experience of men—Jesus of Nazareth, the embodiment of new life. Nothing like it had ever happened before. For nineteen hundred years men have been making history happen because that event gave new meaning to their own lives. The Christian looks back to that event because when taken seriously it always precipitates and defines new and unexpected developments.

History matters to the Christian *because the entire world engenders the person* in the individual. History is personal, not only because it deals with persons, but also because it recounts and sustains the divine-human dialogue which con-stitutes man, a human being, giving him ground to stand on, enabling him to plunge into new and original events with trust and courage.

For the Christian, history is a springboard, and he tests it in order to touch the living, creative force that is at work in events. He finds hypotheses rather than rules, risks rather than certainty. He also finds, frequently, the willingness to take the plunge into the unknowable future, on the chance that God's partici-pation in events will continue to give human life both meaning and hope.

Horace Bushnell, 1802-1876

If Horace Bushnell could have known a century ago that he would eventually be remembered chiefly as the author of *Christian Nurture* and sometimes called "The Father of the Christian Education Movement in America," he would probably have been somewhat surprised as well as pleased.

He was best known in his own time as pastor of North Congregational Church in Hartford, Connecticut. He was an incisive and energetic preacher. Huge congregations gathered to hear him, and most of his widely-read books were largely collections of sermons. His formal theological treatises stirred up a great deal of controversy, and there were repeated efforts to bring him to trial for heresy in his own lifetime. Once, while agonizing in a letter to his wife over the disagreement he knew his ideas would provoke, he illustrated his own need for courage by mentioning Martin Luther. In Hartford he was a public figure, creating its now famous central park, introducing the water system, choosing the site for the state capitol, resisting general panic when the new railroad threatened the river-based prosperity of the city. Bushnell must have sensed that he participated significantly in the making of history as a preacher, theologian, and public citizen, but he seems never to have identified *Christian Nurture* as his major work, and it was not until the twentieth century that Christian Education could be said to have become a movement.

". . . One of God's experimenters."

William Adamson, *Bushnell Rediscovered* (Philadelphia: United Church Press, 1966).
A. J. William Myers, *Horace Bushnell and Religious Education* (Boston: Manthorne and Burack, 1937).

The nineteenth century was a period of change in Connecticut, and Horace Bushnell's life spans three quarters of it. As a boy he was dressed in homespun cloth that his mother had made from the wool produced in his father's pasture, and as a young man he said that the day was coming soon when a man would no longer be personally acquainted with the sheep that provided the wool for his clothes. His father also ran a small factory on his farm, but Bushnell saw the farms near Hartford give way to huge industrial plants. He rode a horse to school, but he watched the country lanes being covered with macadam for the freight wagons. And as a grown man in Hartford he saw the railroad replace the canal and the Connecticut River as the highway from the sea to the Connecticut Valley.

Bushnell grew up in that Valley, from which there was little reason for most people to wander far, but he was off to Yale at twenty-one for an education and to study law, was forced by ill health to spend several summers in Europe and winters in California, and watched young men by the hundreds depart for the battlefields of the Civil War. Travel widened horizons for Bushnell, and the travel of many Connecticut Yankees opened up the Valley. New England sailors had long told stories of the wisdom of the pagan Orient, and the souvenirs of their adventures adorned mantles even in Valley farm houses. But travel in Europe brought back stories of Roman Catholics who behaved like Christians and whose religious experience seemed valid. In Europe Bushnell became acquainted with biblical criticism and

Barbara M. Cross, *Horace Bushnell: Minister to a Changing America* (Chicago: University Press, 1958).

a liberal theology based in German philosophy rather than in Calvin's doctrines. In California he caught the excitement of immense resources and proposed a route for a railroad eastward across the mountains; he saw the dangers of creating a new culture without the support of education and helped select the site and acted briefly as president for the University of California.

The Connecticut Valley was Congregationalist due to the civil establishment of the church of the Puritan forefathers in Connecticut, and Bushnell remembered that as a boy he was sent to a neighboring farm for some apples on a late Saturday afternoon but that the farmer refused to give them to him because he might not be able to reach home with them before the Lord's Day began with the appearance of the first star. In 1818 the establishment was dissolved by a political coalition of Quakers, Baptists, Episcopalians, and Unitarians; after that the Congregationalists joined the Quakers, Baptists, and Episcopalians in a theological coalition against the Unitarians. By the middle of the century, Puritan piety had been largely replaced by political realism and theological debate. Bushnell participated in that, too.

Bushnell's mother was an Episcopalian of Huguenot origin; his father shared the Methodist denial of Calvin's doctrine of predestination, and they all went to the Congregational church because it was the only church available. This put Bushnell on the liberal side of the political issue and on the orthodox side of the theological issue. He never saw any need to change either side, though theological renaissance was coming to New England so rapidly that many of his colleagues in the

John Wright Buckham, *Progressive Religious Thought in America* (Boston: Houghton Mifflin Company, 1919).

ministry were insisting that everyone should be either all liberal or all orthodox.

When he was seventeen, Bushnell wrote a paper attempting to make Calvinist doctrine more human and correcting Paul's willingness to be cursed for the sake of his brethren. While a law student and tutor at Yale College, he and his students stood aloof from a revival conducted along the lines of the New England "Awakening" of the eighteenth century. The theology was rigidly Calvinistic: human beings are depraved and damned, becoming children of God only after being redeemed by the power of divine selection and grace manifested in a visible conversion. Religion was thus a wholly transcendental matter, a revival, a kind of religious epidemic. Bushnell felt that religion came from within and spoke often of "experimental religion." Later, as a divinity student at Yale, he described himself as sound in ethics and skeptical in religion, attributing his soundness to nature and training and his skepticism to the Calvinist theology he was being taught. But of the Unitarian challenge to the doctrine of the Trinity, he wrote: "My heart wants the Father, my heart wants the Son, my heart wants the Holy Ghost—and one just as much as the other."

"I am glad I have a heart as well as a head."

In 1848 he addressed the commencement exercises of the three divinity schools of New England. At Harvard, then completely Unitarian, he preached on "The Atonement"; at Andover, where orthodoxy had emerged victorious, his sermon was on "Dogma and Spirit"; and at his own alma mater, he spoke on "The Divinity of Christ."

Horace Bushnell, *God in Christ: Three Discourses Delivered at New Haven, Cambridge and Andover* (Hartford: Brown and Parsons, 1849).

Though his greatest contribution was to the twentieth century, Horace Bushnell was a man of the nineteenth century and of Hartford, Connecticut. Though at home in the world, his heart was in the Connecticut Valley. Though familiar with the industrial might of steam, he was unable to cross a bridge without calculating the water power of the stream. Though widely published, he was not a scholar; though widely read, he was continually reading new information; though widely influential, he was ready to publish a large revision of a theological work due to "the unexpected arrival of fresh insight." Though intuitional in his approach, he spoke of his theology as a scientific hypothesis. Though orthodox, he was an experimenter with ideas. Though primarily a pastor, he is remembered as an educator. One cannot escape the feeling that he inadvertently addressed himself to the issues that shaped the Christian education movement in the twentieth century. That may well have been because he lived at ease in a world that was changing. However, the cause does not matter now. The result does.

"I cannot believe that [we] will ever perish because of an improvement."

Religious Experience and Knowledge

Horace Bushnell's theological method was rooted in dissatisfaction primarily with the style of New England theology and only secondarily with its content.

The theology that Bushnell learned as a boy at church and encountered full-blown as a divinity student at Yale was the product of many forces: John Calvin's utter devotion to the sovereignty of God in Geneva;

John Calvin, *Institutes of the Christian Religion* (Philadelphia: Presbyterian Board of Christian Education, n.d.).

the early Protestant's toe-to-toe battle with Roman Catholicism during the Counter-Reformation; the Puritan commitment to piety and politics in Scotland and England; the Pilgrim's struggle with forest, Indian, and witch in New England; the Great Awakening under the vivid and vindictive preaching of Jonathan Edwards in Massachusetts. Calvinism had seemed to free man for the dangerous and significant task of pulling down earthly strongholds of persecution and privilege by absolutely turning over to God the care of heaven and hell. But by Bushnell's time Calvinism had become a rigid New England scholasticism, caging the theologian's mind in a web of interrelated logical propositions claiming to represent the whole truth about God: God is the absolute creator. In his inscrutable wisdom man is free only to sin and produce evil in the world. And because of this sin and evil, punishment must necessarily be absolute and eternal for those elected by God to suffer as a demonstration of divine sovereignty. But this did not apply to those whom God had elected, without human justification or reason, to salvation secured by the death of Jesus Christ at human hands, for which God had sent him. For people in the pews of New England churches, this theology meant exhortations to feel sinful, to search the consciousness for signs of a "state of grace," to fear absence of the Holy Spirit as evidence of impending doom in literal hellfire.

The way the doctrine of the Trinity was handled by the theologians particularly troubled Bushnell. It had been the custom to diagram the analysis of the God-

Jonathan Edwards, *Sinners in the Hands of an Angry God* (a sermon). To be found in many anthologies both of literature and historical documents.

head: the word "God" was placed in the center of an equilateral triangle with an arrow and the word "Is" connecting it to each angle; at the apex of the triangle was the word "Father," and at the base angles "Son" and "Holy Ghost"; these three words were connected by arcs forming a circle around the triangle, each carrying the words "is not." The diagram was thus read: "God is Father, God is Son, God is Holy Ghost; Father is not Son, Son is not Holy Ghost, Holy Ghost is not Father." Bushnell objected that the mathematical formula was deceivingly precise. As for himself, he did not know whether this formula was correct because he could not know about the inner nature of God. Indeed, Bushnell found all human categories inappropriate when used to describe God: if, for example, I were to say that *God* reasons, I would necessarily mean that God deduces the unknown from the known, but that assertion would imply that there are some things which God does not know; if I were to assert that God remembers, there would be the implication that he had forgotten something. All Bushnell could conscientiously say of God was that he is *the I am that I am*—eternal and infinite. Nothing less would do; nothing more could be true. But, Bushnell hastened to affirm, my conviction that I know God in the manner that I know trees or propositions does not mean that I do not know him at all: we know God in a different way. This is mystical, of course, because it is not physical knowing, but a mystic quality of this sort seemed to Bushnell to characterize the New Testament. The fact is that I *experience* God because God *discloses himself* to me. Indeed, I experience him in three different ways—which men have named Father, Son, and Holy Spirit—both because of the fragmentation of my experiencing and because of the infinity of his being. The concept of the Trinity is thus a result of the multiple

"Analysis requires dead subjects."

"Fire is the greatest analyzer in the world; and the product, ashes."

"We must fall back on a perceptive power in spiritual life."

"I experience God in three ways."

functioning of human experience held together by the wholeness of God's existence.

In thus attempting to support the functional reality of the Trinity, Bushnell had clearly exposed himself to the charge of *modalism*, an ancient heresy. He had also challenged the whole method of New England theology. He proposed to speak of divine things in frankly human terms, using metaphors from everyone's experience of the family to describe God, of society to explain the Trinity, of the world to present creation, and of personal relationships to talk about salvation.

But Bushnell had only begun: not only is our human knowledge of God inadequate, he continued, so also is the very language we are forced to use when we try try to say what we know. New England theologians had been talking as if the terms they used to describe God—especially those based in Latin and Greek—possessed some special authenticity and actually described divine qualities and attributes. How can one be so certain? Bushnell inquired.

"Words are related to truth only as form to spirit."

Words are symbols, imaging and shadowing realities, which we experience. Words are never exact equivalents of that to which they refer, but always somewhat imprecise, and thus always affirming something which is false to our experience. Further, putting experience into the form of words commits the subtle deceit of suggesting that what was not a form—or reality—in the first place has been given form—or reality—by its use. When we use words to describe God, what they describe is common sensuous experience, rather than divine existence. What happens is that God reveals himself to us, and then we describe our experience of the revelation. In making that

Horace Bushnell, *God in Christ*, a preliminary dissertation on language (Hartford: Brown and Parsons, 1849).

description, what we are actually doing is imposing our experience on the reality of God and suggesting that God exists in the form of human realities. In order to talk of God at all, then, there must be a use of words that corrects for the symbolic and formal nature of language. The *symbolic* correction may be achieved, Bushnell proposed, by piling up symbols, each having a slightly different meaning. In sentences applying to God, this would suggest the use of many adjectives, drawn from varieties and shades of human experience, before pronouncing the apex noun. This is, of course, the way a poet uses words, a musician uses sounds, and a painter uses colors. This impressionistic approach would radically change the methodolgy of the systematic theologians. The *formal* correction could be made, Bushnell thought, by using anithetical words in juxtaposition. Each pair, impinging immediately upon each other, would make it clear that no simple whole had been represented in words which does not exist in reality. This paradoxical approach would change the meaning of formal creeds, which would become comparative rather than definitive and inclusive rather than exclusive.

"The poets are the best metaphysicians."

Some thought that Bushnell had repudiated orthodoxy; he probably only meant to alter its theological style. When the goal of theology is a logically tight system, the method of theology will be rigidly logical and emotionally tight; however, the human mind should be exercised not crucified, the human spirit released not restrained, and consequently the goal of a theological system, as he wrote in one of his own treatises, should be a "wide hypothesis" of the problems of life and sin and redemption such as would "liquidate" the issues between Christians and unbelievers. And the student of theology should be actively a student of divinity, understanding God by being inducted into him by studies that are themselves inbreathings of the divine love and power.

"The exercise of system is a greater benefit than the resulting systems."

"The knowledge he gets will be a Living State not a scheme of sentences."

God, the World, and Man

One of the most heated of nineteenth-century discussions concerned the creation of the world. Early in the century the astronomers led the way, late in the century, the biologists; but for most of the century it was the geologists who provided the excitement by talking about a span of time enormously greater than had ever before been conceived and successive new beginnings and decisive catastrophes that stunned the imagination. The volcanists specialized in fiery cataclysms, the neptunists in aqueous action as an explanation of all this. The latter, of course, appeared to be on the side of the Bible and the flood, but the former could be upheld by biblical literalists for providing the possibility of six successive creative eruptions.

"I want a God relational to my sin and my redemption."

Horace Bushnell, however, seemed not to be interested in the geological data as a way of settling *what* God had done in the creation of the world; he seemed to read geology as a disclosure of the *method* of God, continuously acting creatively and at each stage in the whole magnificent succession providing an anticipatory form of the drama of redemption that would be initiated when the last great creative convulsion miraculously produced man on earth. This view clearly turned the Genesis story of creation into mythology, however grand and theological, an implication which literalists quickly discerned. It also put Bushnell squarely with the orthodox interpretation of supernatural grace. What mattered more, though, was Bushnell's insight that man was the genuinely new factor, a third kind of existant standing between the natural and the supernatural and relating them.

". . . parts of one system"

The human being, Bushnell argued, is clearly physical

Horace Bushnell, *Nature and the Supernatural* (New York: Scribner's, 1860). First published in 1858.

and of the natural world. For the most part he is governed by the laws of nature. But there are significant exceptions. For example, natural gravity would require that my arm hang at my side. But on occasion I lift it, committing a miracle, and this event is occasioned by my will to raise my arm. Thus, though creatures, we can by acts of will and reason set causes in nature to work in new combinations and produce by our action upon nature results which nature herself could never produce by her own internal acting. In this sort of exercise of reason and will man is clearly more supernatural than natural. Indeed, will and reason are spiritual because we see evidence of them in God's actions and creation, and personal because we find them at work in our own experience.

"Personality is a spiritual reality dwelling within nature."

Now, the radical division between two realms—the natural and the supernatural, man and God, reason and revelation—had been characteristic of Christian thought for a long time. The separation had given theology an arbitrary character at the Council of Nicaea, imbued the Divine with an unreal quality in the Middle Ages, restricted revelation to a literal interpretation of the Bible during the Counter-Reformation, and branded the ordinary activities of life as alien from religion in the age of Puritanism. Bushnell does not merely erase the distinction between them: only radical doctrines of divine immanence or pantheism could do that. He agrees that nature and the supernatural are distinct but proposes that they are not separable because a creative act of God in the world holds them together by producing a living being who is both natural and supernatural. Theology thus becomes a task of understanding the meaning and function of personality as a spiritual reality.

"This one point, clearly apprehended, all the difficulties are at once relieved."

The key to this understanding, for the Christian, would lie in Jesus Christ, but the task was not particularly eased. It was clear that the picture presented by formal theology was not very helpful, for there Christ had become primarily a factor in the equation of redemption, more or less mathematically settling divine-human accounts by balancing infinite grace against infinite sin, and Jesus had become quite unconvincing as a participant in human life. Bushnell's picture was "The Gospel of the Face," and the story is that it came to him in a single burst of insight. For Bushnell, the word "face" symbolized the total personal presence of God in human life, "an all-transcending fact-form," making clear to man what God is like by being imbedded in life and character. In short, Jesus Christ impersonated God. Never among men had been seen such a combination of feminine passivity and robust confidence, firmness and gentleness. He seemed oblivious to popularity, incapable of being humbled by ignominy. Yet it is impossible to classify him with the heroes, for he was either no hero at all or else the only hero. In being so completely human there was a unique but recognizable moral power. Christianity is not so much the advent of a better doctrine as of a perfect character, and all the circumstances of our lives are changed by the meaning he showed to be in them. The possibility of bettered lives can only be sustained by "Christed men," those who know who Christ really is and show him forth with a meaning.

But there is still the matter of the equation of redemption in traditional theology to be dealt with. It was generally thought, in Bushnell's time, that Christ paid the penalty for men's sin, satisfied the debt men owed to God, and fulfilled the requirements of justice. The Unitarians had been arguing that there is no justice in punish-

"I have seen the Gospel."

"The gospel is nothing unless it is reincarnated and kept incarnate."

Horace Bushnell, *Sermons on Living Subjects* (New York: Scribner's, 1872). *See* Chapter IV.
Horace Bushnell, *Nature and the Supernatural.* Chapter X: "The Character of Jesus Forbidding His Possible Classification with Men."

ing the innocent in the place of the guilty. Bushnell agreed. He proposed, on the analogy of human experience, that because it is possible for one person to enter by feeling into the sufferings and agonies of another person, it could well be that by his death Christ personally entered into the sins of other men. Jesus knew that his role as Savior required him to bear the sins of the world and in the garden he sweat drops of blood in the agonizing attempt to do what was impossible. But when the crucifixion itself came, Jesus was calm and forgiving because he had come to know that God was suffering, vicariously, the burden of the sins of mankind.

"There was a cross in the heart of God before ever a wooden cross was erected on Calvary."

Further, all men participate in that crucifixion constantly. Circumstances change, and nineteenth-century people no longer conduct crucifixions, but when one comes along who defies conventions and respectabilities, and alienates religious people by superior conviction and morality, they side against him, and that places them in the crucifying throng. "I do not think that I would have driven the nails," wrote Bushnell. "But I would have sided against him. And I tremble." So it is not an ancient event of physical pain that should concern us now, but the continuous suffering of God that simultaneously condemns and forgives us. Using the analogy of human experience, the only appropriate verbal symbol for this improbably divine action is love.

"Look at the anguish in the heart of God and find there your refuge and your peace."

Sin is thus a monstrous thing, introduced into the world and into the life of God by man. Corruption of truth, persecutions, massacres, caste, slavery, piracy, and war among men and the agony of God cannot be dismissed in philosophical terms as the negation of good or lapse into nonbeing, or in theological terms as a debt. Further, man

Horace Bushnell, *Sermons on Living Subjects*.

has demonstrated his incapacity to overcome sin unless there be a new creation. Bushnell suggests that the cure is appropriate to the sickness and that both can be described in sociological terms. Sin is forced upon man by the pressures of family, clan, state, nation, and culture, and his will is not strong enough to overcome them. But the family and the church, especially, because of their awareness of God revealed in Christ, can strengthen the will and support the new being intended by God and intimated in the cataclysms and new creations of the geologic eras, consummated perhaps in a gathering of all the inhabitants of all the planets of all the suns in a company of the redeemed.

"Feeling the air full of wings about me, bouyant and free, I let them come under me and lift."

Nurture

The issue that Horace Bushnell turned into a burning question was the method of entry into the Christian community.

Calvin had taught the doctrine of election: in Calvin's Geneva the sign of election to salvation was regular attendance at divine worship and participation in communion; in Reformation Scotland the moral life was emphasized, in Puritan England the disciplined mind; New England added the conversion experience. After the Great Awakening it was assumed that conversion would be overt, emotional, and under the influence of public preaching. By Bushnell's time the emphasis was on the sinful condition that preceeded conversion and normally came to older adolescents and young adults. Bushnell conceded that it was the primary business of Christians to convert non-Christians, and almost all his sermons end in strong appeals to the Christlike way of life. It was when and how they were to be converted that concerned Bushnell.

"As well might it be said that the great business of travelers is to set out on journies."

It was the popular conception that a child must arrive at an "age of discretion" before he could be responsible for moral choices. Therefore children were neither saved nor candidates for salvation. They were merely left outside the household of faith and no provision was made for them. Bushnell rejected this concept of childhood: his only son had died at the age of four, and he instinctively felt with the French and New England romantics that the simplest form of life is the best. He felt, indeed, that the child was actually closer to God than the adult. He proposed that a child can have a new heart better than an adult. Children act from instinct, impulse, and imitation rather than from reason; they do not have the intellectual capacity to understand and accept the abstract doctrines of the church and they cannot be expected to reproduce, even on a reduced scale, the religious experiences of their elders. Thus the real problem in dealing with children is not that of instilling adult beliefs into the child-mind, but rather of promoting child-religion in the child-mind. Further, when one takes both childhood and religion seriously and in the same breath, he discovers that religion actually goes far deeper than the reason and the deliberate will and is strongest when it is most akin to habit and instinct. On both counts, then, children can be truly religious, because reason and will develop rather late in life and because habit and instinct is the level on which children naturally live and move. The child cannot receive religion as goods are taken into a warehouse, but he can exercise religion as a vital function, like respiration and sense perception, to use Bushnell's own analogies.

Ordinarily the conversion theory required convincing candidates for salvation of their sinfulness. When the theory was applied to children, Bushnell was offended. A popular book for children's reading opened by asserting that depravity is like a poison spreading through the en-

"It would be singular if Jesus Christ, in a scheme of mercy for the world, had found no place for infants and little children."

tire life, corrupting even one's best behavior and producing such a wholly loathsome moral condition that the only cure is to accept, against one's natural wishes, the divine plan of salvation. Adults sang a hymn cautioning, "Little children, stop and think, Turn away from ruin's brink," and the children sang, "Lord, at thy foot ashamed I lie, Upward I dare not look." The logical implication was that the ultimate effect is the opposite of the proximate causes, and that was absurd. The practical implication was that parents should teach their children to lie and steal so that, when they came to the age of discretion, they could more authentically be converted to holiness, and that was monstrous. "I ask you for chapter and verse out of which that theory is derived," Bushnell thundered.

So Bushnell turned against the revivalism that characterized the American church scene, both in New England and on the western frontiers. The strategy seemed to be military, with representatives of the kingdom of God making sallies into the kingdom of darkness, taking captive those who were sufficiently hardened in sin to be converted. Bushnell understood that neither a nation nor a church could expect to thrive merely on conquest. In spite of the dramatic scenes of conversion, the church had worked a vein until it had run out, it had preached too much and lived Christ too little, and it was time to see whether there were not another way—one which takes its method from God's own character and his relations to men.

And, of course, there is such a way: it would be called growth or nurture. It would mean simply training children in the same way they are eventually expected to live. If

Persuasive to Early Piety (New York: American Tract Society, 1831).
Horace Bushnell, Christian Nurture (New York: Scribner's, 1847).

that were done it ought to be possible for a child to develop gradually in love from his earliest years as a person who is continually being spiritually renewed, never having to pass through a conversion upheaval. If the church were to try this method seriously, it might increase its numbers faster than by the revivals, its piety might be more convincing to non-Christians, and children might even grow up never being anything else but Christian.

"The child is to grow up a Christian and never know himself to be otherwise."

Bushnell tried this proposal several times in sermons and articles, and the storm of protest had been immediate and violent. Both he and his opponents knew that these concepts threatened not only New England theology but the life-style of the New England church. But Bushnell was prepared to argue his case and set forth his full position in *Christian Nurture and Views Adjacent Thereto,* a book of sixteen essays describing first the doctrine and secondly the mode, and stirring up a great deal of dust by castigating dissenters, pleading tendentiously for accepted doctrines like infant baptism and the virgin birth, and seriously proposing that Christians conquer the world by outpopulating it with a superior racial stock. His central claims were that a Christian nurture is reasonable, that it has worked, and that it is theologically sound. Whether or not he convinced his contemporaries, he identified the foundations on which modern Christian education would be built.

Logically, the idea of a Christian nurture is merely a proposal that we begin at the beginning. Why is it so difficult to believe that a child can be a Christian? After all, being Christian does not require that one be perfected in goodness, but rather to have begun to love what is good for its own sake. Surely children can begin to love; indeed, it may be easier for them than for adults! Sin is real, and the time to undertake a remedy is precisely when evil is young and pliant. It is at this time that the

"There is no absurdity in supposing that children are to grow up in Christ."

child should be carefully surrounded with human examples of love and faith, and with the sacred and cheerful liberty of the Holy Spirit. Virtue cannot be simply educed or drawn out of a child as goodness from a vegetable, for it must be nurtured and exercised: it involves a real struggle with evil—a fall and a rescue. The only way to achieve this is to support and encourage the child from the beginning with positive influences; to bring up a child for future conversion is unchristian and represents miseducation, a nurture based on the analogy of the ostrich who leaves her eggs in the sand for the sun to hatch and buries her own head in the sand when danger approaches, rather than on what human analogy tells us of the nature of God.

Practically, case studies of successful Christian nurture among both Puritans and Moravians suggested to Bushnell that there was a kind of connection between the character of parents and children as real as the umbilical chord. For many years after physical birth, the child remains within the matrix of the parental life and is not fully born until he emerges to live independently. This spiritual birth is gradual. A Christian education would operate primarily through this organic connection which permits the life and spirit of the parents to flow naturally into the mind of the child, nourishing his incipient intentions with their faith and love, until they become the child's own way of life but still the same in character.

"Children have been so trained as never to remember the time when they began to be religious."

Theologically, such a concept of nurture would appear to be in line with what we know of God and the way he works. Goodness, or the production of goodness, is the supreme end of God. Anything that aids this end must be of God; he could not desire sin for a season and then goodness. Thus God desires goodness in his children, and if he does, we should then train children in the way they should go. In Old Testament times Hebrews became

"Holy virtue is the aim of every plan that God adopts."

Hebrews; in early Christian times children became Christians, and the growing practice of infant baptism was the sign of that intention. One early church father even argued that there was an actual identification between the growing experience of the individual and the developing life of mankind. Religion is learned within the body of believers, and this organic law of relationships would seem to be the way in which God works among men.

Along the way Bushnell offers practical advice to parents and teachers. Christian nurture is no "summary process." Mock piety, sanctimony of phrase, and longitude of face on Sundays will not suffice. The little moral stories usually told to children for their guidance and imitation give the child a dislike for the subject of religion. Lecturing and storming and castigating merely extinguish what we ought to be nurturing. What Bushnell urges is the effort, first, to bear up the child's heart in one's own, to make what is good happy and attractive, to bathe the child in one's own feeling of love to God and contrition for wrong. Then, gradually, the more difficult views of Christian doctrine and experience may be opened, "as the understanding advances." "Your real aim and study must be to infuse into them a new life," wrote Bushnell, "and to this end the life of God must perpetually reign in you."

"Rather seek to teach a feeling than a doctrine."

The Bushnell Legacy

Horace Bushnell's contribution to Christian education may be more in what he talked about than in what he said.

It is easy now to read into his sentences meanings which he did not intend but which have become commonly accepted, and because of that it is easy to brush off the inconsistencies and provincialisms that characterize the

"He liberated the natural life and the natural order of things."

long and involved passages between memorable aphorisms. In the nineteenth century he held attitudes that are often assumed in the twentieth: a positive attitude toward change, a concept of experience as the source of religious knowledge rather than vice versa, an emphasis on the personal rather than the formal nature of the relation of God to man, a defense of natural growth into the Christian life and faith as more valid than a forced conversion experience. There has been as much difference of theological opinion about these specific attitudes in the twentieth century as in Bushnell's own time, but educators have generally sided with Bushnell in the concern for liberating man's life and development.

As it has turned out, however, it has been the identification of the general areas represented by these specific attitudes rather than agreement with his position that has earned the gratitude of Christian educators and the fatherhood of their movement: *historical change, religious experience and knowledge, the God-man relation, and personal growth.* These have become the key questions in developing a philosophy of Christian education. Christian education is not separable from education on the one hand or theology on the other, but insofar as it becomes a distinct discipline, it is as the result of having dealt both educationally and theologically with these issues.

The Emergent Principle

A viable Christian education must demonstrate, both theologically and educationally, that man is a spiritual being at home in a natural world.

Theological Forces

Formal theology seeks not only to know the truth but also to tell it. That is to say, the content of theology is both revelational and relational.

For Christians, the truth refers to the certainty of divine love, its singular concretion in Jesus Christ, and its results in and for human living.

Telling this truth results in theologies. Because one of the purposes of telling is hearing, theologies have been formulated differently in different ages, each culture forcing its own forms on theological truth and exposing new truths. In the New Testament period Christian theology was very simple, reflecting the impatience of the early Christian with this world, his expectation of its soon end, and his personal memory of Jesus, and exposing the saviorhood of Jesus. In the third century theology reflected the demand of the Greek mind for clear-cut, arithmetic precision and exposed the divine-human nature of Jesus and the tri-unity of the Godhead. In the Middle Ages theology reflected the immobility, superstition, and stratification of feudal society and exposed the universality of Christendom. In the sixteenth century theology reflected the Reformers' rejection of earthly authority, their reliance on the Bible, and the sense of God's immediate presence and directing will and exposed the sovereignty of God.

In the hundred years following Horace Bushnell's death in 1876, historical forces which had been gathering in his own day exploded, radically changing the shapes and forms of life and thought. A significantly new culture had come into being. Telling the truth to this new culture required new forms. It also exposed some new truths.

When Robert E. Lee turned over his sword to Ulysses Grant at Appomattox in token of surrender, bringing to an end the first industrialized war of history, the first industrialized society of history began. It was as if a cork had been pulled.

". . . The Gilded Age"

Mark Twain called the postwar period an age of gilt: the apparently limitless resources that had been developed for and then monopolized by the Civil War were suddenly released. Every man who wanted it was handed a farm in the Middle West, and the "iron buccaneers" of railroad, industry, and finance carved for themselves empires of power and wealth.

". . . A world with the lid off"

The lid was literally torn off the old ways of living and the old business morals: the sky was only the nearer limit of the wealth that was to be had by those who would grab with least restraint and hold with most tenacity, taking advantage of the inchoate state of finance and the absence of legal controls. The Erie Railroad paid the governor of New York $20,000 for his signature on one legislative bill; there were 2,000 illegal gambling houses in New York City and some stakes ran over $100,000; Jesse James descended on the Kansas City Fair in broad daylight and escaped with $10,000 in gate money.

". . . The greatest folk movement in history"

Immigrants streamed across the Atlantic, and small communities grew into great, sprawling urban centers. Boys who landed at Ellis Island without a penny became millionaires. During the Panic of 1873, bread lines appeared in all the large cities, and in 1877 the railroads announced a ten percent cut in wages and upped investment interest to eight percent. New York City reported 2,000 cases of smallpox in one winter; garbage clogged the streets of Philadelphia; epidemics in the Nashville Prison threatened the entire city. Mill owners, who once worked beside their help, were replaced by huge corporations, and Americans soon discovered that they were thinking of themselves as farmers, wage earners, industrialists, and financiers rather than as New Englanders or Southerners. The Grange was organized to protect farmers and grew rapidly, the Knights of Labor was organized for "industrial moral worth not wealth," and in the desperate summer of 1877 railroad workers struck and federal troops were mobilized.

All that glittered was not good, and the industrial culture was being shaped.

The enormous losses suffered by both sides on the battlefields of the Civil War haunted families for years. They craved assurance that life is eternal and that heaven is within reach. In 1875 Theosophy was introduced to the United States by Madame Helena P. Blavatsky, the immensely corpulent and romantically hysterical founder of the Theosophical Society. Christian Science, blending Oriental thought with Christianity and asserting that evil is not real, began among the lower middle-class people of Lynn and Boston in the decade following the War, and before the end of the century had become a major religion. The Mormons, who had been driven from New York and Illinois by persecution, were actually building in Utah a new rural society in the desert and mountains. Adventism, which had subsided following William Miller's predictions that the world would come to an end with Christ's second advent in 1843, gained new strength as life on this earth became more uncertain. Dwight L. Moody preached to tremendous audiences in the cities, reiterating the dogmas that had once appealed to the individualism of the frontiersman. General Booth's Salvation Army invaded the burgeoning slum districts with band music, free food, and cheap shelter. The effect was to enhance sheer

"Sin is a lie."

"I will cause the heavens to shake for your good."

"The Bible was not made to understand."

dependence on the supernatural for alleviation of the inevitable injustices of this world.

The industrial culture, however, was here to stay. To tell the gospel meaningfully to such a culture would require an understanding of God somewhat different from that which had been helpful to pioneers, farmers, and small towners.

Humanitarianism

"If I build God a church, it shall be a church to men and women."

As in every crisis, there were many who saw that something had to be done and found things to do. The new thing was that at this time many were moved by a belief in man rather than in God. The year after the dark summer of 1877 had revealed the exploitation of working men; Robert Ingersoll cried out that the only reasonable price for labor was one that would enable a man "to preserve the feelings of a man." His father was a Calvinist minister, and there was bitterness as well as conviction when he also said, "Heresy is the herald of the new day."

The YMCA had been introduced into the United States from England in the 1850s, the YWCA in 1866, and both grew rapidly. However, their programs rapidly moved away from the specifically religious activities of the churches toward literacy, trade training, culture, and recreation. The Society for the Prevention of Cruelty to Animals was formed in Boston in protest to a horse race in the spring of 1868 in which both horses were driven to death. In 1874 the Society for the Prevention of Cruelty to Children was formed in New York City where a parent was being tried by the SPCA for cruelty to her daughter, since the law sanctioned no interference between parents and child. The Temperance Party ran candidates for public office, and in 1874 the Women's Christian Temperance Union was organized in Cleveland as a sign of the entrance of the crusade for women's rights into the political arena.

As a Unitarian, William Ellery Channing had argued the humanitarian principle: "This principle is a ray of divinity in man," he had said. But Ingersoll and many others staked their confidence on man without rays of divinity thrown in. The free man can save himself and his society from the evils which have hitherto beset the race, Ingersoll promised. "We are doing what we can," he said, "to hasten the day when society shall cease producing millionaries and mendicants, gorged indolence and famished industry," and he believed that man could and must achieve a better society. "We are not yet a civilized people," he said. "When we are, pauperism and crime shall vanish from our land."

"My neighbor is as precious as myself."

European Scholarship

A theological revolution was maturing in the old world, also. It was more conceptual than that brewing in the new world. When American scholars turned again to Europe after years of preoccupation with the Civil War and its aftermath, they discovered a way of thinking that was not only new, but already highly developed.

A new approach to the Bible provided the foundation of the movement. Ferdinand Christian Bauer, at the University of Tubingen, probed the question of the influence of the personalities and interests of the New Testament biographers of Jesus on the story they told. The question had never been raised before because it had been generally assumed that the biblical accounts had been divinely inspired. Ernest Renan used this point of view to write a

Edward Caldwell Moore, *An Outline of the History of Christian Thought Since Kant* (New York: Scribner's, 1916).

modern biography, published in 1863, portraying Jesus as an idealistic ringleader, a struggling and erring national hero, always aiming at the highest but doomed to tragic failure by his ideal. For the first time Jesus appeared as a figure freed from the mystery and supernaturalism of biblical literalism. Other scholars accomplished the same emancipation for the Old Testament. Then Egypt and India fell to British conquest, and British archaeologists and anthropologists began to demonstrate that the accounts of deluges, virgin births, crucifixions, and atonements were present in the religious myths of many peoples other than the Hebrews.

"One experiences, in active trust, in patient surrender, in courage, in daily prayer, the reconciliation with God through Jesus Christ."

Albrecht Ritschl, at one time a colleague of Bauer in Tubingen, became a critic of formalized, technical theology. Many Americans studying abroad in the postwar years went to hear Ritschl lecture. Christianity is not theological, he insisted, but an intense practical endeavor. It springs, not from metaphysical speculation, but from the biblical point of view and from a personal experience of forgiveness for sin through faith in Jesus Christ. Ritschl alarmed many Christians by asserting that the divinity of Christ was not a matter of essence or divine function, but a value judgment made by each individual person. In no other way, Ritschl argued, could the experience of Christ be personal. Further, the experience of reconciliation is the slow transformation of the individual through membership in the redeemed community of the Christian church. This gradual transformation is at root an educational procedure, according to Ritschl; even the punishments meted out by God for sin are educative in God's intention. The greatest value in the universe for Ritschl

Albrecht Ritschl, *The Doctrine of Justification and Reconciliation* (Vol. I, 1870; Vol. II, 1874; Vol. III, 1874, and many subsequent editions).

was personality; in the highest sense God is personality, and since this is the same quality of personality as is possessed by mankind, the relationhip between God and man must be that of the family, of fatherhood and sonship —in short, of love. Because Christ is the revealer of this love, we judge him to be divine. And further, because of their kinship, God and man work together to make the world a scene of the Christ-established reconciliation. The essential religious problem, according to Ritschl, is to win a victory over the world, to assert ourselves as beings who can bring better things to pass. The religious ideal for the world is the Kingdom of God—a community of the reconciled in which God's love reigns supreme and unhampered because all men acknowledge their kinship to him. The process of reconciliation which begins with the individual and God has as its goal the transformation of all the world into the Beloved Community. This is man's destiny.

It was perhaps a single English book that combined German biblical and theological studies for American consumption. The book was *Ecce Homo,* published by Sir John Seeley in 1866, and widely read in the United States. "The enthusiasm for humanity," was Seeley's great phrase. He found that "going about doing good" was a far more significant activity of Jesus than his wise sayings. The welfare and happiness of others was for him not a restraint but a motive. He set the first and greatest example of a life wholly governed and guided by "the passion of humanity," and Seeley believed that Christ's passion would move every member of the divine society "to do as much as possible to every other member." As practical applications of his ideal, Seeley suggested medical research,

Sir John Robert Seeley, *Ecce Homo: A Survey of the Life and Work of Jesus Christ* (Boston: Roberts Brothers, 1866).

investigation into the causes of physical evil, and study of the relations of education, labor, and trade to health. Furthermore, he suggested the reorganization of life in accordance with the findings thus obtained.

But if biblical and theological critics worked a revolution within Protestant theology, the Darwinians stormed the whole fort of orthodoxy. *The Origin of the Species* did not become known in the United States until after the War, but the new doctrine immediately became the center of a debate that enlivened the American theological scene for the rest of the century. Some thundered that "evolutionism and the scriptural account of the origin of man are irreconcilable." Others declared that "evolution is the deciphering of God's thoughts as revealed in the structure of the world." Darwin traced the rise of biological species from simple protozoa to complex mammals; Herbert Spencer in England and Lewis Henry Morgan in the United States applied the principle of progression to man and developed the theory of progress from savagery, to barbarism, to civilization. The application of the principle to politics, economics, and institutions aroused wide response in the United States. If survival of the fittest admirably suited the captains of industry who were crushing the little fellows of American finance, it also fitted the new American faith in mankind, and on a much larger scale. In England, Friedrich Engels was delighted with the American enthusiasm for social evolutionism and predicted that it would soon develop into a full-blown Marxian materialism. But in the United States the doctrine of progress furnished the groundwork for a distinctly Christian interpretation called the Social Gospel.

"Some call it evolution; I call it God."

The Social Gospel

The Social Gospel has been called an indigenous and typically American movement. It was called into being by the needs of a newly industrialized society during the Guilded Age. The desperation of maladjustment and injustice was in it and the failure of Puritan moralism. The spirit of humanitarianism was in it and the glaring inconsistency between the public gospel of grab and hold and the teachings and doings of Jesus. The belief in progress was in it, and the faith that the intention of a loving God for man was not poverty and suffering.

It was a gospel emphasizing practical love and hope so strongly that it sometimes made theological qualities of immanence, humanitarianism and progress. It stressed the love of God rather than the transcendental justice and awful majesty that had been the theme of the New England Calvinists. It protrayed God as immanent to the world rather than isolated from it, as permeating every part of human life rather than as separate from human concern. Consqeuently, it rested on Jesus as a man among men who had labored in a carpenter shop and whose words about the dignity of human life and work could be taken as literal truth applicable to human affairs. So it preached a message of the application of the teaching of Jesus and the total message of the Christian salvation to society, the economic life and social institutions as well as to individuals. The new emphasis insisted upon the truth of the obverse of the doctrine of original sin, and pointed in optimism to the inheritance of virtue and imagination by mankind as well as sinfulness. Both of these, the new theology taught, were the product of social conditions as much as inherent in human nature, and pointed out that thus it was man's sacred responsibility to lessen the causes for sin as much as he could and to increase the causes of virtue as much as he might. The Kingdom of God, which has usually been interpreted as the heavenly kingdom of another and far distant future life, was widely reinterpreted

"The Kingdom of God is the first and most essential dogma of the Christian faith."

"It is not a matter of getting individuals to heaven but of transforming the life on earth into the harmony of heaven."

as the reign of the Christian spirit on this earth. All human relationships and institutions should and could be ideally brought under the control of sympathy, love, and service. Divine Fatherhood and human brotherhood, these were the two great principles upon which the Social Gospel rested its theology.

Later it would often be said that this was not profound theology. It was, however, the gospel to which Protestantism was very largely committed as the twentieth century dawned, and it was a theological stance singularly compatible with the attitudes to which Horace Bushnell had inclined Christian education. Some said that the Social Gospel died in the dark days following the Wall Street crash of 1929. But even then the European neo-orthodoxy that took its place was strongly modified by the undeniable American demand for practical and social relevance that created the Social Gospel in the first place. And again it reemerged still later in the very social Civil Rights Movement and the very theological Death of God movement which announced the demise of a deity who had been isolated by the neo-orthodox theologians from the events of this earth. Indeed, it may well be that the American Social Gospel of the nineteenth century was the first truly secularized gospel in Christian history.

But it all started with the force of revelation. "It was not an individualistic piety that appealed to me," wrote Washington Gladden of his interest in the ministry as a young man before the Civil War. "It was a religion that laid hold of life with both hands and proposed, first and foremost, to realize the Kingdom of God in this world." Shortly after the War a sensitive young Californian tramping the streets of New York City suddenly saw before him

Walter Rauschenbusch, *Christianizing the Social Order* (New York: Macmillan, 1912) and *Christianity and the Social Crisis* (New York: Macmillan, 1907).

a vision: "Every nerve quivered and then and there I made a vow." It was to a theologically based program for the correction of economic evil, the single tax. Late in the century, while Walter Rauschenbusch was the pastor of a German Baptist church in New York City, he met what he called "a terrifying insight into the conditions of the working classes." He emerged from this baptism into reality convinced that society must be remodeled, through Christianity as a philosophy, by the church as an agent, and with the Kingdom of God as a model.

The revelation was relevant. New circumstances had exposed new truths in the old gospel.

The Impact of Science

All in all, the outstanding theological phenomenon of the twentieth century has so far been not so much the fading of faith as its transfer from a metaphysical to a scientific object. The harmony between science and Protestant orthodoxy achieved during the nineteenth century rested chiefly on the facts that Newton's celestial mechanics did not specifically challenge any important biblical doctrine and that Newton was himself a devout Christian who had no intention to upset the Christian tradition. Further, in America Protestantism was more interested in the New Testament than in the Old and had not been much concerned with either scientific or Old Testament cosmology. Darwin's theory of evolution was successfully transmuted into the doctrine of social progress. "All these facts in their natural connection," wrote scientist Louis Agassiz of Harvard, "proclaim aloud the One God, whom man may know, adore and love." American theologians were gen-

". . . Analysis of the thoughts of the Creator of the Universe as manifested in the animal and vegetable kingdoms."

Washington Gladden, *Recollections* **(Boston: Houghton Mifflin, 1909).**

erally inclined to adapt convictions rather than to jettison them, and Americans as a whole were generally inclined to accept science as a technology—a way of getting things done easier and faster—rather than as an alternate philosophy, but the result of the scientific movement in American theology was not to simplify it, and the result in American life was a new style of faith.

The Passing of the Biblical Cosmology

Americans had been reared on the ancient language of the Bible. They named their children Patience, Grace and Prudence, their towns Providence, Hope and Paradise. The speeches of their orators were redolent with Biblical phrases. But the great modern task of theology was to learn to speak of and to the world revealed by science.

"The sun sets and hastens back to the place where it rises."

Biblical scholars were plunged into the necessity of understanding the Bible as reflecting a pre-scientific world-view, and as a result of this discovery to retranslate the biblical materials in terms of the reigning scientific world-view of the twentieth century. This was indeed a monumental task, threatening, it appeared, many of the essential concepts of the biblical material. The biblical writers unquestionably conceived the world to be solitary and unique, certainly not a minor unit in an extensive solar system. The sun and moon seemed, according to the Bible, to be lights fashioned by a benevolent God to illumine his chief work by day and by night. If one reads the biblical accounts literally, he discovers that its writers conceived of the world as flat and stationary. Somewhere above it was heaven where God and his angels dwelt, and to which in the future the fortunate would be removed. Beneath this flat earth was the place of punishment to which sinners would eventually be consigned. There were no immutable laws, and stones fell down and not up

"He stretched out the heavens like a tent; is not God high in the heavens?"

because God momentarily willed them to do so, and the sun moved across the heavens daily for the same reason. If God chose to alter that arrangement, as occasionally he did, on behalf of his friends, he could do so. Direct petitionary prayer with the confidence that divine forces could be influenced was perfectly natural and proper in these circumstances. Society seemed organized in a feudal manner from the top down—God, kings, high priests, local lords and priests, and the common people.

The problem at the beginning of the twentieth century appeared to be that Christianity's entire religious terminology stemmed from this earlier thought-world in which no twentieth century citizen of the world would find himself at home. The very titles for God reflected the difficulty, especially in a self-conscious democracy: King, Lord of Lords, Lord of Hosts. Older versions of the Bible taught men to address God as "thou" in an archaism that seemed in itself to suggest that God was no longer an active reality in the new kind of world that science was revealing, where the regularity of the universe observed by everyone and explained by science seemed more meaningful to the conduct of daily life than a capricious God could possibly be.

If the only way to solve the problem were to live in two thought-worlds at once, constantly juggling terms and concepts, many were ready to give up the effort. Some merely contrived thought-tight compartments for religion and life and shifted from one to the other as infrequently as possible. Most Americans, however, settled for the possibility of one final translation. It would be from theology to science, making this ancient religion not only speak the language of the twentieth century, but changing its essential concepts where necessary so that it could be at home in the scientific world.

"And the sun stood still and the moon stayed."

"The Lord has established his throne in the heavens and his kingdom rules over all."

"The scientific method is my guide, I shall not err."

Douglas Clyde Mackintosh, for one, devoted his considerable skills to the proposition that theology could become an empirical science. He began with carefully identified propositions, the most important of which is that God exists as an object of theological science. This assumption may be made on the basis of religious experiences. The second step is to analyze the empirical data of theology in order to distinguish "the divine elements within human experience, the qualities or events which are to be regarded as the immediate products of the divine activity," and hence as "revelations" of God to us. Having examined the data, the scientific theologian turns, third, to discovering theological laws, "generalizations as to what the divine being does on the fulfillment of certain

discoverable conditions." The method Macintosh followed was to postulate the dependability of divine activity, then to examine the possible hypotheses about God and his activity reared on the basis of these postulations, and finally to verify these hypotheses experimentally by acting upon them and attaining "immediate awareness" of the reality of what was supposed in the hypothesis. A theological law, the goal of theological science, describes the dependable working of God under suitable conditions; it also gives us the power to predict the result of right religious education, evangelism, or prayer. "On condition of the right religious adjustment with reference to desired truly moral states of the will," wrote Mackintosh, "God produces the specific moral results desired."

It was a fascinating possibility, and many who had neither read Mackintosh nor stated it so unequivocally, opted for the same sort of adaptation.

Douglas Clyde Macintosh, *Theology as an Emperical Science* (New York: Harper, 1919).

Science affects everything. So does the past. During the 1920s and 1930s religious thinkers began to develop different ways of responding to the challenge of science. They called on Plato and Aristotle for the distinction between theoretical reality and mathematical reality. They referred to Spinoza's concept that God is substance, to Hume's that causality is final, to Kant's that God is unknowable, to Locke's that knowledge is objective, to Bacon's that knowledge is power. It is possible, however, to group their philosophical responses into three trends. There were those who saw scientific method to be the clue to the present and the builder of the future; some found their primary stimulus in the discoveries and methodologies of the physical sciences, and some found most help in the methodologies and discoveries of the life or personal sciences. A third group understood scientific method to be the clue to all discovery, past as well as present. The last group tended to translate ancient religious truth into the language of a scientific world. The first two groups tended to adapt religious concepts to scientific truth. Those who have been most helped by the physical sciences may be called "experimentalists." Those who have been most helped by psychology and sociology may be called "personalists." Those who have understood scientific method as a universal methodology may be called "essentialists."

The experimentalists are the "tough-minded" among religious philosophers. From the beginning their world view has been Copernican, and their devotion is to help man take his place in the scene of things resulting from this point of view. There has, therefore, never been the strong anthoropocentric bias among experimentalists that

"Science has been the major transforming agency in modern culture."

"We take our science straight."

John Herman Randall, Jr., *The Making of the Modern Mind* (Boston: Houghton Mifflin, 1940).

has usually characterized traditional theology. Their primary insight concerning personal reality is in line with the understanding of the world of matter revealed by physics. Reality is a business of energy, entities in motion, of matter and antimatter, of stress and repose, cause and effect in constant change and flux. One speaks of predictability rather than of law, of reasonable assurance rather than of reliability.

There is a direct feeding from the findings of the scientists into the thinking of the theologians. Experimentalist philosophers tend to dub overtones from prescientific supernaturalism as irrational. Wherever there are overtones of mysticism in religion, these are open to exploration, in the anticipation that they will disappear with the discovery of more knowledge. Knowledge is to be found through the application of observation and experimentation which aggressively quests for data, and through the application of reason which refines and gives order to data. The result is not an idea but an active agent in the lives of men. Mind is an experience, "an instrument for advancing discovery." Experimentalist philosophers are, above all, practical in their motivation. "Truth energizes and does battle," William James used to say, "in the midst of life." John Dewey would say, "Truth is meaning in practice."

According to most theistic experimentalists, God is primarily thought of as a cosmic force supporting the changes and precipitating the flux described by the scientists. They tend, however, to be agnostic about God, and concentrate on achieving a positive and experimental attitude by man, as part of the process, toward his world.

The personalists begin with self-experience as the ultimate basis for understanding all reality. They tend to criticize the experimentalists for ignoring the productive role man plays in the world and find their most help from

"Knowledge is not a system, but a way of doing things."

"An idea is true so long as it is profitable in our lives."

psychology, personality theory, as well as psychoanalysis and sociology. Knowledge, they remind their readers, is a distinctively personal or human achievement. "The self is the source from which we know." We understand the world not only in accordance with the data that comes through human senses but also according to the whole organization of human thought and feeling through which it is systematized and interpreted. Indeed, they say that we are able to understand the world only inasmuch as it is like us. It is of utmost importance, therefore, to understand the process by which one senses and relates one datum to another. Sociology, however, corrects the individualism and subjectivism that may be suggested by psychological studies alone. There is the public checking of data and reasoning, and there is the interaction of many individuals that develops common laws and meanings, common ways of behavior and interpretation.

"The self is the datum."

"Selfhood is more than the sum of its parts."

According to most theistic personalists, God is the one absolute personality. Human beings are imperfect and incomplete personalities, but it is because both God and human beings are personal that we can know anything at all about God. Even physical matter is knowable as a certain kind of willed organization of divine consciousness. The aim of religion is the attainment of common human purposes by the cooperation of free moral cooperation with God.

"The universe is a society of selves."

The essentialists begin with the objective world and are inclined to say that it will tell us what we need to know if we are receptive and unbiased enough to accept it for what it is and to get along with it. This is the way man has always done through the ages, and what he has learned has not been new so much as more skillful. They often call themselves "realists," tending to take all facts as real, making no necessary value judgment among them by saying that one kind of reality is more important

"Things are essentially what they seem to be."

than another. They therefore tend not to be enthusiasts. Scientific method is merely a refinement of man's instinctive acknowledgment that he is surrounded by realities which are there and continue to be what they are whether he acknowledges it or not. He does not change them when he knows them; indeed, knowing them changes him, as he learns to take their stubborn reality into account as he steps over rocks, separates positive from negative poles in an electric circuit, deals with the emotions and fears of men in a heavily overpopulated world. Knowledge is a series of facts which intelligence may put together usefully. Science is a discipline for finding out how things actually are.

"God is the religious object."

According to most realistic theists, God is an objective fact which sustains and accounts for religious attitudes and activities. The fact that religion has survived many great changes in belief indicates that it possesses some objective validity. But God is not necessarily manlike or especially interested in man. Indeed, one of the greatest causes for disenchantment in religion, especially among liberal theologians, is the unfounded assumption that man is God's primary concern. God is probably something so thoroughly other than man that the only way we can know anything of him is through his own act of self-revelation. This comes, often enough, through the objective world, but when it does it is incumbent upon us to hear exactly and only what is said.

For the most part, present ways of thinking about the world, God and education were formed in the crucible of science as a way of thinking.

The Electronic Age

When George Warrington Steevens returned to England after covering the presidential election of 1896 for the

London *Daily Mail*, he described the American as "an electric Anglo-Saxon." He was impressed by the volatile energy of Americans in everything from personal relations to problem-solving. He thought it remarkable that the tangible evidence of the five senses was much more convincing to Americans than logical demonstration. It was an exciting election. The observations were accurate. The metaphor was prophetic.

The electronic American, however, the possibility of whose emergence began to cast its shadow on history sixty years later, is no mere subspecies of Anglo-Saxon. He may, indeed, be the prototype of a new world culture brought into being by his own invention, television. It would be comprised by the ultimate extension of the qualities Steevens had noted—made possible by the use of electricity for mass communication and problem-solving, characterized by energy rather than direction, and given its new form by the multidimensional quality of the five different senses used simultaneously. It would be the result of the applications of scientific technology rather than of the implications of scientific philosophy, and might cause more dramatic adjustments in theological truth-telling than did the challenge of the new scientific cosmologies and philosophies. Marshall McLuhan, a professor at University of Toronto, has been one of the most persuasive in describing it.

The new electronic culture is multidimensional. Until now the Western world has been linear, dominated by the technology of reading and writing. In a book the line of type goes straight across the page, and the content goes from subject to verb to object in a single forward line. With the invention of printing and the multiplication of

Henry Steele Commager, *America in Perspective* (New York: Mentor, 1948).

books so that everybody could and must read, lineality became the way in which man thinks and understands reality. Linear thinking has controlled logic and education and feeling for four hundred years.

But the world of electric circuitry proceeds in many directions simultaneously for a nonfragmented, integral, and organic purpose. The intricate process of television communication is a supreme illustration. The television screen does not present a single picture electronically, but 240 separate lines of black and white, a mosaic which the human experience organizes instantly into one picture which is received and responded to as a whole. Thus, in television communication, the human receiver is deeply involved in the action, producing himself the end result of the communication process. In response to this change in technology, argues McLuhan, man's experience is changing, and in response to change in experience his thinking is changing: it is becoming multilinear and instantly whole.

"A profound incubus of information has settled on our nervous system."

Further, electronic communication is simultaneous the world around: the same experiences of electronic logic as well as of news and events may be universally shared. Simultaneously, electronic circuitry had been applied to information gathering and storing so that the human mind may be released from the time and energy consuming tasks of accumulating and recalling data for the much more productive task of producing new combinations of data, which may in turn be permanently stored and instantly shared when relevant.

A new world-culture may be in the process of formation by these changes—more native and Oriental and tactile than Western culture. Education may be called upon to

Marshall McLuhan, *The Medium is the Massage* (New York: Bantam Books, 1967) and *Understanding Media* (same).

teach thinking rather than reading: "Instruction is obsolete," says McLuhan, "and discovery, a much more fruitful form of activity, has taken its place." The content of communication may become less important than the method by which it is achieved. "The medium *is* the message," argues McLuhan, and adds, "regardless of content." The interpersonal chasms may be between the young and the old—between linear thinking and multilinear thinking people—rather than between classes or nationalities or races. "The generation gap is always the result of some sort of technological innovation," says McLuhan, "but in our time it is spectacular." Theology might find it necessary to become more multilineal and sensory, which might be to say more Hebrew than Greek and perhaps even a little Oriental. As Professor McLuhan once said in a public discussion, "Good news upsets everybody." A long time ago Jesus and the early Christians discovered the same thing.

"The only thing to program is sensory life."

The Importance of Art

One of the most important contributions of the artist is offering an alternative way of understanding to that produced by the scientist.

"Science" is the title of a poem by Robinson Jeffers in which he warns that man may destroy himself by his own scientific discoveries. The poetic allusion is to the classical legend of Actaeon, who surprised the Goddess Diana bathing in a forest pool. As punishment he was turned into a stag, chased down by his own hounds and killed. In April of 1937 the nonmilitary Spanish village of Guernica was obliterated as an experiment in air-to-ground military tactics by German bombers flying for Franco; in May, Pablo Picasso expressed his abhorrence in a mural that immortalizes the dead town in figures of agony, terror, and brutality. It was said of Martha Graham that "she forsook the outside shell and danced the reason why."

It is perhaps in centering on human feelings as the clue to understanding that the artist offers his distinctive views of the world. By depersonalizing knowledge, science has produced technology, and technology has become an automatism, a process to be carried on regardless of the results. Many of its products are pleasant to have, but poems and plays, paintings and music have begun to inquire how human qualities function in the equation of facts and inventions. The question seems to show that the exclusive loyalty of science is to fact—what it is possible to know must be known—and of technology to invention—what it is possible to do must be done. Human beings, who were supposed to manage the process, having produced it, seem to many artists to have become merely the consumers of its products. Rather large numbers of them, both in their life-styles and in their artifacts, have begun to reject the cliques, conveniences, and comforts the runaway technological process has showered on the affluent masses. They have withdrawn into enclaves visited by the tourists, but in the act have become the secular conscience of a secular age.

"We are the hollow men."

Prophecy

Artists, of course, are not uniquely endowed with pre-science, nor would they often claim to be "spokesmen for the Lord." They are neither, that is to say in the word-play of the theologians, "foretellers" nor "forthtellers." They tend to be more truthsayers than soothsayers. Artists often say that they "tell it like it is," which may be the secular way of saying "thus saith the Lord." Nonetheless, equipped with artistic hypersensitivity to human feelings in common situations, they have often condensed the truth about the present into images so vivid and unexpected that they seemed to be telling the world about things it didn't yet know. That is, perhaps, the role of the artist in any society. Most people are so preoccupied with the pleasures and details of living that they must rely on somebody else to point out what is going on and what it may mean. In a highly technological and comfortable society it may take something of a kook to drop out, to probe around, and to find out what is going on. Consequently, much of what he has to say sounds to many people like protest. That, too, is a form of prophecy.

The art of the twentieth century clearly suggests a shattered age. Painters, especially, have worked in so many different styles and created so many different movements in such rapid succession that the very lack of the focus or direction that characterized other centuries and their paintings must be regarded as significant. Painting has ranged from machine-like motifs to psychological reflections, from expressionistic social-realism to complete nonobjectivism, from material and form to psychic content.

Twentieth-century painters have developed ways of warning the commonsense people of a technological age that things are not always what they appear to be on the surface. Cubist painters showed the importance of stopping the increased pace of thought and movement that was threatening to thin out life fatally with a technique called simultaneity: a teacup or a woman's face is shown from two points of view simultaneously, the succession of

"The artist is the only person actually in contact with the present."
McLuhan

"Art is a lie that makes us realize truth."
Picasso

John Canaday, *Art in the Contemporary World*, Portfolio L, Metropolitan Seminars in Art (New York: Metropolitan Museum of Modern Art, 1960).

a figure's movements in descending a staircase are shown at once. The concern for what lay behind appearances led to painting the dynamically interlaced planes beneath a hill rather than its somnolent surface, or to attempts to understand the complexity of a solid form moving through space. Their probings suggested that the insides of things were more important than their outsides.

The theater has given contemporary society a truer-than-life picture of a culture careless of human values. Some characters in plays speak a series of non sequiturs that are contagiously amusing onstage but enough like actual everyday conversations to stop the laughter in mid-breath. Others find themselves in commonly experienced situations that can turn out to be nothing but absurd when played out to their logical end. Antonin Artaud talked of a theater that would reflect the truth about the world by being deliberately cruel to its audience: "The theater is a plague in that it exteriorizes a depth of latent cruelty by means of which all the perverse possibilities of the mind, whether of an individual or a people, are localized." The theater drains such "collective abscesses," as he called them, because it releases the repressed conflicts, and liberates the possibilities of a demon-dominated culture.

"It is through the skin that metaphysics must be made to enter our minds."

Thus, by responding to what is in the air, the artist has at times anticipated the general nature of things to come. In 1911 Pablo Picasso painted a picture called MAN WITH A VIOLIN that many historians have understood to be a prophecy of the atomic bomb: a painting of common objects in a pattern of geometrical shapes that merge, overlap, and break against one another, destroying

Antonin Artaud, *The Theater and Its Double* (New York: Grove Press, 1958).

them. A little later Georges Seurat created paintings by using dots of complementary colors in juxtaposition to create a mosaic very much like the principle of the electronic dots of the television tube that McLuhan theorizes about. Before World War I, Luigi Russolo showed a racing car and the geometric lines of force around it in a pattern precisely forecasting those photographed of the pressure waves caused by an airplane passing through the sound barrier. For seventy-five years, art has been making it clear that life would become dominated by the emotionally deprived straight lines, hard textures, reflecting surfaces, harsh sounds, and exposed nerves of an urbanized and engineered existence. A survey of theater, poetry, and painting reveals that it has been a long time since God was thought to be alive.

Communication

Though many people claim to find much of it incomprehensible, art is basically a form of communication. The difficulty lies primarily in the fact that many people insist on reading art as they would a newspaper or a chemical equation. Art does not seek to communicate facts—objective truths perceptible to any who will undergo the necessary intellectual discipline, and the same for all—so much as experience—subjective recreations of meaning available only to those who are free to respond personally, and different for each. When artists talk about communication, they tend to speak of how it has broken down, paradoxically, in a world of increased geographical proximity and technical facilities. They also tend to speak

"I never see sunsets like that."

"Don't you wish you did, Madam?"

Allen Leepa, *The Challenge of Modern Art* (New York: Thomas Yoseloff, 1957).

of it as an extended and creative interpersonal process and to use feeling-words rather than thinking-words.

"The substance of art is the human being himself," says an artist, and the artistic understanding of communication begins and ends in experience. It may be said that the artist is merely a more sensitive experiencer than other people. He undergoes the same stimuli—colors, patterns, sounds, movements, rhythms. He responds by pondering about their relation to himself. This pondering tends to be more intuitional and emotional than analytical and intellectual, but sometimes it involves a great deal of probing, exploring, researching. When insights come from this engagement between the ego and the world, the parts are related to each other, elements that are unnecessary or confusing are pushed aside, and a design emerges. Sometimes all this happens instantly and effortlessly, and sometimes only after considerable calculated effort. As it comes clear, images and metaphors are selected and clarified. A new thing is emerging: a creative transformation of experience into perception.

Expressing the perception is sometimes thought of as the whole of the artistic process. It is only the fulcrum on which the process is balanced, but it is the point at which the artist becomes craftsman. Externalizing what is personal and private is a formidable task. It means that he must choose a language—shapes, tones, textures, movements—and master it, so that he can productively combine inner personal experiences with the objective nature of the language he has chosen. Indeed, there is the live possibility that putting perceptions and experiences into a medium may change the character of the initial experience. At the end he says, "Here is a new thing I have made, and it is a summary of what I see and feel."

But the goal of the process of expression is not the

"Art stems from meaningful experience."

"The act of expressing means to make known one's thoughts and feelings through a medium."

artifact so much as the artifact's impact in the experience of the viewer. The artist's challenge is how to give the greatest vitality to what he wishes to say so that his communication will live for the spectator. The hope is that the viewer's perception will be altered or sharpened in such an internal and personal way that he will never experience his relationship to the world in quite the same way again. It is thus that works of art often appear to be more significant than the impersonal findings of science. Art involves a deep human involvement in reality, from beginning to end. It implies, in short, a personal development.

"The substance of art is the human being himself."

Celebration

In a society dedicated in general to things as they are, events of communication deserve notation. It is a creative process throughout, from beginning to end intensifying and disciplining personal qualities so that new things happen. It is the inclination of the artistic community to celebrate both the possibility and the event of creativity. Protestantism has long been wary of celebrations, discerning in them a tendency to lay undue emphasis on material rather than spiritual things. And, of course, the beginning of a new thing implies the end of some old thing. Science, with which Protestant theology is beginning to establish a truce, is always wary of anything that tends to lay emphasis on feelings rather than on facts. Art, however, has a way of suggesting that there is a life-style characterized by joy and productivity as well as one characterized by earnestness and conservation. This is heady stuff for those stifled by factuality and precision. It constitutes a humanism often attempting to practice a priest-craft for which it is unprepared and discovering truths which are only partly manageable, while insisting with considerable attractiveness that there is a distinctly alternative way to

". . . the discovery that other human beings are contributing to life society and culture."

deal with life which science has apparently rejected and theology seems to have forgotten.

The Emergent Principle

A viable Christian theology must demonstrate that the truth it tells is relevant to man in his present circumstances because it is true in more than present circumstances.

Education seeks not only to enrich the learner's life now but also in the future. Of course teachers cannot know what the future will be. It is difficult enough to understand the learner's life now. However, as a discipline perhaps more systematically concerned with the life of the young than any other organized social activity, education needs some sense of the drift of history.

The twentieth century has been an extraordinarily self-conscious period. Its citizens, with their varied interests, have called it "the end of the Protestant era," "the beginning of the atomic age," "the space age," "the beginning of the postscientific era." It has been dubbed, "the Age of Education," of the child, of the pocket edition, of the man in the grey flannel suit, of the organization man. It has been described as a period of rapid social change, irreversible urbanization, instant information, the world village, secularization, religionless religion, the death of God. An impressive number of historians have thought it important to interpret the signs of the times. Many philosophers end their weightiest works with guesses.

It has been the custom to read the trends of history somewhat as a glacier, irrevocably shifting toward the sea but so slowly that the movement itself is perceptible only after long time lapses. Sometimes the metaphor has been of more rapid movement, as a river accepting its many tributaries, laden with the sediment and flotsam, with many eddies and currents, meanderings and rapids. Interpretations of recent history suggest a snowball, picking up momentum and bulk, careening more and more rapidly, to end either resting magnificently in the valley or spectacularly disintegrating.

"Human history becomes more and more a race between education and catastrophe." **H. G. Wells**

Whatever may be the direction, the pace of recent history seems to be one of geometrical progression. Each new secret unlocked seems to provide the key for not one but a dozen others and the solution of each old problem seeems to reveal many new ones. The tilt of history increases constantly.

Progress and Optimism

"Unquestionably, the outlook on the threshold of a new century is exceedingly bright."

The lead editorial in the New York *Times* for Monday, January 1, 1900, anticipated a new century with unhesitating optimism. The city, with its 3½ million inhabitants, had had a gay time the night before with the celebration jammed into the square in front of Trinity Church. Seventy-six million Americans in forty-five states had joined in the event. With the tin horn "at its highest altitude of evolution," reported the *Times*, high carnival ushered in the end of the nineteenth century. The editor's optimism was shared by men in all walks of life. A midwestern newspaper said that the century just closed had been significant for "the improvement in the condition of the working classes." A minister had said in his sermon the day before that the past century was "one of the most fascinating chapters in the story of man's upward progress."

New Year's dinner was being served at the Broadway Central Hotel for 75 cents, a business house was looking for a stenographer at $7 a week, and the wage for a week of fifty-nine hours of work was $13. Men's shoes were advertized at $2.50, roast beef at 8 cents, gingham at 5 cents. Women's muslin corset covers were advertised at 14 cents each, and a cambric undershirt, "trimmed with tucks, lace insertion and ruffle of lace," was selling for 49 cents. The big bill before Congress was to appropriate $50 million for the Army, most of it an emergency measure on account of the unexpected resistance of the Aguinaldo rebels in the Philippines after the Spanish had been defeated.

The front page carried the news that the British Navy had siezed a German ship for carrying volunteers to the Boer War. Kaiser Wilhelm was reported to be angry about it and had ordered two German cruisers to Delagoa Bay in Portugese East Africa to protect German shipping. The German press was demanding a larger navy to match England's. John Jacob Astor, one of the richest men in the United States, predicted that "war will become so destructive that it will probably bring its own end." In September of 1905 the war between Japan and Russia ended with Japan emerging as a world power.

A newspaper in Providence, Rhode Island, predicted that the day would soon come when nearly every household would have a telephone. Early in 1901 Marconi transmitted the first radio signal across the Atlantic. A scientist in the Smithsonian Institution said that airplanes could be built "to travel at speeds higher than any with which we are now familiar." The *Popular Science Monthly* urged "extreme caution" in a field "where success is doubtful and failure is likely to bring discredit." H. G. Wells could not believe that the airplane would ever develop "as a serious modification of transport and communication." In 1903 the Wright Brothers made their first successful air flight at Kitty Hawk. Late in 1899 the *Literary Digest* said that "the horseless carriage would never come into as general use as the bicycle," but in 1903 Thomas A. Edison dared to bet in Chicago that he could go home to his workshop in New Jersey and prepare a car of his own design that would make a return trip to Chicago at an average speed of 25 miles an hour. Mr. Astor said that the keeping of horses in large cities should be prohibited.

President McKinley was about to enter the White House. Queen Victoria, ailing at eighty, was resting in her country place on the Isle of Wight and died on January 22nd. There was a severe snowstorm in the Southeast, and a man in Georgia had been frozen to death.

When the Archbishop of Canterbury was asked his opinion of the greatest menace to the twentieth century, he is reported to have replied, "I have not the slightest idea." In 1906 a world convention of Christian youth in Tokyo announced as its goal "the Christianization of the world in this generation."

"Public education has become the American religion."
Henry Steele Commager

In this period the educational philosophies of the twentieth century were conceived, tested, and formulated. They so much embodied the spirit of the time that they may be said to be products of it. They so much influenced the lives of the young that education may still be said to be the embodiment of an optimistic faith in progress.

Crisis and Uncertainty

"There is only the question 'When will I be blown up?' "

Where there are silver linings, however, there are clouds. They were heaviest in Europe, where World War I seemed to many to be a warning of things to come. Nicolai Berdyaev observed in Moscow in 1919 that "Man's history has been a series of failures and there is no reason to think that it will ever be otherwise." In England, George Bernard Shaw quipped that if the rest of the universe were inhabited they must be using this planet for their insane asylum. In America, H. L. Mencken called man "a sick fly taking a dizzying ride on a gigantic fly wheel." The Hitler nightmare revealed that societies as well as individuals may become paranoid. On August 6, 1945, President Harry Truman announced that a Japanese city had been destroyed by a single bomb. Most people who read the news probably heard of both Hiroshima and atomic energy for the first time. Columnists talked about "the basic energy of the universe." One commentator noted "the fulfillment of the strangest, most dreadful dream that has ever entered the mind of man." A war of nerves followed the end of the open fighting of World War II. Russia made an atom bomb. The United States tested a bigger one. Nuclear scientists revealed uncertainty about the control of chain reactions and the effects of increased radioactivity. A speaker on Easter Sunday, 1950, referred to the Four Horsemen of the New Apocalypse— "inflation, unemployment, hunger, the atom bomb." In receiving the Nobel literary prize, William Faulkner said that "there are no longer problems of the spirit," only the question of when the end will come.

The New York *Times* editorial for Easter Sunday, 1950, verbalized the uncertainty many felt. Noting that the world had been laid into two competing parts by the success of Communism, it pointed out that "dreadful doctrines and weapons have been invented," and "in some ways the earth is not so happy and safe as it was a century or several centuries ago." However, "When this spring has withered there will come other springs." A professor at Cambridge said that "our brightest hope is that the hydrogen bomb will very nearly, but not quite, work." A minister in Colorado called for a national defense system that would "panic-proof civilian personnel." Robert Frost declared that he was about to resign as a poet, indeed, that he was "resigned to everything." John Foster Dulles talked of peace as an arrangement whereby the Soviet leaders "would promise not to wage a war they do not plan with weapons they do not have." Archibald Macleish lamented the disappearance of "confidence in peace, confidence in the future, the natural, normal decent confidence of men of courage and character in their country and in themselves." Herbert Hoover remarked that at about the time people thought they could "make

"We Americans have 7½ billion headaches a year."

ends meet, somebody moves the ends." A sales executive defined durable goods as "goods that will last until the time-payments are concluded." The newspapers were filled with stories of flying saucers, the Air Force reported that it had examined hundreds of cases and that many of them could be accounted for as misinterpretation of conventional objects caused by "a mild form of mass hysteria," and President Truman said that he was as puzzled by the damned things as anybody else.

For modern theology it was a significant period. The Nazi philosophy and the National Socialist machinery made it clear in Germany that the church must choose between Germany and God. There were many German Christians, of course, who thought that some sort of compromise could be made, and there were some who thought that it was a spiritual movement with which Christianity should identify. But there were others who understood that a national spirit which claims exclusive allegiance cannot tolerate the Christian doctrine of God as universal Lord and Judge. In that crisis they were driven relentlessly back to the fundamentals of an ancient faith which had no dependence on immediate cultural situations. Karl Barth began to each a system of "revealed theology" as distinguished from the "natural theology" of the prewar period, affirming the absolute transcendence of God and speaking in terms of despair for man because of his manifest sinfulness. Emil Brunner began to speak of man's relationship to God as "confrontation" with a Being who is "totally other." The German crisis showed that the Bible, in spite of its prescientific world view, points unequivocally to the Holy God through its essential content—Jesus Christ. "When Christ stands before Pilate," said Barth, "the Word of God is there in one man." The truth which the Bible proclaims has become the last line of defense against modern lies and man's in-

"God is in his heaven and you are on the earth."

"One does not speak of God by speaking of man in a loud voice."

humanity in the name of science. Exiles from Germany won large followings in the United States. An American, Reinhold Niebuhr, began to say with increasing clarity that the hope of a kingdom of God on earth was not immediately realizable by human efforts. Out of the German situation came a new revelation of the power and authority of the biblical message that lies back of much that happened in theology. Then, in mid-century, American servicemen, returning from the combat zones with inelegant lingo and a passion to forget violence and death, flocked to the churches. There was what was called a "Return to Religion." Theology became set in the crisis-and-certainty mood of its hour of greatest relevance.

American education at mid-century, however, seemed not to share the public uncertainty. An article in the *Journal* of the National Education Association for March of 1950 proclaimed that the American people are "in the midst of the most amazing century in the long upward struggle of the race," that they need have no fear of the future. In the May issue, a University of California professor pointed with pride to the public school as "the greatest agency for citizenship which the American people have developed," claiming that it had "contributed to the moral and spiritual development of youth, given the people of this country a very high literacy rate, tended to raise the standard of living and to improve physical well-being and health and safety habits, and was teaching more efficiently than ever before." A historian of education marked the achievements of education in statistics: the number of children in schools had been multiplied twelve times in fifty years, expenditures per pupil eleven times and for school building construction twenty times.

Education's own crisis was only being postponed, however. In 1954 the United States Supreme Court ordered

"There are no problems which high ideals and intelligent persistence will not solve."

the racial integration of the public schools, challenging the assumption that the public school system was socially adequate and plunging schools throughout the country into the racial crisis. In 1957 Russia lofted the first man-made satellite into orbit, challenging the assumption that American education was educationally adequate and plunging the schools into a crash program to overcome the demonstrated educational superiority of the Russians. Education became big and public business. In 1966 there were 125,000 separate educational institutions with more than 60 million students and nearly 2 million teachers, spending approximately 45 billion dollars annually, not counting adult education and extension courses and educational television. One out of three persons in the country became directly engaged in the educational system. Ninety-nine percent of the children from six to thirteen were in elementary schools in the United States in 1960, ninety percent of those between fourteen and seventeen were in high schools, and nearly forty percent of those between eighteen and twenty-one were in colleges. Educators entered the public consciousness, and their opinions became quotable: William H. Kilpatrick said that the purpose of education was to assure the good life; James B. Conant said that it was to secure marketable skills; Robert Hutchins said that it was to achieve intellectual power. But it continued to be the American faith that education would solve the remaining problems.

"Most students have scarcely learned the Three Rs."

Change and Ambiguity

When uncertainty arises from crisis, stasis results, and the historical process comes to a halt. But when the momentum of the process increases in a period of crisis, an increase in the rate of change results. In a technological society, the solution of every crisis is to increase the pace of productivity. And when the uncertainty that prevents stasis is carried over from a period of crisis into a period of rapid change, ambiguity results. Man cannot produce new value judgments as rapidly as technology can make new products. Thoughts do not keep pace with things. In a time that combines rapid technological change with a mood of ambiguity, revolution takes form as the shape of the future. Rapid change is somehow transmuted into radical change.

The conformist morality of an industrial culture is currently exposed to radical criticism. Art and literature have been giving American values a thorough drubbing. Automation and prosperity have tended to make all Americans fat, comfortable, and dull. Abroad they all seem ugly, and at home they drive new automobiles that look very much alike, aspire to split-level ranch houses and read the magazines of their in-group. The caricature appeals to the intellectual and the rebel. There are few real intellectuals, so poetry becomes more esoteric, music more abstract, the novel more nihilistic, the theater more bizarre. There are few real rebels, so they find each other where they can and express their rebellion to each other by adopting a common style of nonconformist language, dress, and life. In both cases the moral criticism loses its bite by being disposable as merely oversophisticated or far out. The intellectual criticism produces ambiguity by happy acceptance of the comforts produced by the industrial culture it criticizes. The rebel criticism produces ambiguity by use of synthetic excitement while criticizing a synthetic society, the exotic instruments and ideas of the Orient while rejecting sophistication, divisive tactics in support of togetherness.

The ideological struggle has moved from confrontation to ambiguity. During the 1950s, the cold war and scientific

"What is different now is the pace of change, and the prospect that it will come faster and faster, affecting every part of life."
Max Ways

"Why do you have to be a nonconformist like everybody else?"

competition brought into sharp focus the philosophical
differences between Communism and democracy. With
coexistence, however, it has become clear that both
produce materialistic cultures promising power, wealth,
and standard of living as the chief tangible evidences of
success or failure. Both tend to assume that man is the
product of society, that man's nature can be improved
by the improvement of social conditions, that man will
become more intelligent and moral with increased material comforts. The result has been to bring the two most
materialistic cultures together in an ambiguous alliance
against the world's less materialistic cultures. The same
shift has occurred in interracial as well as intercontinental
issues: beginning with a clear drive for personal equality
as a moral principle (clearly dividing the conservative from
the liberal), the civil rights movement has tended to judge
separation, hatred, and power to be morally good if they
will produce work, housing, and education (alienating
both the conservative and the liberal and throwing them
together in an ambiguous alliance). When disputes that
began in difference of principle end in the question which
is more likely to produce the kind of society both parties
aim at and are actually in the process of achieving, ambiguity is the result.

A radical revision of Newtonian and Copernican concepts of a rigid and predictable universe has been necessitated by developments in subnuclear physics and astro-
mechanics. Putting the two disciplines side by side is one
evidence of the rapid changes occurring in the advanced
sciences. A new ambiguity is introduced when the physical
scientists, who have traditionally dealt with hard reality,
tend to accept the proposed flexibility, but the life scientists, who have traditionally concerned themselves with
"soft" reality, tend to reject it. The physicists and the

mathematicians are saying that their subjects cannot be profitably studied with the mechanistic models of a generation ago, while the sociologists and psychologists seem unwilling to apply the same assumptions of mystery and freedom to their less mechanistic subject matter.

Education maintains officially a progressive philosophy dedicated to the gradualism of evolutionary change and the assumption that all directed change is an improvement. In attempting to meet the population explosion, public education has, in the local school districts, so far relied on a stand-pat program of more of the same kind: bigger buildings of the same design and higher salaries for the same teachers who are required to have more of the same kind of training. Simultaneously, it is engaged in a crash program to produce technicians for the international space race, which is in fact more ideological than technological in origin and which will certainly be more revolutionary than evolutionary in result.

"In the future education and technology will be much like love and marriage: you can't have one without the other."
Jackson Grayson, Jr.

In short, the reaction of American society to intensified change seems to be confused and ambivalent. Since change and ambiguity is the seedbed of radical readjustment, the question is what kind of new world it will be. If the tilt of history is onward, it may be a new Golden Age to replace the old gilded one. If the tilt is reversed, it may be a new Dark Age. Neither can be predicted. Neither will be final. Neither can be assured by education.

Education has passed through two phases in the United States. The first was the achievement of quantity. Everyone was to be provided the chance for an education of some sort. That phase began in the colonies and is almost completed in the schools and is on its way in higher education. The second phase is equality of opportunity. That phase is under way now and was begun in many areas only after the Supreme Court decision of 1954. The third phase

"The educational pattern of the past is no longer valid."
Robert Theobald

is yet ahead and revolutionary in nature: the achievement of quality. The rapidly increased pattern of change makes it necessary. "The goal of education," says Carl Rogers, "is to develop people who can live more comfortably with change than with rigidity." Young people have lived a larger proportion of their lives in the new world of change than have adults and may already be more at home in it than those whose thought patterns were established in a world of crisis and uncertainty, with its vestigal remains of progress and optimism. In any case, it is they who will create the culture of the new environment. The implication, of course, is that it might be better for the teachers to attempt to join their young pupils in the struggle to understand the new world they live in than for them to say, "Listen to us and learn about the old world." It appears that a school composed chiefly of classrooms and libraries may soon become obsolete. The introduction of information banks and computer-programmed learning may be necessary if for no other reason than that the world today's learners will eventually live in as adults may be one making common use of electronic intelligence. Indeed, as Lynn White, Jr., has written: "Our revolution is so new we really do not know what a high democratic culture would look like much less what its formal education would be."

The Emergent Principle

A viable education must learn how to help learners live meaningfully now in an ambiguous situation and eventually in one that will probably be revolutionary.

The Christian Education Movement

Modern Christian education is as American as ice cream and the separation of church and state. A great deal of Christian education in the United States has been as informal and folksy as the Sunday school picnic, of which the ice cream was an indispensable element. The "wall of separation" between church and state has given to Christian education its distinctive form in the United States, though, of course, Christian education existed before that principle was ever conceived.

". . . an American phenomenon."

Development

Early in the colonial period, the New England Pilgrims founded schools so that the children of the community could learn to read the scripture and to love God and glorify him forever. The village parson was often the village schoolteacher, and the school stood next to the church on the village green. So that he might be trained to carry on his tasks in both pulpit and school room, Harvard and Yale were established, and in the eighteenth and nineteenth centuries frontier preachers left behind them a string of colleges reaching to the Pacific. All that, in turn, began in Europe with the Protestant Reformation which depended upon teaching men to read so that they could know the Bible for themselves and not be dependent on churchly authority for either faith or doctrine.

"Education is an inherent necessity in Christianity."

Frontier life was not conducive to thorough education, however, and many visitors from abroad noted the ignorance and roughness of American life. For instruction in religion, most Americans were dependent upon the

Lewis Joseph Sherrill, *The Rise of Christian Education* (New York: Macmillan, 1944).

long and often evangelistic sermons of the local preacher. During the Revolutionary War both general and religious education sank to such a low ebb that a remedial program was one of the primary needs of the National Period, and when this need became gradually linked with the principle of political separation between religion and government, the United States was committed to a free or public school system. An absolutely nonsectarian secular education turned out to be an elusive ideal, but by the 1830s it had been effectively decided that while tax-supported schools should be responsible for some kind of moral training, religious education was not the province of the state.

Robert Raikes, a businessman of Glouchester, England, is traditionally credited with inventing the Sunday school idea. During the year 1780, he noted that children who were employed in his factory six days a week were running dangerously and unproductively loose on their day off. He began gathering them into his home on Sundays for instruction in reading. The Bible was the textbook. Other Sunday programs began about the same time, some of them quite independently, for much the same purposes. In the United States, however, with its new concept of public school committed to nonreligious instruction, Sunday became the day for religious instruction and the church the supporting agency. The teachers were church people, not educators. The Bible—often begun at the beginning and worked straight through—was the curriculum. Rote knowledge of the material seemed to be

Walter Scott Athearn, *Religious Education and American Democracy* (Boston: Pilgrim Press, 1917). William Bean Kennedy, *The Shaping of Protestant Education* (New York: Association, 1966).
Henry Frederick Cope, *The Evolution of the Sunday School* (Boston: Pilgrim Press, 1911).

the goal. It was the desperate need for improvement that created the American Sunday School Union in 1824, which for forty years held conventions and training sessions, published books and lesson materials. By the time the Civil War broke the organization apart, the Sunday school had been defined: an activity of the local church, conducted for children and adults for an hour or two on Sunday, by nonprofessional volunteer teachers.

The pluralism and growth of the period following the war was reflected in the Sunday schools, but without altering their lay character or the growing enthusiasm for them. In 1873 "uniform lessons"—one lesson for all ages in all schools—made their appearance, in 1892 a "graded" series —separate lessons for different age-groups—and before the end of the century a "closely graded" series—separate lessons for each year of childhood. In New England the United Society for Christian Endeavor moved into the youth-vacuum in 1881 and rapidly became a national movement. In the middle west some churches moved out of the Sunday limitation: in Wisconsin, Bible schools were started during the long public school summer vacation, and in Indiana, classes were held on weekdays after public school dismissal. A World Sunday School Convention began meeting in 1889.

"The adoption of the Sunday School by the church marked a new era in religious history."

It was during the period preceeding World War I that Christian education became a professional movement. In 1903 a distinguished gathering of professors, college presidents, and church educators met in Chicago to organize the Religious Education Association, "to inspire the educational forces of this country with the religious ideal; to inspire the religious forces of this country with the educational ideal." They founded experimental schools and the science of teaching; they established laboratories and the study of religious psychology; they created and occupied the first chairs of religious education in the country's

"1903 may be taken as a convenient date to mark the rise of the Religious Education movement."

theological seminaries. They gathered about them the resources of other disciplines and in time could begin to speak of the history, the psychology, the philosophy, and the theology of Christian education. In their own bridging between the fields of education and religion, they pioneered the development of other practical theologies, such as psychology-and-religion and sociology-and-religion.

In 1922, under the influence of this professional development, the International Council of Religious Education was organized in Kansas City to train and assist laymen teachers in the local church schools. The council was responsible for turning the work of the professors into new curriculum materials. Through its journal it brought teacher-training to thousands of volunteer teachers in their own homes. It took over the publication rights of the American Standard Version of the Bible and was instrumental in producing a significantly new Revised Standard Version. It brought the denominational agencies together for coordination and planning.

By the mid-1920's, with a history, an intellectual discipline, a following, and a mission, education in the churches could be said to be a movement.

Achievements

The change from 1900 to 1950 was spectacular, by any accounting.

According to a widely accepted statistic of the 1950s, 41 million students attended classes on Sunday mornings in the United States, 8 million more young people

Adelaide Teague Case, *Liberal Christianity and Religious Education* (New York: Macmillan, 1924).
Robert W. Lynn, *Protestant Strategies in Education* (New York: Association Press, 1964).

gathered on Sunday evenings, and 10 million adults were involved as leaders. Frequently there were more people learning in the church schools on Sundays than worshiping in the church services. Usually there were more church members actively involved in Christian education than in any other program of the church. Often churches in the new suburbs built the educational unit first. Many of these plants surpassed the local public school in attractiveness and facilities, and many of the churches put off building the sanctuary so as to be able to add a trained minister of education to the staff to guide the program. Some churches even paid their teachers.

The major denominations invested millions of dollars in preparing and printing new curricula and by the second or third revision were able to present their teachers and learners throughout the United States with materials that rivaled those of the public schools in both educational design and effectiveness. Public school educators began to talk about "moral and spiritual values in the public schools," and some held conferences with church school educators. Every theological school had its department of education, most offered specialized degrees, and some professors of Christian education became deans of their faculties. High-level committees studied the professional difference between a director of education and a minister of education. The International Council of Religious Education became one of the founding bodies of the National Council of Churches.

The educational system stretched from womb to tomb and from the simplest introduction to highly technical graduate studies. Church schools not only provided three or four years of Sunday morning programs before kindergarten, but many offered specifically Christian prenatal instruction for expectant parents and conducted Christian-oriented nursery schools in the church facilities on weekday mornings. The problems of senior citizens prompted studies of the religious problems of aging as well as activity programs in the church during the week. Beginning in the kindergarten class, it was possible for a learner to pass through six years of elementary study, graduate into the junior high school program and complete a high school curriculum before going on to a church-related college, where he could take a rigorous sequence of religious subjects qualifying him to enter a theological seminary, after completion of which he could achieve a doctor's degree in one of the branches of formal or applied theology. Along the way he could enlarge his fun and learning with an extensive series of camps and conferences, many of which would provide a demanding depth-plunge into personal and theological issues. If he chose not to study Christianity vocationally, he could find lectureships and special courses through his home church and the local council of churches which would, in time, provide him with most of the subjects of a theological seminary. A vast range of literature became available, much of it in paperback form, ranging from Christian classics to current theology and from biblical study to social issues.

Education had become one of the primary occupations and methods of the American church.

Problems

"My son did not miss a session of Sunday school for ten years," wrote a puzzled mother to a seminary professor. "How could he fail your course in New Testament?" About the time parents were discovering that the elementary public school had not taught Johnny to read, and a widely quoted study demonstrated that four years of higher education did not significantly change the attitudes of college students, Christian educators began to suspect that American Protestants as a whole were biblically illiterate and ethically uncommitted. If, indeed, some sixty million hours were devoted every Sunday to Christian education in the churches, much of the energy seemed to have been wasted.

Closer investigation revealed even more extensive wastefulness. Many of the stunning new curriculum materials languished on Sunday school room shelves unappreciated. An alarming proportion of the teachers were completely untrained; somewhat overwhelmed by their task, they tended to revert to the rote memory methods of their own Sunday school days, and when faced with theological issues they tended to recall the aphorisms and fables of simpler times. Even a casual glance at the street in front of the church on Sunday morning revealed that many parents were dropping their children at church school and spending their own Sunday mornings at home with the television set or Sunday paper. Attendance charts showed that not only were these young adults missing from most church activities, but that the adolescents who had just graduated from the boredom of church school were ducking further exposure to Christian education.

Even the one hour of the typical Sunday school session was cut into by announcements, taking roll and collections, and many nominal Christians were living from Sunday to Sunday without contact with Christian thought. Clearly, if Christian education were to become a significant force in people's lives, it needed more than five or ten percent of the time children needed for general education. Some countered by wondering if even the one hour in 168 were worthwhile and pointed to the handicap of sporadic attendance that would stagger the secular educator. And if conditions that had already demonstrated themselves to be ineffective were to be unchanged, the mere increase of time spent in them would only increase the quantity of ineffectiveness. Some became enthusiastic about special techniques as a cure: audiovisual aids, group dynamics, team-teaching, experimental worship services, home involvement. But the basic difficulties did not seem to curl up and die. Others hoped that the public school interest in moral and spiritual values would significantly supplement the efforts of the church schools, but the interest often turned out to be superficial and short-lived.

"Secularization has occurred because we wanted it." Martin Marty

In the seminaries, theologians began to question the depth of the return to religion in general and of the Christian education movement specifically. It seemed to some of them that at the local level the gospel preached was "It pays to be nice," the intent was "not to offend anybody," and the goal was "to build a tower higher than St. Babel's down the street." Once again David had met Goliath, but this time "Goliath yawned." The failure of the churches to make of religion's popularity anything more than a mild religious kick could be traced to a demonstrated biblical illiteracy on the part of church-goers, and the responsibility for that could be laid directly at the door of the church schools. Christian education seemed to be taking many of its cues from secular education; talking about science, common sense, the Golden Rule, and sportsmanship, and joining in the creation of a semisecular faith in democracy as an object of religious dedication.

Meanwhile, denominational and ecumenical strategists saw that professionally trained ministers could not possibly meet the administrative demands placed upon them by the increasing number of programs for which they were responsible, and be the parish teacher as well. That, obviously, would necessarily be the task of the laymen of the church, and an impressive "doctrine of the laity" was developed to support the authority and responsibility implied. The lay movement, however, did not develop in the United States as it had in Germany following World War II, partly because conditions were different and partly because American adult education had not supplied laymen with biblical knowledge, theological understanding, and communication skills. Without them laymen preferred to exert their new ecclesiastical authority in secular areas where they were skillful, such as building maintenance, financial management, legal advice. These interests of the laymen demanded the pastor's time, giving a sort of evidence to ministers that laymen were not interested in theological and social issues. Prevented from using their own hard-won theological skills in the local church, the more gifted and less patient pastors began to look for unconventional ministries outside the parish or for ways to get into full-time teaching. In the seminaries, Christian educators divided their labor into practical and theoretical, and a new crop of specialists began to do scientifically designed experiments on cognitive theory and computer-programmed teaching. Ironically, the chasm between specialist and layman was either widening or closing in the direction of apathy toward the theological issues, rather than closing in the direction of the priesthood of all believers.

Sometimes, to a Sunday school teacher exhausted after an hour of wrestling fruitlessly with wandering and disinterested child-minds, and to a church school superintendent discerning that despite his efforts most of the children in the school average only two Sundays in a month, the effort seems unjustified. But the parents continue to send the kids on Sunday mornings, the pupils once again appear expectant, and almost every Sunday some Johnny or Mary responds directly to an idea or

"Only an all-wise God could utilize the Sunday School to change the course of so many lives!"
Ronald C. Doll

conviction, and they go on. There is some sort of indestructible confidence that if one knows the biblical story, the life, death, and resurrection of Jesus Christ, the history of the Christian movement, and the basic tenets of its faith, God will be known personally and individuals will respond to God's acts of love.

Directions

So, in the light of all these achievements and problems, what's to be done?

Some suggest that the Sunday church school as it is now conducted be closed and laid away before it closes itself. They argue that this decisive move would make room for a new form of Christian education.

"Sunday schools that pervert their function should go the way of other decadent institutions."

One proposal is for an in-family education to take its place, with parents contracting to lead the program. The time might be perhaps an hour daily, in which the family participates as a whole, guided by material supplied by the denomination—a transformation of the presently disappearing family devotions into a disciplined educational process.

Another proposal is to concentrate on age-groups other than children as an alternative to the traditional church school. Some think that adult education is the answer, because theological study demands adult thinking skills, because there are more adult years than childhood years available for education, and because the church has historically been an adult rather than a children's movement. Another concept calls for the creation of youth and young-adult schools to take the place of children's education. Its proponants cite current examples of programs enlisting the enthusiasms and dedication of young people. A training for evangelism could be adapted from the Mormons, for social action from VISTA, for missionary work from the Peace Corps.

Some would shift the entire educational program of the church from Sunday to other times, concentrating on summer schools both in the community and in resort areas, or special retreats and conferences throughout the year. Boy Scout, Chatauqua, Ashram, and other movements provide possible models. Church camps have demontrated the effectiveness of short but concentrated periods of instruction in which the entire environment and the whole day is devoted to the program. University extension programs, among others, have shown the possibilities of securing attendance and attention for special courses and lectureships in town during the year.

Another proposal is to do away with all traditional educational programs to concentrate on the mass media. The phenomenal success of the paperback book industry is cited. It would be possible, through an extended program of publishing and distribution, to make available most knowledgeable and interesting interpreters of the Christian faith to the mind of every Christian layman, and perhaps to the non-Christian as well. The facilities of television, both local and national, have been untapped by Christian education as yet. Resources now poured into the Sunday schools could be pooled to develop programs, ranging from Romper Room to University of the Air, paralleling educational programming with religious instruction. Broadcast publicly for home watching or prepared on video tape for group use, these programs would become the new forms of Christian education.

Others suggest that the Sunday church school be transformed into a real children's school. This might be achieved by applying public school practices to the church: professional teachers and staff, compulsory attendance, with classes meeting a full day on Saturday or a half-day

"The church is being killed by her own failure to take the shape that the world needs."
Stephen C. Rose

on Sunday or an hour a day after school on weekdays, with examinations, grades, and promotions. The practices of Reformed Synagogue schools and of Catholic parochial schools are often cited as examples.

Still others suggest solving the problems raised by the American constitution and the traditional interpretation of the separation between church and state so that religion can be taught in the public schools by professionals. They cite the example of religious instruction in free schools in England since the Education Act of 1944. Not only would the churches be freed from the tremendous financial burden of special religious education, but the instruction would be linked directly with the child's entire learning experience. The character education movement of the 1930s was dropped in mid-development, losing the opportunity to exploit its possibilities, which many feel are great.

"God leads his people in every age in unpredictable ways." **Gordon Cosby**

All these programs might become little more than relatively unproductive tinkering with techniques, however, if they were applied as stopgap measures substituting for more radical measures. If, on the other hand, the controlling purpose is to illuminate the entire life of the Christian person and through him the life of the non-Christian, both in the church and in the world, new specific programs as well as some adjustment of old ones will result. Along the way Christian education may find itself associating with other disciplines in the development and understnading of strategies. It is even possible that what is now recognized as Christian education may disappear in a new grouping of forces and disciplines. Meanwhile, the nature and development of the Christian education movement may be such as to fit it uniquely to stand at the heart of the revolutionary task of the Christian faith.

Christians believe that the presence of God in human life is so potent and his will for human life so creative that if they were taken seriously the entire world would be refashioned. They think that God is actively at work in human history, constantly addressing man in love and in grace enabling the sort of response that would eventually create a new way of life. They see the possibility implanted in human nature of construction as well as destruction, of cooperation as well as competition, of trust as well as suspicion, of concern as well as power, of peace as well as war. They hold the faith that man can respond to God in love and joy, releasing an ontologically new being in human life. They believe that this new creation can be enabled by offering to stand beside another human being in the sorrows and joys and events of his ordinary living, offering one's own convictions about the nature of love and redemption because this is the way God chose to teach men when the time had come for the greatest lessons to be taught. They remember that Jesus went about changing individual lives and talking about God and man. And they remember that he gathered a basic group and patiently explained to them his principles and convictions, illustrated for them his understanding of God as he met people from every walk of life, demonstrated to them his commitment to the will of God as he died.

"If the gospel is from God, why is it not more effective?"

Within that faith, Christian education is apt to place special emphasis on the four areas identified by Horace Bushnell.

Christian education is apt to emphasize *change*. It is difficult to believe that all the loneliness and estrangement and despair of human life are precisely what the loving Father that Jesus revealed intended for man. To be devoted to change is not to think that God's work is progressive so much as to believe that God's work is continuous. It is not to suppose that God changes so much as to take seriously the fact that man changes. To be dedicated to a strategy for changing human beings is not so much to believe in salvation by education as to admit that when man voluntarily and consciously exposes himself to God the change will be radical.

Christian education is apt to emphasize *personal knowledge*. The very content of the gospel and the Christian faith are constituted by the personal Word of God addressed to man. The incarnation demonstrated, to anyone who understands the ultimately personal language, that to know is to be known. Thus the community of those who need each other and worship with each other in the name of God is the home base and the context of Christian education. It is a fellowship with depth and joy, enabling men to build strength into their lives quite beyond their individual resources.

Christian education is apt to emphasize the possibility of the *encounter between God and man*. The peculiar promise held out by the Christian faith is a mysterious and redemptive camaraderie between divine and human in daily life. Undeserved it may be; unexpected it need not be. It is, wondrously, not completely unlike the relationship of trust and discovery that is sometimes between man and man. It sometimes occurs, even more mysteriously, where man resists man and man rejects God. It is the possibility that sometimes makes life endurable, and at other times makes it believeable.

And Christian education is apt to emphasize *personal growth and nurture*. To be devoted to an educational strategy is not to believe that classrooms and curricula produce a relationship between God and man, but rather to trust that one man can conduct another to the threshold of the redemptive encounter by exposing his experience to the reality of God. And educators tend to feel that an informed Christian is a more effective Christian than an ignorant one, that the data of the Christian faith have some relation to the living of a Christian life.

By putting its own special emphases to work, Christian education places itself at the disposal of the Christian movement and its total goal of enlisting and supporting a life-wide, week-long, world-around reconstruction of life according to God's will and under his direction.

". . . to move to Servanthood."
Don Benedict

The Emergent Principle

A viable Christian education movement will devote itself to the development of a total approach to the task of the church in the world, based on a deepening understanding of the nature of spiritual communication and the radical nature of the Christian faith.

Alternatives

Educators tend to work in a cumulative way. In teaching, everything that may possibly contribute to the proximate goal in a discussion period or to the ultimate goal in lesson-planning is related to the developing process. The irrelevant ideas and unproductive activities are dropped and forgotten. The suggestions that help the learning experience along are kept and emphasized. Historians and philosophers of education tend to work in the same way. For them history is evolutionary, the educational process progressive. The logic tends to be straightforward, the method eclectic.

Theologians tend to work in a dialectical way. In preaching, everything possible is done to make clear the need for a choice between the religious and the non-religious ways of life. The principles and practical consequences are separated into two groups, and the differences between them are emphasized. Ideas that are irrelevant or activities that are unproductive are demonstrated to be negative or harmful. Historians and philosophers of theology tend to work in the same way. For them history develops through crises, doctrines through conflict. The logic tends to be paradox, the method selective.

The educational way runs the danger of oversimplifying. It sometimes gives the impression that everything runs along smoothly, developing naturally from step to step. The theological way runs the danger of overintensifying. It sometimes gives the impression that nothing is achieved except by unusual and decisive struggle.

Another way, which understands history and ideas to be the product of several constantly interacting forces, might run the danger of overcomplicating. It might sometimes give the impression that nothing is ever permanently achieved. It might also provide a way of relating educational and theological history and ideas in Christian education. The selection of three alternatives from among many is somewhat arbitrary. Theoretical categories cannot actually be mutually exclusive: centers of gravity in thinking produce fields of influence throughout which forces interpenetrate and areas which near their peripheries overlap. At the edges the distinctions break down. Educators tend to sound a little alike because of their common specialization. Philosophers invade each other's domains. Theologians are drawn together by claiming a common enemy. History produces new constellations of ideas. Inevitably the possibility of still another distinctive category is suggested.

However, three focuses are clear enough. Education is activity-centered, child-centered, and content-centered. Learning is by doing, by becoming a person, by knowing about things. Philosophy is pragmatic, idealistic, realistic. It is grounded in three commonsense hunches: "Truth is what works," "Truth is more than it appears to be," "Truth is exactly what it appears to be." Religion is life-oriented, person-oriented, truth-oriented. It draws its insights from the physical sciences, the life sciences, the methods of the sciences. Theology is progressive, liberal, traditional.

The three categories are here named Experimentalism, Personalism, Essentialism. Each has a personal archetype in the first decade of the twentieth century, has reached full intellectual development in the first half of the century, and is now undergoing serious challenge.

EXPERIMENTALISM

". . . we take our science straight"
. . . pragmatism
". . . truth is what works"
. . . activity-centered education
". . . learning-by-doing"
. . . life-oriented religion
. . . progressive theology

John Dewey, 1859-1952

"John Dewey," said the distinguished professor of education as the first sentence of a university course in the philosophy of education in the fall semester of 1948, "is education."

"John Dewey," said the bright young high school teacher at a conference on moral and spiritual values in the public schools in 1955, "is democracy."

"John Dewey," said the rector of the University of Paris in a somewhat freely translated condensation of an elegant Gallic introduction presenting him for an honorary degree in 1930, "is America."

One of his favorite students said that John Dewey was "an average American," and another said that to look at him one would never expect him to be brilliant. He would come to class with his necktie out of contact with his collar or a pants leg caught up on his garter, his hair looking as if it had been combed with a towel, his black moustache unruly, and his eyes seeming to search for an idea.

A critic once said that Dewey published 38 books and 815 articles and pamphlets, producing a pile 12 feet 7 inches high, and that "if he ever wrote one quotable sentence, it has got lost in the pile." At least one, however, has been widely remembered: "I would not have a child say 'I know,' but 'I have experienced.'" With that principle he probably did more than anyone else to save children from dying of boredom in school. The *Encyclopaedia Britannica* put it more carefully: "He changed the school from a place where children prepare for life into a place where children live."

It has even been said that in Pragmatism he created the

". . . the most profound and complete expression of American genius."

Sidney Ratner, ed., *The Philosopher of the Common Man: Essays in Honor of John Dewey to Celebrate his Eightieth Birthday* (New York: Putnam's, 1940).

first and only system of philosophy entirely native to America.

Growing Up American

"Hams and Cigars— Smoked and Unsmoked"

John Dewey was born just before the Civil War in a small town in Vermont where his father ran the general store. As a boy he delivered papers after school for spending money, and since he was a great reader it must be assumed that he read, more than most lads of his time, the news of the Reconstruction period. However, he did not receive high marks in school, and later people remembered him more for his personality than for his brains.

In later life Dewey could not remember why he had gone to college, but there was one close by in Burlington, and he "slid," as he said, into it. He joined the White Street Congregational Church in Burlington, was a most conscientious Sunday school teacher, and held an uncomplicated adolescent's version of the New England theology. He said that he "slid through" college without "throwing any sparks." However, his marks rose steadily, and he graduated at the head of his class with the highest record in philosophy yet achieved at the University of Vermont.

A year after graduation he borrowed $500 from an aunt and went off to continue his study of philosophy at Johns Hopkins University in Baltimore. He studied political and institutional history, psychology, and philosophy. Among his teachers were G. Stanley Hall, who was a pioneer in a new field called educational psychology; George S. Morris, who has been called "the American Hegel"; and Charles S. Peirce, who later coined the name "pragmaticism" for

The Saturday Review, November 21, 1959, the John Dewey Centennial Section.

his philosophy. The philosophy department, like most in the country at the time, was under the influence of German Rationalism, especially as developed by Hegel and turned by him into Absolute Idealism. Dewey apparently accepted Hegel's concepts of absolute Mind and of the actual and conceptual unity of the universe, together with Hegel's dialectical method of thesis-antithesis-synthesis. His early essays assumed a theistic stance and he opposed Herbert Spencer's hypothesis of social evolution as destroying the foundations of ethics. When he graduated with his Ph.D. in 1884, the president urged him not to be too bookish: "Don't live a secluded life," he said. "Get out and see people."

"Whatever banished God from the heart of things with the same edict excluded the ideal."

Mystical Experience

The year after he graduated from the University of Vermont, Dewey went to Oil City, Pennsylvania, to teach in a high school run by one of his cousins. One evening, while reading, he had what he called his "experience."

"Everything that's here is here, and you can just lie back on it."

Two years before, during his junior year in college, he had experienced something of an intellectual awakening while reading a physiology textbook by Thomas Henry Huxley. He felt swept off his feet by the rapture of scientific knowledge. In the months that followed he worried a great deal over the chasm between this scientific vision and what he was telling the boys in his Sunday school class at the Congregational church, but for the most part he devoted himself with new vigor to his philosophical studies and left the chasm gaping.

The experience at Oil City, however, was more personal. "What are you worrying about, anyway?" was the way he described his feeling later. One can simply trust things as they are, not only to be what they are but by their reality to give guidance to man in his moral quest.

"I've never had any doubts since then," he said, and added, "or any beliefs." He concluded, "To me, faith means not worrying."

At the end of the year his cousin resigned his position at the Oil City school, and Dewey returned to Burlington for the summer. He felt at peace, but he also felt the chasm between the moral and material sciences, as they were called then. During the summer he focused his aim on closing the chasm. Since that was the task of philosophy, he determined to become a philosopher.

The Experimental School

When he graduated from Johns Hopkins, Dewey took a position at the University of Michigan as an instructor, and there he met a coed named Alice Chipman who began to exert a strong influence on John Dewey and in time became Mrs. Dewey. She was an ardent woman suffragist, moved by religious convictions but a member of no church, partly because of her scorn of sloppy thinking and easy answers. She admired Dewey's intellectual brilliance, but was impatient with abstract philosophy. Using a homely metaphor, Dewey said she put reality into his intellectual method. She wanted a place for him to try out his developing theories, and when, in 1894, an opportunity appeared for them to move to the University of Chicago, they went. The chair was to be philosophy and education, an unprecedented combination precisely suited to the Deweys' rebellion against the old system of education summed up by the infamous Mr. Dooley, that "it doesn't matter much what you study so long as you don't like it."

". . . stuffing and guts"

Soon the Deweys had determined that the only appropriate laboratory for the testing of educational theories would be an actual school. In January of 1894, together with some of their neighbors and under the auspices of the University of Chicago, the University Experimental School was opened. It was destined to change schools throughout the world.

The beginning, however, was slow and tentative. The neighbors supplied the pupils. Dewey's classes at the University provided the teachers. Later Dewey remembered the difficulty he encountered even in securing the equipment he wanted. He described his needs to a number of salesmen in Chicago's school supply houses: "desks and chairs thoroughly suited from all points of view—artistic, hygienic, and educational—to the needs of little children." Finally one salesman blurted, "I am afraid we do not have what you want. You want something at which children may work; these are all for listening."

For the school, itself, a "plan of organization" was formulated, "not to give a rigid scheme," as Dewey said, but "to define the general spirit in which the work was undertaken." The children ranged from four to fourteen years of age. They were divided into small groups—eight to ten in each—but not according to the traditional grade levels. The teachers worked directly under Dewey's supervision. The method was rigorously inductive and began with questions, of which there were four that were basic. "What can be done to break down the barriers which have come to separate the school from the rest of the everyday life of the child?" "What can be done in the way of introducing subject matter in history and science and art that shall have a positive value and real significance in the child's own life?" "How can instruction in the

"The teachers started with question marks rather than with fixed rules."

John Dewey, *My Pedagogic Creed* (University of Chicago Press, 1897) and several subsequent editions.

formal branches—the mastering of the ability to read, write, and use figures intelligently—be carried on with everyday experience and occupation as their background and in definite relation to other studies of more inherent content, and be carried on in such a way that the child shall feel their necessity through their connection with subjects which appeal to him on their own account?" "What can be done to give individual instructional attention to each child?"

". . . the most effective instrument of social progress and reform"

The ideal, said Dewey, is that the school should be "an embryonic community, active with types of occupations that reflect the life of the larger society and permeated throughout with the spirit of art, history and science." When the school helps the child learn how to live in a community of service and self-direction, "we shall have the deepest and best guarantee of a larger society which is worthy, lovely and harmonious." Dewey believed in "the ability of individuals to live in cooperative integration with others," and that the Experimental School was the place to begin.

"Out of it came the phrasings of a new philosophy of education."

From the beginning, this experiment in new educational methods produced phenomenal results. The children learned with unprecedented rapidity and effectiveness, and in later years its students provided the talent for a nationally broadcasted radio program called "The Quiz Kids." Educators from throughout the country, and eventually from all over the world, visited the school and went home to begin similar experimentation. It also provided the workshop in which Dewey clarified his understanding of the processes of education and verified the principles on which he built his philosophical struc-

John Dewey, *The School and Society* (University of Chicago Press, 1899) and innumerable subsequent editions.

ture. Eight years of the Experimental School equipped Dewey with the foundational material he needed.

University Teaching

In 1904 Dewey moved to Columbia University in New York City. "Ideas were sprouting out through the bricks at Columbia in those days," said one of his friends, "and Dewey's mind was happy there."

He established a home on Long Island where he maintained a small farm, raised a family of five children, and did a great deal of his studying. The mixture was productive. He boasted that he actually earned enough from his eggs and vegetables to pay for his keep and delightedly told a story of one of his wealthy neighbors who exclaimed as he rose to speak at an exclusive women's club, "Why, he looks exactly like our egg man!" He also told of being disturbed in his study one day by a stream of water from the bathroom above and dashing upstairs to find his son Fred with sailboats in the tub desperately trying to shut off the water. "Don't argue, John," shouted Fred. "Get the mop!"

At the University, Dewey seemed to teach from experience rather than from books, was quickly recognized as a character, and soon thereafter regarded as a prophet. In class he would sit with an elbow on the desk, purse his mouth and look vaguely over the heads of the class as though he might find an idea on the ceiling. He talked slowly, as if searching everything he knew for each sentence and with frequent glances to the spot on the ceiling as if to check what he was saying. For some time

"Life is the stuff of philosophy."

Oscar Handlin, *John Dewey's Challenge to Education* (New York: Harper, 1959).

one of his favorite subjects, usually in a critical vein, was Theodore Roosevelt; a student prankster posted a picture of Roosevelt on the ceiling, but there was no comment. Another tried a sign lettered "John's Spot." Others followed. There was no sign of recognition. One day, however, following a vitriolic attack on religious superstitions, a picture of an angel appeared, and Dewey is said on that day to have recounted the entire series of jokes, making a philosophical point of each.

"The problems with which a philosophy relevant to the present must deal are those growing out of changes."

During the historic quarter of a century that he taught at Columbia, Dewey influenced changes as much as he mirrored them. He was a consistent relativist. He opposed the idea of fixed value systems in any human area. He joyously attacked everything fixed and sacred in both education and religion. He urged "the expansion of critical inquiry to all problematical situations." He was happiest when he saw ideas in action. He was eager for the demonstration of possibilities. For him truth was a series of dynamic processes by means of which the purposes of human life could be achieved. The tone of his dynamic and pragmatic attitude was perfectly suited to America, and the tonic of his freshness and freedom swept through American philosophy and education. In 1919 he was invited to lecture at the Imperial University of Tokyo. Later he taught for two years at the University of Peking. The Turkish government requested him to reorganize its school system. At eighty years of age he headed a commission to investigate the Stalinist "purge" of 1936-1938, interviewing Trotsky in Mexico and rendering a verdict against Stalin. Simultaneously with the release of the thousand-page report of the inquiry of the commission, he published his own philosophical interpretation of method: *Logic, The Theory of Inquiry*. During the Second World War, he and his second wife adopted two war-refugee children from Europe. At a party on his ninetieth birth-

53276

day he made the most vigorous speech of the evening. The same day the New York *Times* said that he was regarded by his disciples as "the nation's most characteristic intellectual expression, notably in its emphasis on practical reasons for ordered change."

Roots of Experimental Principles

"... A new name for an old way of thinking."

When William James introduced the word "pragmatism" in a lecture at the University of California in 1898, he referred back twenty years to the use of it by Charles Sanders Peirce, and three centuries to the thought of Francis Bacon. He said that "the term applies itself conveniently to a number of tendencies that hitherto have lacked a collective name." When Dewey was a student at Johns Hopkins, Peirce was one of his teachers, and when he lectured in Tokyo, he referred to William James. The tendencies had been about since ancient times, but it remained for John Dewey to put them together for the first time and shape them into a comprehensive system of thought viewing all philosophy as a way of applying the scientific method to solving problems and influencing individual and social behavior. A distinctively American and twentieth-century phenomenon had occurred.

William James, 1842-1910

William James was a teacher, that rare combination of original thinker, persuasive interpreter, and irrepressible popularizer. He is remembered for describing God as "unthinkable, unknowaboutable, nohowaboutable," and as "surely no gentleman." He spoke of "moral flabbiness" and of success as a "bitch goddess." He summed up the impact of experimentalism in daily thought by describing a hypothesis as "a candidate for anybody's opinion." There is "one primal material" which he called "stuff"; consciousness is "the name of a nonentity"; but "pure experience" is stuff, "the immediate flux of life which furnishes the

"Truth happens to an idea."

William James, *Pragmatism* (New York: Longman's Green, 1907); *see also* a paperback edition of selections (Chicago: Henry Regnery, 1955).

material to our later reflection." An "option" exists when two or more hypotheses seem attractive; "experience" forces a choice, "willy-nilly," and when one cannot be made scientifically, "our passional nature must decide." Thus truth "happens," and there can be no true idea which does not make itself felt in a concrete result: "There can *be* no difference anywhere that doesn't *make* a difference somewhere."

No matter how he is quoted, William James comes out part empirical psychologist and part intuitional philosopher, and the latter almost always wins.

He traveled widely as a boy, attending schools in New York, London, Bologne, Geneva. He studied painting furiously in Paris as a teenager. His formal study was of medicine. He taught only at Harvard, but he moved through three departments: from physiology to psychology to philosophy. He was very Protestant, democratic, and human, and it was in regard to religion that his principles really came home. Early in the 1870s, he experienced deep depression. His health was frail, philosophical doubts plagued him, he considered suicide. Later he said that the memory of comforting scripture texts kept him from insanity. But the solution came in the realization that in suicide he had the option of doing something specific about his condition. Thus, even in his depression he had freedom of will. The only way to test the idea of freedom, however, was to put it to work in life. The story is that his father came home to find him pacing the floor, saying jubilantly, "It's the difference between life and death!" William James had discovered that the idea of free will was true because it had saved him. Experience had laid the groundwork for the principle that ideas are true insofar as they help us get into satisfactory relation with other parts of our expereince. "An idea," he said, "is made true by events."

"An idea is true so long as it is profitable in our lives."

". . . looking
forward
into
facts"

For William James the discovery constituted a change of direction. For the most part, philosophy had been interested in the past and present and in discovering ideas that would always be the same. Freedom of the will, appeals, however, only as a relief from a past and present in which things are not as we would like them to be: if everything were satisfactory, what reason would I have for wanting to be free? Free will is the hope to make things better; ideas are put to work for the purpose of realizing higher values. James called this "the growing edge" of experience. The really vital questions are "What is this world going to be?" and "What is life eventually to make of itself?"

In this way, theories become instruments for change, not answers to enigmas. "The true is the expedient in our way of thinking," said James and added, "in the long run and on the whole, of course."

Belief in God becomes meaningful in precisely the same way, that is, as "the idea of God" is "projected" into the thick of experience where it can make a difference in actual living and display its "stuff" by its "consequences." It is the business of philosophy to find out what differences it makes to you or me if this or that world-formula is true, and it is the business of religion to find out what difference it actually makes if this or that idea of God is true. "We cannot reject any hypothesis if consequences useful to life flow from it," James wrote. "If the hypothesis of God works satisfactorily in the widest sense of the word, it is true." James sets out to show, in his monumental book *The Varieties of Religious Experience*, that the hypothesis of God does work. He examines conversion experiences

"Higher
powers
exist."

William James, *The Varieties of Religious Experience* (New York: Longmans, Green, 1902) and many subsequent editions, some paperback.

and concludes that "conversion is the process, gradual or sudden, by which a self hitherto divided, and consciously wrong, becomes unified and consciously right, superior and happy." He examines beliefs and lives and concludes, "We may well believe, on the proofs that religious experience affords, that higher powers exist and are at work to save the world in ideal lines similar to our own."

Charles S. Peirce, 1839-1914

Recognition of the importance of the man who coined the name "pragmatism" for an experimental epistemology has been slow in developing. During his own lifetime he could get only one of his books published. He wanted to be a professional philosopher, but for thirty years he worked for the United States Coast and Geodetic Survey. Indeed, he held but one professorship and that but briefly, but it happened to be at Johns Hopkins while John Dewey was a graduate student there, though it seems that Dewey did not find him interesting. Now his papers have reached over six published volumes, and one biographer has called him "one of the greatest philosophers America has thus far produced."

His training began while he was young, and it was rigorous. His interests inclined him to the study of knowledge and logic. His father was a Harvard professor of mathematics, and under his direction as a boy he read Kant for two hours a day for three years. But Kant left him with no content or essence of an idea because for Kant the thing-in-itself was unknowable. For two years,

"Truth is meaning in practice."

Philip P. Wiener and Frederic H. Young, eds., *Studies in the Philosophy of Charles Sanders Peirce* (Cambridge: Harvard University Press, 1952).

1872-1874, he and William James were the leading lights
of the Metaphysical Club which met in Cambridge, and
together they hammered out their principles. Later Peirce
added James's name to his own, becoming Charles S.
Santiago (St. James) Peirce. Their thinking is similar,
especially when contrasted to the abstractness of the
philosophy of the time. Peirce is concerned with the

*"The
essence
of an idea
is identical
with its
consequences."*

"upshot" of ideas "in the event of someone actually taking
a decision how to act." Indeed, he proposes that "our
conception of these effects is the whole of our conception
of an object." Ideas can only be known, as a matter of
fact, when they are put into relationship with actual
things: "To determine the meaning of any idea, put it
into practice in the objective world of actualities, and
whatever its consequences prove to be, these constitute
the meaning of an idea." We cannot know directly anything about such an elusive quasi reality as "essence," but
it may be said that the consequences of an idea are
identical with its essence, and thus practically and indirectly we may know what we need to know about
philosophical essences. Practical meaning may be determined by habit and result, but truth is a more rigorous
word and is determined by careful experiment: it is "the
opinion which is fated to be ultimately agreed to by all who
investigate." Truth is, therefore, indeterminate in the
present moment.

Auguste Comte, 1798-1857

Comte was an unhappy man. He alienated peers, teachers,
benefactors and a wife. His philosophy was nonpersonal,
nonspiritual and nonmetaphysical; he was one of the first

Charles S. Peirce, "The Fixation of Belief" (November, 1877),
and "How to Make Our Ideas Clear," *The Popular Science
Monthly* (January, 1878).

to propose that all life and thought be built on objective scientific method.

Mathematics, he assumed, is the basis of all trustworthy thought. There are other kinds, of course, which must be passed through and left behind. One is theological, which believes in supernatural powers and regards them as the foundation of all existence. A second is metaphysical, which believes in substances and powers, but does not regard them as supernatural. Positive thought, however, is based on the laws revealed by the exact sciences and regards them as constituting the final and ultimate structure of things.

". . . progress"

With mathematics as the basic discipline, Comte arranged the sciences in the order of necessity: inorganic sciences, astronomy, physics, chemistry, biology, and sociology. He made no place at all for psychology, incidentally, because it was too "metaphysical." While sociology is the most important, it depends upon all the others, becoming, thus, a matter of straightforward action-and-reaction. The summit of intellectual insight is the discovery that man can cope with society by discovering the laws of society and working in harmony with them.

". . . Positivism"

Sociology is a positive religion—replacing theological and metaphysical religions—of humanity and altruism on a scientific and experimental basis. Comte felt that it would be possible to rebuild society with a genuine science as the base: "to generalize our scientific concepts and to systematize the art of social life." Thomas Huxley once called the idea "Catholicism minus Christianity." It had much in common with Dewey's faith in man's capacity to solve social problems by application of scientific method to all problems.

"Sociology is the queen of the sciences."

Auguste Comte, *Positive Philosophy* (New York: Calvin Blanchard, 1855).

"His acute sense that science means invasion of the unknown, rather than repetition in logical form of the already known," said John Dewey of Bacon in Tokyo, "makes him the father of induction." He also called him "the great forerunner of the spirit of modern life." Francis Bacon was a career politician, entering Parliament at twenty-three and becoming Lord Chancellor; he was banished from public life for taking bribes. He was a scholar, producing brilliant essays on science, education, and utopia; he was suspected of having written Shakespeare's plays. He died of pneumonia contracted while experimenting with refrigeration alongside the road by stuffing full of snow a chicken his carriage had killed. For his restlessness and brilliance he may be said to illustrate the spirit of renaissance life. He appealed to Dewey because he knew that knowledge is "the power to effect all things possible" and that knowledge comes by experiment.

Bacon's explicit aim in writing the *Novum Organum* was to work a revolution in human knowledge. He regarded the beliefs of men as too much the invention of their own minds. The great body of learning inherited from the Middle Ages he called "pseudo-knowledge," "pretentious knowledge," because it did not "give power." It tended to be either "delicate" (attempting to be decorative but not actually effective), "fantastic" (attempting to gain control of natural forces but by magical and deceptive means) or "contentious" (attempting to gain control over other men's minds by clever hairsplitting and scholastic disputation). All this "not knowledge" had little if any relation to actual facts and had resulted from the "bad knowledge habits" of spinning learning out of one's own insides, like a spider: he called them "tribal thinking" (imposing on nature the inherited judgments of one's group), "cave thinking" (imposing individual judgments on the outside world), "marketplace thinking" (imposing a deceptive exactness of words on another man's meaning), "theater thinking" (imposing an unreal system of thought on reality), and "school thinking" (imposing blind authority on children's minds). All these produce "cobwebs of learning," admirable for the fineness of thread and work but of no substance or profit.

Bacon simply and sweepingly proposed to replace all these deductive systems of logic with inductive thinking. We should seek knowledge, not because it will preserve what men have learned but because it will seek new truth, not because it will give some men power over others but because it will give men power over their natural environment. The only way to achieve this kind of knowledge is to see and deal with things as they are. Rather than like the spinning spiders, we ought to work like the ants, collecting all kinds of things for their use, and like the bees, both collecting and arranging. It is true that Bacon's method of induction was elementary: if he wished to discover the nature of heat, which he rightly assumed to consist of rapid and irregular motions of the small parts of bodies, he would make a list of hot bodies, another of cold bodies, and one of the bodies of varying degrees, hoping that these lists would show some characteristic always present in hot bodies and always absent in cold bodies, and thereby arrive at some general conclusions concerning the nature of heat. This is, of course, simply induction by enumeration, but it is the beginning of the modern scientific method as contrasted to the medieval philosophical methods of seeking truth and was used most brilliantly by Charles Darwin.

Francis Bacon, *Novum Organum* and *The Advancement of Learning* (available in World Classics and other paperback editions).

"Knowledge
is
power."

In his own description of utopia Bacon suggested that power over nature is collective. An English ship, making one of those Elizabethan voyages of high daring on the open seas, comes upon an island nation in the South Pacific whose chief institution is a great establishment devoted to scientific research. The ruler takes the travelers through this island paradise, saying "The end of our foundation is the knowledge of causes, and secret motions of things; and the enlarging of the bounds of human empire, to the effecting of all things possible." The nation maintained a spy system throughout the world for the purpose of gathering scientific information, which was pooled at home where scientific work was carried forward as one united social plan. The "Empire of Man over Man" had at last been replaced by the "Empire of Man over Nature."

Protagoras, 480-410 B.C.

Bacon despised the Platonic and Aristotelian ways of thought that had so much dominated medieval thinking. The famed Greeks "assuredly have that which is characteristic of boys," he wrote. "They are prompt to prattle but cannot generate; their wisdom abounds in words but is barren in works." It was the same sort of impatience with formal Greek thinking that led to the modern rediscovery of the Sophists. They were a sort of third force in classical Greek philosophy, suspected of many deviations by established members of the Athenian Academy because they free-lanced for pay among commoners. This was enough to endear them to Dewey, who said that their chief value was their "disconcerting effect

Francis Bacon, *The New Atlantis* (available in World Classics and other reprint editions).

upon the traditional system of religious beliefs," and credited them with originating "philosophy proper."

Protagoras of Abdera is one of the best known of these ancient mavericks. There is a story that he taught a young man on the terms that he should be paid his fee only if the pupil won his first law-suit, and that the pupil's first suit was one brought against him by Protagoras for failure to pay his fee. The story that he was convicted of impiety in Athens may or may not be true, but he did write a book which began, "With respect to the gods, I cannot feel sure either that they are or are not, nor what they are like in figure." The difficulty lay both in "the obscurity of the subject," he said, and in "the shortness of human life." Man, he suggested, is thus the judge of the reality of the gods.

"Man is the measure of all things."

All one can know, argued Protagoras, is what he himself can verify through his own experience, for example, when a man has jaundice everything looks yellow. This is the basis for a thorough relativism, for there is no sense in telling him that things really are not yellow but rather the color they appear to be to a healthy man. While it can be said that one opinion is better than another, it cannot be therefore said to be truer: we can only say that since health is better than sickness, the opinion of a healthy man is better than that of the man with jaundice.

"Knowledge is sense perception."

Heraclitus, ca. 540-470 B.C.

Most of what is known about Heraclitus is contained in what Plato and Aristotle said about him in the effort to refute him. From their accounts, he was not an amiable character: he said that his own city would be better off if left to "beardless lads"; he suggested that Homer ought to have been "turned out of the lists and whipped"; he at-

tacked all his colleagues but one who said that "most men
are bad."

He was a mystic who apparently believed that change
was the basic characteristic of the world. Consequently he
regarded fire as the model of existence, because a flame is
born by the death of something else, and would make
propositions that seemed obscure: "Mortals are immortals,
and immortals are mortals, the one living the other's
death and dying the other's life." The world is composed
of endless sets of opposites and all apparent forms in the
world are but stages in the continual change of one into
the other—day and night, winter and summer, water and
earth, moist and dry, cold and warm, waking and sleeping,
young and old, living and dead, satiety and hunger, war
and peace. "This world," he summarized, "is an everlasting fire, with measures kindling and measures going
out." God is also contained in all these dialectical forms,
for "all things come out of the one, and the one out of
all things." God assumes various forms, "just as fire, when
it is mingled with different kinds of incense, is named
according to the savor of each."

Man's life has always seemed fleeting and elusive, like
time itself. For most men in most ages, this awareness has
created a need to find something permanent and abiding,
and for the most part philosophy, education, and religion
have been built on the search for it. There have always
been those, however, who found meaning in the change-
ableness itself and sought to understand and utilize it.
They have tended to concentrate on method rather than
results. In the modern world, Experimentalism in science,
philosophy, religion and education has furnished a method
of coping with a world in which change seems more
universal and rapid than it once did and the permanent
verities of philosophy and religion less relevant.

The Experimental Nature of Pragmatism

Traditionally, philosophy begins with the ontological question: What is meant by the verb "to be"? If the answer is that "being" consists of the embodiment here and now of some preexistent form or idea, the philosophy that results will be "idealistic." If the answer is that "being" consists really of the things and events that are here and now what they appear to be, the philosophy that results will be "realistic." The entire history of Western philosophy, back to Plato and Aristotle, who answered the ontological question differently, may be said to be the story of the competition between Idealism and Realism.

Pragmatism, however, begins with the epistemological question: What is meant by the verb "to know"? From a theory of knowledge, Pragmatism builds a complete philosophy, but by the time it gets around to dealing formally with the ontological question, it does not seem to be very important. By beginning with a different question, philosophy is given an entirely new feeling.

Perhaps the great change had come between Hegel and Darwin in the nineteenth century, but they both contributed to Pragmatism: beginning with ontological assumptions concerning the absolute "being" of substance and thought, Hegel had made the contradiction between them the source of his entire method of philosophy; beginning by observing and cataloging biological development, Darwin had come to the conclusion that the struggle for survival between different forms of life produced the basic characteristics of "being"; beginning with the processes of experimental thinking, Dewey came to the conclusion that "being" occurs in a condition of suspenceful uncertainty.

John Dewey's claim was that he turned from "the problems of philosophers" to "the problems of men." It was a shift from ontology and metaphysics to epistemology and ethics, or, less technically, from theoretical to practical issues. Philosophy was, for Dewey, a way of dealing with the problems of living. Man's own experience, as it occurs day by day, thus was for Dewey the "stuff" and the "sole object" for philosophical study. The purpose of philosophy was to guide man's day-by-day experience "to more satisfactory levels." And the first and most obvious thing to be noted about actual experiencing is that it is constantly changing, producing new experiences, new problems, new thinking. Indeed, it might be said that man probably would not think at all were there not some sort of difficulty. As problems are solved, a man comes to some awareness of what it means "to be." "Being" is thus understood as the continuous result of constantly solving new problems.

"Thinking begins in dilemma."

Mind and Knowledge

"Mind is built in the process of experiencing."

For centuries philosophers had been talking as if the mind were some transcendental faculty or inherited structure. It had seemed to them to have little connection with the rest of the body and its sensations. Dewey, however, began with man's universal experience and concluded that mind and intelligence have evolved in a purely natural way.

In daily life, knowledge is the result of activity, that is to say, the original activity undergoes a change because of the results which follow it. Dewey's favorite illustrations

John Dewey, *Reconstruction in Philosophy* (New York: Henry Holt, 1920).
John Dewey, *How We Think* (Boston: D. C. Heath, 1933).

were simple: a child thrusts his hand toward a flame, a sharp pain follows, repetition of the act is inhibited, the next time the child sees a flame he knows the results of the experience. An experience may be described as the whole flowing sequence of action, sensation, perception, modification of action. Knowledge may be described as the modification of action. Mind may be described as a way of solving problems.

It is in this same way that mind has come to us out of the distant past experience of the developing human race. It has evolved because of the activity of human organisms in meeting the varied practical and social situations of life. Human beings discovered that perceiving objects, remembering them, and reasoning about them greatly increased their power to control them. The exercise of mental powers in connection with the ordinary activities of daily existence brought results which could not have otherwise been enjoyed. Mind is thus an effective tool or instrument. By use of it man has raised himself above the other animals. A being of lower intelligence was not able to resist the fascination of the flame or to deal productively with new situations. *"Mind is a process of growth."*

Knowledge is thus the by-product of action. Action is spontaneous and primordial, and as a consequence of taking actions knowledge arose. Thus knowledge is not something apart from experience, as bits and snatches of data to be itemized and handled as if possessing an independent existence of their own. Ideas are modes or activities of the problem-solving process, and they are developed in order to assist man in dealing with the objects of his environment so as to avoid pain or to secure satisfaction. *"Mind is not a content."*

Knowledge is therefore purely utilitarian, resulting from the struggle for survival. The dominant attitudes in that struggle were devoted to securing shelter, food, and clothing. These activities exerted by our ancestors have *"Mind is not inherited."*

resulted in powerful tendencies which emerge in us today as impulses and interests. Dewey hesitated to use the word "instincts," for he regarded these tendencies only as general urges that respond to the stimulation that comes from the environment. The most continuous form of knowledge comes from human interaction. This exchange not only prevents simple dissipation of knowledge but supplies the framework in which knowledge may be communicated and tested. Therefore, education becomes one of the characteristic human functions and is requisite to the further development of experience.

Inquiry

When René Descartes in the seventeenth century wrote the sentence, *Cogito ergo sum,* "I think, therefore I am," he both summarized ancient Greek thought and established the basis for modern rationalistic philosophy. Dewey proposed an antecedent formula, "I experience, therefore I think."

"Thinking is an inventive process."

Thinking does not just happen or result from pure contemplation as some of the Greeks had thought. Nor does it come from amassing sensations and assorting them into categories, as Bacon had suggested. There must be something to cause thinking, some change in circumstances which causes habitual reactions to be inappropriate. In short, man thinks when he is challenged. Thinking, therefore, takes place when a problem arises.

"A question to be answered, an ambiguity to be resolved," said Dewey, "sets up an end and holds the current of ideas to a definite channel." When a problem presents itself to experience, one begins to analyze the situation to discover what adjustments must be made. Soon or perhaps even immediately some suggestions will occur for solving the problem. Thereupon one actually tries out the most likely of these hypothetical solutions until something works. When it does, activity moves ahead again serenely until some new difficulty arises. Meanwhile, experience has been enriched.

Thinking is thus a universal and continuous process of experimentation. When highly refined, Dewey isolated five logically distinct steps which became the basis for what he called the logic of inquiry.

"Inquiry is the essence of logic."

First, there is the indeterminate situation, which is always problematical. Activity, as it flows in experience, is always more or less disturbed, troubled, ambiguous, confused, characterized by conflicting tendencies. In the optimal circumstance, these conditions are not sufficient to cause panic, but do set up dissatisfaction with things as they are going. There is a "felt need," a consciousness of a difficulty.

. . . problem

Next comes the brooding of the mind over the total situation, until by an analysis of its various elements, the mind locates what seems to be the heart of the difficulty. The problem, in short, is defined. In the well-formulated problem, of course, the pattern of the solution is already taking shape.

. . . analysis

Dewey calls the next step "the determination of the problem-solution." Ideas for possible solutions come out of the situation itself and thus are relevant to the entire experiential situation. Formally he calls them "indigenous ideational-existent emergents."

. . . hypothesis

Significantly, Dewey terms the actual application of hypothetical solutions the reasoning process. Traditional philosophers would have applied the word "reason" to the analytical or hypothetical steps of the process. Of course, as Dewey warns, problem-solutions are not blindly applied and some choice is exerted, but it is in the

. . . experiment

John Dewey, *Logic, The Theory of Inquiry* (New York: Holt, 1938).

submission of the probable solution to action that reason reaches its supreme moment. This is, indeed, "Experimentalism."

. . . solution

Further observation and experimentation lead to the acceptance or rejection of the hypothetical solution. At last the problem is solved, in action, and experience resumes its flow toward the next problem.

Dewey says that this is the course that all healthy minds pursue in the practical affairs as well as the theoretical issues of life. It is, of course, the scientific method applied to thinking. Highly refined, this process determines logic itself. As Dewey said, common sense and scientific inquiry are really the same thing, and the difference is of subject matter not of logic. Dewey provides his own definition: "Inquiry is the controlled or directed transformation of an indeterminate situation into one that is so determinate in its constituent distinctions and relations as to convert the elements of the original situation into a unified whole." And so that one cannot miss the negative implication concerning abstractions, he adds, "inquiry is concerned with objective transformations of objective subject matter."

Truth

"The hypothesis that works is the true one."

Facts and meanings, Dewey insisted, have "an operational character." By operational he meant overt and observable, and he meant to say that facts have meaning only as they have effect in some actual circumstances. Facts do not have abstract existence, but exist only as they "work" in actual experience, altering the flow of events in individual and social activities. In placing comparative value upon working facts, one says that "truth is the insight that solves problems." In short, truth is "what works," and there is no way of knowing in advance of actual experimentation what the problem-solving insight may be. Thus "warranted assertability" is dependent upon "effects." "Truth," says Dewey, "is an abstract noun applied to the collection of cases, forseen and desired, that receive confirmation in their works and consequences."

In this view, action is essential but always perilous. Judgment and belief can only be regarded as actions to be performed and tested, never as rigid guides developed in the past and applicable to new situations. The most they can achieve is a precarious probability. Logic may reduce the possibilities of future error, but the uncertainty of actual experimentation cannot be evaded by the substitution of abstract thinking. Truth is always a futurity and a challenge to be acted, and the quest for solutions is the only certainty there can be.

"The scientific method is my guide, it leadeth me into changing experiences."

Pragmatism in Education

For John Dewey, the school is the indispensable laboratory for both philosophy and society, and in the school the theoretical concerns of philosophy and the practical needs of society meet in a radically experimental way. It is there that both individual and social problems are solved. "Education," said Dewey, "is efficiency in solving problems in a social context." It is the testing ground for new ideas, an experience in individual growth, a process by which civilization is preserved, a means for the orderly development of society. Philosophy is nothing more than "the general theory of education." Individual growth is the human characteristic, and education is the most significant of all the activities of society. "Growth is intelligence," Dewey summarized; "intelligence is freedom, freedom is education, education is growth."

John Dewey, *Education and Democracy* (New York: Macmillan. 1916).

Dewey's educational philosophy is a direct application of his theory of knowledge. He defines education is "the process of the reconstruction or reconstitution of experience, giving it a more socialized value through the medium of increased individual efficiency." The definition is repeated throughout his published work. It is a specific repudiation of the older definitions which spoke of "drawing out" what was innate in the child, or of "pouring into" the child what he did not yet know. Dewey's definition refers to the changes in activities required by constantly changing experiences and new situations. There are always problems to be solved, choices to be made, readjustments to be achieved. These changes bring about an increasing diversification and enrichment of experience: experience is revised, reorganized, reconstructed. This growing, changing, and revising of experience is the heart of education. It is a process because it is continuous. It is social because it can take place best only in interaction with others.

The implications of Dewey's definition were far-reaching. It suggested that "the meaning of education was within the process itself." A pupil was no longer to learn Latin because the discipline and system sharpened the wits for some other activity. It also challenged the formal notion that education begins when the child enters school and stops when he withdraws. Dewey's concept suggested that education begins when the child is born and proceeds throughout life. It will even take place outside a schoolroom. It challenged the classic idea that education was a preparation for life. Education, indeed, is defined by Dewey as living at its fullest, and the schoolroom

John Dewey, *Experience and Education* (New York: Macmillan, 1939).

PRAGMATISM IN EDUCATIONAL PHILOSOPHY

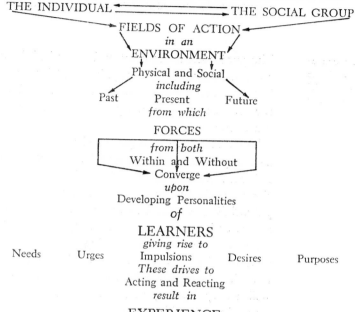

THE INDIVIDUAL —————— THE SOCIAL GROUP

FIELDS OF ACTION

in an

ENVIRONMENT

Physical and Social

including

Past   Present   Future

from which

FORCES

from both

Within and Without

Converge

upon

Developing Personalities

of

LEARNERS

giving rise to

Needs   Urges   Impulsions   Desires   Purposes

These drives to

Acting and Reacting

result in

EXPERIENCE

a process of, "being, undergoing, and doing"

LEARNING THROUGH ACTUAL LIVING

poses the

EDUCATIONAL PROBLEM

of providing for

Continuous Reconstruction of Experience

on

progressively higher levels

This may be solved by

FORMULATION OF PURPOSES—ORGANIZATION OF MEANS AND RESOURCES

plus

CONSISTENT MOVEMENT IN DIRECTION DESIRED

Which, in American Education

is

DEVELOPING CITIZENS EQUAL TO RESPONSIBILITY
OF CONTRIBUTING EFFECTIVELY

to the

PROGRESSIVE REALIZATION OF DEMOCRATIC IDEALS

experience ought to be as much like life as possible. It is even possible that education might be enjoyable.

. . . a center of experience in a social context

The pupil's life is the heart and ground of the educational process. Learning is the pupil's idea. The initiative comes from the needs and powers of the child rather than from the teacher. It is necessary, therefore, to understand the life of the pupil.

The classroom is not peopled by resistant lumpy things naturally averse to learning and therefore to be tricked or bullied. Pupils are rather living beings, reaching out tentacles of individuality to procure the materials that their potentialities demand in order that they may come into action and find satisfaction. They are distinct centers of experience in an all-embracing flow of biological and sociological and historical currents. Their biology demands that they be active, learning by touch and movement as well as by hearing and looking. Their wriggling and squirming is evidence of potential receptivity, not of disobedience. They are in the process of development from animal to person, needful of communication and therefore of language and information. They are ready to gather in clusters of meanings to assist in their individuation and to relate their selfhood to other dveloping selves in a group.

The Objective

. . . an added capacity for growth

It has been customary for educators to set up aims, both ultimate and proximate, for the process of education. Dewey does not. "It is nonsense," he said, "to talk about the aim of education." The child lives in the present. He

John Dewey, *My Pedagogic Creed* (New York: E. L. Kellogg, 1897).

knows nothing about the faraway future when he will become a man. It is absurd to require him to do things today for the sake of a tomorrow in which he has no interest. The child acts only in the living present, readjusting experience as he goes along. So Dewey speaks of the "episodic character" of experience: learning situations are always problem-solving episodes in the continuing movement of experiencing, and effectiveness in dealing with ever-changing experience is the only residue a person carries from one experience to another. Because experiences are always so new that they cannot be typed and solutions carried over, the pupil learns neither a content nor a conditioned response, but practice in coping with indeterminacies. Whether in infancy, youth, or adulthood, what is really learned at any and every stage constitutes the value of the experience. The objective of education is, therefore, to be found within the process itself. Education proceeds by constantly remaking or reconstituting experience, and it is precisely this reconstitution that constitutes its value and accomplishes its aim. Dewey said that the objective of education was "to give a learner experience in effective experiencing." His critics alleged that he meant only that "the general objective of education is more education." Permitted his own definition of education, which those critics usually did not, Dewey would, of course, have agreed.

The Process

Learning follows the same pattern as effective thinking, according to Dewey. It never begins from a static lag line, but always in movement. The educational process begins in experience going on, and opens with the discovery of a problem to be solved. If pupils are not aware of a problem, they will be encouraged to study the situa-

. . . a process of living

tion until they discover one that is of interest to them. Then they will examine the problem, recognize relations within the situation, discover similarities and differences with other experiences, uncover and discuss relevant data, formulate hypotheses, and test them in action. The continuous enrichment of experience by readjusting to the complexities of the environment constitutes both life and the educational process.

The process of education begins in the life of the child. "The primary root of all educational activity is in the instinctive, impulsive attitudes and activities of the child," wrote Dewey, "and not in the presentation and application of external material." Dewey suggests four basic childhood activities: conversation, finding out things, making things, artistic expression. The language activity, Dewey calls "perhaps the greatest of all educational resources." But all four relate to the fundamental racial activities, such as getting food, securing shelter, making clothing. Education seeks only to "know what these activities mean," in terms of "their social equivalents": "what they are capable of in the way of social service," as the "inheritance of previous race activities," and "what their outcome or end may be."

To these individual life activities, education adds the social experience. Existing life is too complex for the small child, so the school is, at first, "a simplified social life," reduced to "embryonic form." The first school experience is simply an enlargement of the child's home life. The child engages in home activities because he discovers that they have a social meaning outside the home. Little by

"The root of all educational activity is in the activities of the child."

"Individual mind is a function of social life."

John Dewey, *The School and Society* (University of Chicago Press, 1915). The three basic lectures were first published in 1900, a year after their delivery to workers and friends of the Experimental School.

little, the capabilities of intelligence are developed as the child enters into relations with other children his own age and with adults other than his own parents. "The primary business of the school," said Dewey, "is to train children in cooperative and mutually helpful living." The educational process becomes gradually an intensified process of social living, concentrating in the school all those experiences which will assist the child in sharing in the inherited resources of the race, and to use his own powers for social ends.

The Method

"The first approach to any subject in school," Dewey wrote, "should be as unscholastic as possible." Methods of unscholastic approaches were one of Dewey's primary concerns as an educator. Experience, after all, is unscholastic, and the search for teaching method is the search for meaningful experience. Dewey believed that careful investigation of methods which are permanently successful in formal education revealed that they depended for their efficiency on the fact that they go back to the kind of situations that cause reflection out of school. Learning results from naturally induced reflection —actual problem-solving. Further, experiential learning comes as a by-product of action, not as a thing aimed at for its own sake. The Egyptians learned arithmetic and surveying from their need to reset the boundaries of farms after the annual inundation of the Nile. The Phoenicians learned to write because of the necessity for keeping their commercial accounts and contracts accurately over long periods of time. Necessity is not only the mother of invention, but of learning as well.

Educational method, for Dewey, was not a matter of discovering how best to make a child learn a specific content matter chosen in advance by someone else, but

"Methods give the child something to do not something to learn."

rather a matter of discovering how to stimulate the child so that he would best exercise his potentialities for problem-solving. It is interested in discovering the child's own problems. It concerns itself with methods of attack rather than the communication of specific solutions. "That our children shall think rather than what they shall think must be our first concern" was the slogan. The teacher thus is a pilot rather than a commander, and it becomes one of his responsibilities to assist the pupils in taking over their own steering.

The Curriculum

"The center of correlation of subjects is the child's own activities."

It does not come as a surprise to discover that Dewey had little sympathy with traditional curriculum structures. The mind of the child, he felt, does not make divisions of experience into subjects and branches. These are forced on the child by the adult mind. For the child, the correlating center is his own living, the problems confronting him. Thus the school should not begin with the classic three Rs, but with the activities of the child which reflect the great racial functions: housing or carpentry, clothing or sewing, food or cooking. These activities, which Dewey called "direct," will in their own time demand the "derived" activities—speech, writing, reading, drawing, molding, modeling. In the first six grades, Dewey emphasized the occupations: numbers, music, art, shop, cooking, sewing, reading, history, and gardening. But none of these things was taught as a formal subject. The food interest led to cooking, baking, studying sources of food supply, health and nutrition, and so on. The clothing interest furnished opportunities beyond hand work for the study of fabrics, their origin and manufacture. From these basic

John Dewey, *The Child and the Curriculum* (University of Chicago Press, 1902).

activities, the pupils went on naturally into agriculture, transportation, industry, distribution, buying and selling. They were led back into history to find the origins of all these activities in primitive life and their development through succeeding cultures. Incidentally—which is the only way anything is really learned—in the course of these activities the children acquired the facts of arithmetic, geography, history, botany, chemistry, language, and other formal subjects.

Dewey called this an "occupational" curriculum. The school should furnish the child with "sufficiently large amounts of personal activity in occupations, expression, conversation, construction and experimentation," so that his individuality would be challenged. The experiences of others, which is all that text books can contain, will only swamp him. But if he is encouraged to experiment sufficiently with his own present needs and aims, he will naturally resort to "the traditional social tools." Thus language will be learned as "the organic outgrowth of the child's experience." History will be learned as the activity of the child "reproduces or runs parallel to some form of work carried on in social life," and it becomes, not a matter of dates and names, but "the recapitulation of past important activities of the race." A detailed observation and discovery of nature—an ant hill as a home or factory—will lead him from the known to the unknown. This vision of children and teachers at work together, developing the curriculum as their mutual experiences led them, Dewey once called the "Kingdom of Heaven in Education": "If we seek it, educationally all other things shall be added to us: i.e., if we identify ourselves with the real instincts and needs of childhood, and ask for its fullest assertion and growth, the discipline and information and culture of adult life shall come in their due season."

. . . not algebra, bookkeeping, rhetoric, and spelling, but a play city, a study of wool, tree people, and caring for a flock of chickens

If the cycles of learning were to have the same freedom and flow as experience, the schoolroom itself would need to be flexible and functional. Desks and stationary furniture are no longer appropriate, for there must be open space for movement and activity. The building should give easy access to the out-of-doors. There would need to be things for working with, and the equipment not only for cooking but also for designing and building. Indeed, the pupils should have a hand in producing their own school world. Books are available for research and free reading. The school would provide "a child's world in a child's size environment."

To many, it would not seem to be a school at all. Dewey's disciples enthusiastically drew the contrast. The "listening school" is a place where the chief weapons of education are chalk-talk on a dismal blackboard, a few intensely dull required texts, and a teacher's tired voice in continual strident pursuit of elusive young attention. Here children are "sent" and school "keeps" until four o'clock. In contrast, they picture the children of a "new school," busy and hard-working youngsters who seem to play all day, who do not seem to have lessons and recitations, yet who do not wait for teachers to make assignments. They dance, they sing, they play house and build villages, they keep store and take care of pets, they read and write and make up stories and dramatize them, they work in the garden, they churn and weave and cook: they live in "a democracy of youth."

"Life," Dewey wrote once and said many times, "is the great thing after all." And the school, he believed, was the place where it could be best enriched by being freed:

Harold Rugg and Ann Shumaker, *The Child Centered School* (New York: World Book Company, 1928).

"the growth of the imagination in flexibility, in scope, and in sympathy, till the life which the individual lives is informed with the life of nature and of society."

Pragmatism and Religion

When discussions came around to the subject of formal religion, John Dewey could be counted upon to be on the negative side. It was generally understood at Columbia in the twenties that Dewey's thought represented an alternative to traditional theologies. It was taken for granted among Dewey's students that religion was no more than an interesting survival of an earlier period in mental evolution, a touching expression of the native longings and poetic imagination of primitive man, which through the church had induced a cultural lag in the scientific revolution by emphasizing sin, the soul, and absolutes, but would be overcome in a free society on earth of which Professor Dewey was the true prophet. As for himself, Dewey tended to be both less orthodox and less antireligious than many of his students. He regarded traditional supernaturalism as a dangerous threat to the experimental method in science and society, and hopefully noted the "decay of cohesion and influence among religiously organized bodies of the familiar historic type." But he also suggested that their decadence might be the result of their replacement by a free and open attitude toward spiritual insight and aspiration "too religious to tolerate."

Christianity

Dewey was inalterably opposed to the classic metaphysics of the Greek Golden Age and of the European Middle Ages. One of the chief characteristics of the pragmatic

". . . pretentiously unreal"

notion of reality, he insisted, was that a metaphysical world-view—indeed, an *überhaupt* of any kind—is neither possible nor needed. For Dewey, philosophy is a mode of knowing not of being, and it would be self-contradictory for an experimentalism devoted exclusively to the reality of solving problems to supply a theory of being. As far as Dewey was concerned, classic Hellenistic metaphysics and Christianity were synonymous. He was against both on four counts.

"Dualism" was one of Dewey's dirtiest words and to label a view dualistic was to condemn it. All classic philosophies have made a distinction between two realms of existence and the Christian theology adopted and sacralized it. One of these is the ordinary phenomenal world of everyday experience, the other is a special noumenal world of ideal existence. This distinction was invented by the Greek philosophers and arbitrarily rendered complete: the ideal was said to be ultimate and rational and absolute, the actual to be immediate and empirical and relative. Of the two, the ideal was said to be the more real, knowable only by special revelation or the disciplines of metaphysical philosophy. Time, movement, and change became signs of non-being somehow infecting daily life. And Dewey lumps Plato and Aristotle, Plotinus and Marcus Aurelius, Augustine and Aquinas, Spinoza and Hegel as sharing this classic Christian tradition. All forms of supernaturalism, he says, place God completely outside nature, fixing an impassable and ultimately disastrous gulf between sacred and secular, between philosophy and daily life.

Belief in a supreme being is the result of moral laziness, for, having made this dualistic distinction, man places

John Dewey, *Reconstruction in Philosophy* (New York: Henry Holt, 1920).

God over on the side of the ideal as something which he can fall back on for emotional support in times of difficulty with this everchanging, here-and-now, real world. Fear of life, inability to cope with problems, the sense of human incompetency account for man's creation of supernaturalism; he merely projected a reality that could accomplish what he in his love of ease would not attempt to do. Ideals he does not really want to live with are projected into a supernatural order for support, safekeeping, and sanction. Man would be much more moral if he were to "hoist the banner of the ideal and then march in the direction that concrete conditions suggest and reward."

In actual fact, knowledge comes only the hard way, Dewey is convinced, by scientific analysis, hypothesis, and experimentation. Religion, grounded in its dualistic distinction which supports its moral laziness, also is mentally lazy: it slothfully posits a reality and then claims to have special knowledge of it through mystical and other special experiences. When it defends these special insights it becomes intolerant of all others, calling in the forces of heaven and morality against the more strenuous but more productive methods of scientific inquiry. The doctrines and dogmas of religion must therefore be swept away. Indeed, as science gains ground, theological dualism will become less and less tenable.

And, because of the assumed dualism, supernaturalism isolates man from nature and from other men. The drama of sin and redemption as described by Christianity goes on within the lonely soul of a man, removing him from the social context that Dewey regarded as all-important. If man is directly related to the noumenal realm of the ideal and absolute, he is thereby isolated in his daily

". . . desire for irresponsibility"

. . . obstruction of science

". . . man in isolation"

John Dewey, *The Quest for Certainty* (New York: Minton, Balch, 1929).

life from the phenomenal world of change and relativity.

As far as Dewey was concerned, traditional Christianity is inescapably and fatally prescientific and antiscientific, and he knew—or admitted—of no other kind.

Nature

John Dewey's rejection of classical metaphysics does not mean that he had no metaphysics of his own so much as that it is not classical in content and is to be discovered indirectly through implications and interpretations more than in primary assertions. Method is primary, even though it is "dogged by a pack of metaphysical consequences."

". . . fidelity to the nature of things"

Dewey is not at all concerned with anything supraphysical, and his notions of "being" are drawn from nature itself. Man must learn to live and think within the bounds and according to the limits set by his natural environment. This acceptance, however, does not imply surrender to nature but rather rising to the challenge of nature. Human desires and ideals are to be revised according to the ways and means which only nature makes possible. This process of constant revision is the definition of both reason and faith. It leads to a wholeness, also of the kind which nature makes possible. But the "wholeness of things" is present not futuristic and factual not moral. Man does experience infinite and enduring relationships, but they are with men and nature and are infinite because of their vast plurality, enduring because the present is the only dimension of actual experience, obligatory only because they exist and cannot be escaped.

Dewey believed with metaphysical fervor in an open universe. He viewed "the cosmically real" of traditional

John Dewey, *Experience and Nature* (Chicago: Open Court, 1925).

philosophy as one with "the finished, the perfect or wholly done," and rejected it in favor of the anthropological concept of "the precarious." Peril makes every significant human event possible. It even brings religion into being as an effort to deny the uncertain character of the world. Science broke away from all static assumptions of universal law, inherent rationality, and natural uniformity and set man free for unlimited inquiry in "a universe with the lid off." Change is all-inclusive. Uncertainty is inevitable. Nothing is lasting. There can be no complete security: "it will crumble before the gnawing truth of time as it exceeds a certain measure." There is nothing permanent, even in the background, to provide fixed perspectives or the materials for an abstract system of ideas. The world is all foreground and movement. It is no machine, but rather organic, growing, and unfinished, with room for additions and improvements. It is incomplete and indeterminate and all existence has an "eventual character." It is like a flowing stream, full of eddies and swirls. Society is also like a river in which discernible currents occur but merge back into the flow. Individuals emerge momentarily as events in the everchanging process. Because each event has its own validity, the world is radically pluralistic, and it can neither be reduced to a single basic substance nor unified. It is a multiverse rather than a universe.

"Every existence is an event."

But the pluralism means that we are not completely at a loss, for there are many different rates of change. The very slow and the comparatively rhythmic have all the advantages for us of stability and may be interpreted meaningfully as structure. The more rapid rates of change may be understood as process. The important thing, therefore, as Dewey said, is knowledge of the comparative tempos of change.

"The important thing is relation, ratio."

Knowledge can only deal with relations, which make themselves evident, in one way or another, to the senses through changes. Matter is not solid and lumpy, as science has amply demonstrated since the seventeenth century. But there is, in every event, "something obdurate, self-sufficient, wholly immediate, neither a relation nor an element in a relational whole, but terminal and exclusive," and in every thing are some "irreducible, infinitely plural, undefinable qualities." As it turns out in actual experience, it is precisely these indefinable, terminal, and relational qualities that are most unstable and most precious to man. It is to savoring and enriching their possibilities that man should devote himself rather than to attempting to find behind them some abstract "reality." The end is not guaranteed, not even progress in discernible directions, only change; the world is indeterminate even in regard to values; but there is a moral imperative to engage in the flow of events, turning new experiences into new knowledge by the diligent application of experimental methods to objective reality.

God

When John Dewey published *A Common Faith* in the mid-thirties, a reviewer in *The Christian Century* welcomed him into the Christian faith. The "Letters to the Editor" section of the next issue contained a note from Dewey acknowledging the review but declining the welcome.

The book begins by accepting the Oxford Dictionary definition of religion as "man's recognition of a relationship to some Unseen Higher Power." By definition he then rejects religion as "inadequate" and characterizes it as "superstition." Historically, Unseen Powers have been conceived in a multitude of mutually incompatible ways, forms of worship directed to them have been incompatible, and no discernible unity exists in the moral motivations appealed to in their names. After all, if there actually were some singular Objective Unseen Higher Power, as traditional religion claims, men's concepts, worship, and morals would be the same. Religious experience therefore cannot point to a reality outside the human self.

There are, however, religious experiences which do not have a transcendent reference. Ideals are real enough in themselves, needing no theological justification, and religious experience may be defined pragmatically as any kind of experience that especially inspires imagination, evokes deep responses toward life, channels energies into fruitful directions, and focuses the ideals and purposes common to human existence. The shift in this definition is from content to result, and the result has for Dewey, as always, an experimental validity. It suggests a shift to the adjectival form of the stumble-word religion: "religious," a quality of life rather than a church or doctrine, an instrumental attitude enabling the actual achievement of ideals and goals.

Now, for Dewey, the ideal is not something that exists independently: the ideal exists only as man experiences it. However, a theoretically conceptualized ideal does perform a valid function if and when it becomes a symbol making more possible the actual achievement of a hope or desire. As man's ongoing human life thrusts into the unknown future, the ideal becomes an actual part of the life of men when the indeterminate future becomes a present actuality, providing there be a relation between the present and the ideal which makes experience flow in the direction of the ideal. This functional relationship, uniting the ideal and the actual in the experience of man, Dewey is willing to call God. It is not necessary to use that word—indeed, Dewey would a bit rather not—but

Religiousness: "*attitudes taken toward every object and every proposed end or ideal.*"

God: "*a legitimate way for the religious mind to symbolize its faith in the reality of life.*"

John Dewey, *A Common Faith* (New Haven: Yale University Press, 1934).

its use may serve to protect some men from a sense of isolation and from consequent despair or defiance which would only make impossible the desired functional relationship between the present and the future. God is thus a symbol, lacking objective reality, and functional, lacking a priori existence—both of which are demanded by traditional theologians. It is always a bridge to a further, presumably larger, good, and is to be used only "insofar as such symbolism satisfies and helps."

Man

In the Humanist Manifesto, released in 1933, Dewey announced that "the complete realization of human personality . . . in the here and now" was the goal of man's life. But there was little sentimentalism in the vision. Man is a product of nature through the long and difficult process of evolution, and is therefore now a part of nature with all its surging push and pull. He is thus neither totally depraved nor all sweetness-and-light; his goodness consists of acting purposively in meeting problems and tensions, his evil in his failure to stand up to life and face its difficulties. In fact, he does not even actively initiate changes in this world of which he is a part, but is capable only of interacting with the world in its own constant changes. However, this is enough. What man needs to do is to settle for this situation and to apply his natural intelligence to it. "The humanist," the Manifesto concluded, "finds his religious emotions expressed in a heightened sense of personal life and in a cooperative effort to promote social well-being."

Art

It is when Dewey talks about art rather than when he talks about religion that he sounds most religious. Art is the concrete proof, according to Dewey, that man uses the materials and energies of nature, in accord with his own brain, sense organs, and muscular system, to transform mere interaction with his environment into participation and communication. This transformation is an actual "intervention" by imagination and construction into the uncertainty, mystery, doubt, and half-knowledge of experience, and it turns experience upon itself to deepen and intensify its own qualities.

". . . the deep realization of intrinsic meanings"

Experience occurs continuously, because the interaction of live creature and environing conditions is involved in the very process of living. But experiences ordinarily fall short of their potentiality for meaning. Art consists of leading the "unit of experience" to fulfillment. It involves, first, a "passionate perception," which means an active ordering or reconstructing of seeing and feeling. The perception is ordered, abridged, concentrated, and finally expressed in a "work of art," and all this requires a great deal of craftsmanship and special skill. "A poem and picture present material," says Dewey, "passed through the alembic of personal experience." But the artistic experience is not complete until the beholder or reader creates his own perception, and this perception is fed into his private experience, recreating and changing it. "The medium," Dewey says, "is the mediator." It is a go-between of artist and perciever. It is the "work" of art to present the world in a new experience which those who enjoy it themselves undergo. "The work of art is a challenge to the performance of a similar act of production, organization and perception through imagination."

". . . the transformation of experience"

The logic of science leads to an experience; the logic of art constitutes one. Knowledge becomes more than data-knowing because it is merged with nonintellectual

". . . that which unites"

John Dewey, *Art as Experience* (New York: Minton, Balch & Co., 1934).

functions and elements. It is "religious" in Dewey's own terms, because change in the climate of imagination is the function that unites the future to the present. It is prophetic, because it insinuates possibilities of human relations not found in rule and precept and provides the first intimations of a better future. By enlarging man's capacity for experiencing, it is "more moral than moralities." "The prophets have always been poets," he observes. By affecting an immediate form of communication between the experience of the artist and of the viewer, art becomes the incomparable organ of instruction, though far above what we are apt to think of as education. It is a more universal mode of culture than language. It breaks through the barriers, impenetrable by ordinary association, which divide human beings. "In the end," he says, "works of art are the only media of complete and unhindered communication between man and man that can occur in a world full of gulfs that limit community of experience."

Pragmatism for Religious Education

As John Dewey kept talking and writing, it became clear to many that he meant for his views of epistemology, education, and metaphysics to coalesce into a life-style. He once described it as "the ordering of life in response to the needs of the moment in accordance with the ascertained truth of the moment." His name for it was democracy. With the experimental method as a guide, it is a way of problems and hypotheses, tested solutions, and the warranted acceptance of consequences, literally making ideas true day by day as we go along: "the surrender of fixed, all-embracing principles to which, as universals, all particulars and individuals are subject for valuation and regulation." This democracy of knowledge can only be achieved in a democracy of life, a society of free interchange in which "one experience is made available in giving meaning and direction to another." Any program, he concluded, which develops the power to share effectively in the extension of social life is moral: "it forms a character interested in that continuous readjustment which is essential to growth."

There were some who understood this kind of thing to be a direct and serious threat to everything Christianity stood for. There were others, however, who thought that it provided not only the challenge but the basis for retooling for the contemporary world a faith crystalized in prescientific and autocratic ages.

A Value-Theory

William Clayton Bower spent a summer at Columbia in 1916 and most of his teaching career attempting to reinterpret Christianity as a program for giving religious value to democratic change and individual growth. His baccalaureate degree was in education, and he had been a pastor of several congregations. He became professor of religious education at the College of the Bible in Kentucky, where he was subjected to the suspicion of heresy in the twenties, and later at the Divinity School of the University of Chicago, where a number of distinguished theologians were developing a theology of process in the thirties. His students called him "The Deacon" and remembered him lecturing formally before the blackboard on which he repeatedly drew a single diagram showing "experience" as an arrow moving from left to right, encountering a solid line labeled "problem," making repeated assaults on the "problem" until one arrow of "experience" skirted the lower end and passed into the open space to the right.

Personality

"A living person is growth."

Personality is essentially a process, Bower taught, in which continuity and change are indissolubly united. It is basically physical in nature, which means several things. It means, at the beginning, that a person is an organization of physico-chemical elements. The organization shows itself in reflexes, habits, ideas, and attitudes. But these are all undergoing continuous change. It means, at the ending, that personality is an integral part of the physical universe, which science has shown to be itself probably composed ultimately of energy—"or even mind," Bower adds. A living person is, therefore, a becoming, "like reality itself of which he is a part."

Experience

The source from which all experience derives is the interaction of the person with his objective world. Experi-

William Clayton Bower, *Character Through Creative Experience* (Chicago University Press, 1929).

A THEORY OF VALUES
William C. Bower

Experience and Character
The dynamic human being (HB^d) in constant reciprocal interaction with the dynamic outside world (OW^d).

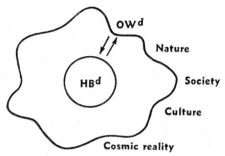

The Unit of Experience
Human experience (E) encounters a complex situation (S^{a-n}), to which a multitude of possible responses (PR) may be made. However, between situation and response there is a gap (G), filled with thinking (t), impulsive (i), reflexing (r) psychological processes.

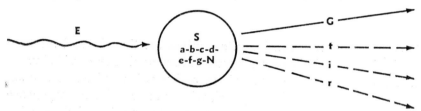

Values and Experience
Human experience (E), embodied in a dynamic human person (P^d), encounters a blockage (B) obstructing the end sought (ES), with all its projected values (V^{1-N}). There ensues an interval of delay (ID) between desire and realization, heightening the value of the end sought.

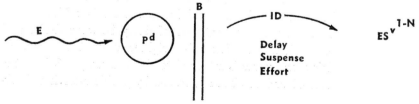

William Clayton Bower, *Moral and Spiritual Values in Education* (Lexington: University of Kentucky Press, 1952).

ence is thus bipolar: there is a sensitive, responding, and forthreaching organism; there is a stimulating, dynamic, and expanding universe. The dynamic outside world is composed of the natural world (which is the immediate environment for the child but expands as the child grows older and his knowing processes become more scientific), the society (which with the child is also immediate and personal but also enlarges), the culture (which is the accumulative result of man's interaction with the natural world), and the cosmic world (which is continuous with our immediate known world, but is also "the locus of those creative forces that have brought the universe into being and sustain it within a vast comprehending framework of a rational and moral structure.") Both the human being and the outside world are processes in which continuity and change are constantly united. Neither is imposed upon the other. In the interaction both are changed and something new emerges. One of those emergents is personality.

Value

If moral and spiritual values are thought to have their origin in some supposed supernatural order outside human experience, they will be authoritarian and foreign, Bower felt. But, he proposed, values inhere in human experience and grow out of it. Indeed, the psychological situation in which values arise is precisely the same as that in which reflexive thinking arises. At the animal level, experience passes directly from yearning to satisfaction without coming to awareness. But at the human level a gap occurs between impulse and fulfillment: there is a blockage of experience and an interval of delay between desire and realization. The desire is heightened by the degree of delay, and value is attached to the end sought. When the delayed end has been achieved by problem-solving think-

"Personality is the outgrowth of experience."

". . . the capacity to sort experience"

ing, a value is attached to both the end and the process. Thus values may be defined pragmatically as "the capacity to sort one's experiences, to project near and distant goals, to devise means for their achievement."

Education

The task of education, concluded Bower, is to help the growing person understand his experience and bring it under the control of ideas and values. And the way to do this is to help the growing person understand the structure of experience so that he can consciously and intentionally select or modify the factors that determine the ways he reacts to situations. The basic concept to be understood by teachers is "the unit of experience." In it there is "an identifiable situation," which is, of course, extremely complex. There is an "identifiable response," some sort of overt action. It then becomes necessary to understand the psychological processes that unite the situation and the response: they may be reflexive (impulsive and irrational) or reflective (rational and purposive). The correct reading of this whole unit of experience, with its multiple factors in every given situation, and its relation to the pupil, is the task of education.

". . . to bring experience under the control of values"

Learning

Learning is a process of making choices, carrying through decisions from intention to action in specific and concrete situations, and building up the many specific decisions and actions into generalized attitudes toward all situations and into dependable patterns of behavior. Bower's steps of learning include Dewey's steps of thinking and add to them Bower's own emphasis on the learn-

". . . to help pupils experience values by making choices"

William Clayton Bower, *Moral and Spiritual Values in Education* (Lexington: University of Kentucky, 1952).

ing of value as both the method and the goal of education. In explaining them, he makes it clear that in experience the steps will overlap and that learning may begin at any point to leap over intervening steps as the situation demands and the capacity of the learner makes possible. They are: realizing the situation, defining the problem, searching the learner's past experience, searching racial experience, analyzing the situation, analyzing the response for outcomes, identifying possible outcomes, evaluating possible outcomes, choosing of an outcome, appreciating the outcome, experimenting, generalizing of the outcome, reducing the outcome to habit. The last two receive special emphasis as the keypoint of method and the goal of character growth. "Learning is moral," Bower said, "when it is a choice of possible outcomes in the light of the growing ethical insights of mankind and in the light of the personal and social demands of the situation itself." It is spiritual when it takes place "in the widest perspectives of the world of reality and at the highest level of the capacities of the human spirit."

Curriculum

"The school becomes society's most dynamic and effective instrument for guaranteeing progress."

The usual way to teach values is to import a teacher or subject into the school from outside or to release students to go elsewhere to study them. Bower contends that moral and spiritual values are indigenous to the school itself, especially by participation in the school as a living community with its sports and recreation, ceremonies and celebrations. The teaching of values is a matter of emphasis rather than of new subject matter; it is not something that can be done for the pupils, but only with them. Thus, the study of every subject, from the arts to science, becomes the curriculum for spiritual education; all that is needed is the spiritual approach: discovery, identification, development, symbolic expression, and sharing. In these ways the school becomes a laboratory into which experience is brought for redirection in the light of the moral and spiritual insights of mankind through countless generations in the struggle for the good life.

A Functional Theory

Ernest J. Chave was a Canadian Baptist minister who earned a doctorate at the University of Chicago and did graduate work at Columbia under Dewey. He taught at Chicago and was one of the leaders of the International Council of Religious Education, exerting a tremendous personal influence through his committee work and a series of little books aimed at church school teachers. Gradually he became deeply disturbed by the ineffectiveness of organized religion. Diffusion and obsolescence had become its chief characteristics, he felt by 1947, and churchmen were spending far too much time keeping machinery from falling to pieces and discussing outgrown ideas. What was desperately needed was some direct help enabling people to organize new ideas and to effect new programs. Religious education was his proposal, "a planned procedure for making religion effective."

Criticisms

Chave's critique of Christianity was as forthright as Dewey's and perhaps more incisive because it came from inside. Christianity is rendered ineffective, he said, by its institutionalism, theologicalism, and supernaturalism. The organizations and agencies of Christianity exhaust its strength and dissipate its influence by diverting energies

". . . very little unifying power and just a pathetic demonstration of socially transforming power"

Ernest J. Chave, A Functional Approach to Religious Education (Chicago University Press, 1947).

and attention to endless discussions of theoretical issues. Tragically, this is happening just at a time when spiritual forces are emerging in all areas of life quite independently of ecclesiastical sanctions. Meanwhile, preoccupation with theology is merely propagating traditions and keeping people divided on doctrinal issues. Even when formal theology does address itself to the nature of man and God, the result is a debilitating sense of intimacy with him. Children ought not to be taught to think, Chave argued, of the spirit, "who has moved through the vast realms of time and eternity, and whose handiwork is in the processes of nature," as a kindly old man to whom they can chatter. It is more important to have a good working-view of the universe and its processes than to be able to use theological terms for God in a familiarly vague way. The roots of religion lie deeper than any system of doctrine, in "the spiritual resources of our natural world." Supernaturalism is a prescientific world view, and no matter how it may be rationalized to make it seem to fit a modern world, only a blurred theism can result. What is needed is a growing faith, unhampered by an ancient theoretical supernaturalism.

Affirmations

"Religion arises in the primary adjustments of life and is pervasive of all of life."

Each of these three rejections implies an alternative, and Chave forthrightly affirms all of them. He had once believed, he says, that the world was to be saved by the preaching of "the faith once delivered to the saints," and was confident that he had "the gospel of salvation," but he has come to know that "there never was a faith once delivered which could be propagated as a magical formula for salvation." True religion, he affirms, cannot be confined to an institution, because "religion is latent in all of life." "Latent" is a key word. Religion arises from what is going on in the organizing and evaluating experiences of individual life, in meditation and reflection, in the instinctive drive for nobler and more satisfying forms of social living. Religion cannot be caught in a system of theology, he affirms, because "religion is constantly changing like the experiences out of which it arises." Most theologians do not do justice to the creator and sustainer of the universe. They suggest that religion demands a blind faith in a fixed order, whereas religion is actually dynamic. "God," he wrote, "is always a reflection of world views." It is as reasonable to expect growth in religion as in other fields of human experience. And religion cannot be supernaturalistic, he affirms, because "religion rests on nature as man experiences it." He feels free to use the traditional word "God" to refer to "the creative order," but only "when there is clear reference to identifiable and experiential phases of universal processes." No special systems or revelations are necessary: "The marvels of the ordinary natural world are enough to inspire man "to share in the cooperative enterprise." We live in a dynamic world, he affirms, "not of one Book but of many books, not of one religious culture but of plural concepts and practices, not of one God but of many gods."

Analysis

The question is, therefore, whether religion will become "a sideshow of antiquities," or "an integrating spirit ever rising to higher levels of vision and purpose." Most studies of religion have been historical or doctrinal, concerning themselves with the by-products of religion—creeds, rituals, institutions, customs—and they lead to museum pieces. Chave's study, however, is genetic and functional,

". . . a constantly changing creative attempt to adjust ideas to changing experiences"

concerning itself with religion as it operates in growing lives and leads to the integrating spirit.

Over the years, with persons of different faiths and cultural backgrounds, Chave discovered ten types of experiences which describe religion "as it operates." The *sense of worth*: man is the one being in nature capable of cooperating in a developmental process, thus finding worth in himself but also giving worth to the whole. *Social sensitivity*: the desire to help others realize potentialities is seen everywhere in life and is probably the primary test and ultimate goal of spirituality. *Appreciation of the universe*: faith in the resources and processes of the world in which we live produces an enhancement of personal and social values. *Discrimination in values*: readiness to sacrifice lesser values for the sake of achieving greater is the test of spiritual progress. *Responsibility and accountability*: each man's freedom is bounded by the next man's right to freedom. *Cooperative Fellowship*: the vision is of a social order in which each and all have the best conditions possible for realization of their several possibilities. *Quest for truth and realization of values*: the quest for knowledge in all areas of life yields a spiritual interpretation of life. *Integration of experiences into a working philosophy of life*: in solving life's problems, anywhere and everywhere, religion is emergent. *Appreciation of historical continuity*: religion is a product of social interaction. *Participation in group celebrations*: any celebration has a religious quality when it gives incentive to discriminating, cooperative commitment to a worthy cause or course of living.

Education

When religion is understood to be "a growing faith in the spiritual resources of our natural world," religious education can no longer be identified with biblical knowledge and theological fluency, but must be thought of as 'the total comprehensive plan by which leaders in all realms of life cooperate to further the growth of personal-social values and attainments." It will stimulate thought, reconstructing concepts of god, redefining spiritual objectives, and reorganizing religious programs. It will seek to identify the growth factors of experience, to clarify the best conditions of spiritual development. It will emphasize the responsibility of man for a large share of his own salvation by systematically releasing the latent capacity to function as an intelligent, discriminating, self-conscious being. It will place emphasis on creative experience. And when it does, there will be a basis for integrating religion into general education. There will also be some hope that it may expect the cooperation and intelligent interest of thinking men and women in every sphere of life. While theologians and philosophers struggle for an adequate metaphysics for an expanding universe, a hopeless task in Chave's view in any case, "let educators move forward with working functional concepts and values to help organize personal-social living on a world scale of relationships."

A Research Program

Ernest M. Ligon, a professor of psychology at Union College in Schenectady, New York, applied the experimental method to the education of character. For two decades, at least, he provided a storm center for religious educators in the churches, some of whom viewed him as a sort of devil's advocate challenging the church school to more scientific approaches, and some of whom viewed him as the devil himself. Ligon was a character in his own right, beginning from his own assumptions and doing things in his own scientific way, from coast to coast supervising with great personal charisma the work in churches participating in his Character Research Program, restlessly testing, experimenting, publishing. The validily of his research methods has been widely criticized and his theological assumptions have drawn considerable fire, but many of his methods have become accepted emphases in denominational programs of Christian education.

Assumptions

"... to be sought and discovered like any other laws of the universe"

The project began in research, through the extensive testing of hundreds of children attempting to develop a measurement of the elements of character as they appear and develop in childhood. It was a more extensive and elaborate program than any that had ever been undertaken. At the beginning, it was not certain that such a measurement could be achieved, but Ligon was convinced that effective character education required some objective standards. It was assumed that while character traits can have no meaning apart from the individual of whom they are characteristic, it was nonetheless possible to isolate, observe, and measure them. As the data flowed in from trained observers in the field and was tabulated in the laboratory at Union College, Ligon concluded that an objective description of character traits and measurement of personality development was appearing. From this profile it was at last possible to state the aims for a program of character education "with a high degree of precision and scientific objectivity."

Character

The unit of character is, according to Ligon, the evaluative attitude. An evaluative attitude is an element in the

Ernest M. Ligon, *The Psychology of Christian Personality* (New York: Macmillan, 1935).

working philosophy of life of the individual which represents his evaluation of some object, person or event in his environment. Character is the sum of the effect of these attitudes. These attitudes are formed toward everything in one's environment, including those things we ordinarily think of as universal, such as good and evil, life and death, achievement and failure. Building on the definition of character, religion may be said to be the sum of the effect of all of one's universal evaluative attitudes. Every man has religion, differing as his universal evaluative attitudes differ, but religion has always been a powerful force in the building of character and should not be ignored. Because in the United States the basic religion is Christianity, Ligon examined the teachings of Jesus "to discover what universal evaluative attitudes were included in them pertinent to the development of character and to evaluate them from the point of view of personality integration." Eight general attitudes were selected from the Sermon on the Mount and stated as traits appropriate for psychological refinement and educational development. There are four "traits of experimental faith": vision, love of righteousness and truth, faith in the friendliness of the universe, and dominating purpose. There are four "traits of fatherly love": being sensitive to the needs of others, forgiveness, magnanimity, and Christian courage.

". . . the total effect of one's evaluative attitudes"

Data

The next phase in the development of an educational program was to integrate the traits with what can be known about them and about children. One task was to search for and catalogue attitudes—positive and negative, healthy and unhealthy, aggressive and submissive, introverted and extroverted, social and seclusive—which might have value for charcater education and to organize them about the eight general traits. It was assumed that this was to be

". . . to know precisely what we are trying to accomplish"

viewed as a positive and additive process, not as a fear-inspired or negative one. Another task was to arrange the attitudes thus selected into age-level groups, using the results of various child study institutes. When these two tasks had been accomplished, it was necessary to study the children in the project in order to determine which of these attitudes were most in need of development. Questionnaires were devised and revised for parents of children of all ages, and from an analysis of many hundreds of them Ligon selected those most needing development at various age-levels: "these are the ones which in the very nature of the children themselves constitute the most efficient possible program of character education."

Individual Development

". . . to proceed with confidence that the basic laws of personality are not violated"

With this material in hand at the laboratory in Schenectady and the file of data on the child in one of the participating schools, it was possible to draw up a plan for the child's own development during the next academic term. An example could be John, age ten, grade four, number X123. *The undesirable attitude to be changed* is the idea that failure is a disgrace; *the desirable attitude to be developed* is that failure is really a road to success. John has been observed to be a boy who is *most mature* in athletic persistence and sharing home responsibilities, *medium mature* in team play and social adjustment with peers, *least mature* in reading and spelling, causing disciplinary problems in school and football. His *interests* are baseball, football, and model airplanes. His *vocational interest* is aviation. In *natural endowments* he is *strongest* in height, coordination, and intelligence; *medium* in vision, memory, and mechanical aptitude; *weakest* in

Ernest M. Ligon, *Their Future Is Now* (New York: Macmillan, 1940).

DIAGRAM FOR INDIVIDUAL CHARACTER EDUCATION

name _____ age _____ school grade _____ number _____

B_1 Situation in which adjustment is in-adequate	C_1 Undesirable interpre-tation of situation	D_1 Undesirable tensions aroused	E_1 Resultant undesirable behavior
objective S situation	perceptual PS situation	tensions T aroused	adjustment R reactions
B_2 Desirable changes in situation	C_2 Desirable interpre-tation of situation	D_2 Desirable tensions aroused	E_2 Resultant desirable behavior

Om

TRAIT FOR IMMEDIATE EMPHASIS

A_1 Undesirable attitude to be changed		A_2 Desirable attitude to be developed	
F Character traits and attitudes		G Interests and activities	Vocational Choice
most mature	medium	least mature	
I Natural endowments		H Skills and achievements	
strongest	medium	weakest	best	medium	weakest

$Oí$

Oi—Innate Organism
Om—Modified Organism

By permission of Ernest M. Ligon.

stamina, hearing, and music. The *objective situation* is that he is being over-challenged in school and competing unsuccessfully on the playground. His *undesirable interpretation of the situation* is that he is of inferior caliber, and this leads to *undesirable tensions,* namely avoiding difficult tasks, and *resultant undesirable behavior* such as nervousness, temper tantrums, laziness. The *desirable interpretation* would be to see difficult tasks as opportunities for high achievement and to show courage even if unsuccessful, leading to *desirable tensions,* such as love for trying the difficult and desire to prove courage, and *resultant desirable behavior* such as trying cheerfully even if failure is inevitable. The teacher now has an objective view of John's situation and knows precisely what to try to help John to do.

Curriculum Plan

". . . more to be discovered than created"

Having discovered what attitudes need development, their organization into a curricular outline was a relatively straightforward task. Departments were set up into two-year groupings, and six trait-attitude aims selected for each level in terms of the developmental data. The first responsibility of the curriculum builder is to understand the selected attitude precisely and definitely. The next step is a series of interviews with parents of the cihldren of the age-level being considered. Enough data is to be gathered so that the teacher can construct a plan of individual development for each child. Suggestions by parents concerning materials for the curricular unit are also solicited. The curriculum builder searches the literature for useable materials. By this time a file of materials will have been gathered, and the next tasks are to select those most appropriate to the age-level and to unify them into curricular units. Each day's program is organized both in terms of the different kinds of children in a class and the needs of some particular child. Then these units are ordered into a logical sequence. In addition to this classroom schedule, a parent's calendar is prepared, for it was one of Ligon's basic principles that parent cooperation is indispensable in making character education a seven-day-a-week process. And, finally, the actual process of class education is recorded, together with the learning experiences of individual children, and then both forwarded to Schenectady for analysis and evaluation.

Personality Research

For thiry-five years the research and analysis have gone on at Union College. In the early stages the concentration on "testing for individual differences" focused attention on the study of individual personality. During the sixties Ligon moved from "trait analysis" to a "cluster analysis" of personality characteristics and a complex concept of "Uniqueness" as a dynamic pattern of several interacting personal elements. As data came in from extensive youth studies, it began to appear that character "elements" gathered into series of clusters with sufficient regularity to constitute a mathematical commutative group, and that the Uniqueness element always appeared in all of the clusters, constituting an Identity Element, thus suggesting a formal "Group" as described in Mathematical Group Theory. This mathematical theory has been applied to other complex fields (such as number, space, time, motion, relation, play, work, sense data, and ideas) with unexpectedly systematizing results. As Ligon's research team has experimented with applying this theory to character development, the concepts have shifted to the current language of mathematics, though some of the language from Ligon's earlier theories has persisted (vision of destiny, courage to strive toward maximum potential, growth and achievement of maturity, judgment and wis-

"Group Theory has helped to catch glimpses of innermost patterns and relationships."

dom, and so on). The new model from the new math gives a degree of flexibility and interaction which the Ligon trait theories never provided. At the beginning of the seventies, the mathematical analysis of data is in full swing and the hopes for increasing the effectiveness of character education through experimental research run high in Schenectady. "I am convinced," writes Ligon, "that if enough of us use this model we can make significant contributions to the search for insights which will make it possible for man to achieve his maximum potential."

Recent Experimentalism in Education

While Western culture is thought to be technological, there will be many convinced that education and religion are best understood and developed experimentally. As is the way with intellectual movements, some of the children of the third and fourth generation do not seem to know the father of their ideas or to attain his level of competence. Educational experiments, ranging from Summerhill Schools in England to a hippie Freeschool in the hills north of San Francisco, are hailed as radical new developments, though exploring for themselves principles and practices applied by Dewey in the Experimental School in Chicago at the turn of the century. Others, however, are very conscious of their debt to Dewey, and, convinced that he was basically right in his insistence on the experimental method, are continuing to refine and apply it. They share the conviction that education and religion must be integral to life as it is lived and that in a scientific world this principle demands that both be scientific in orientation.

Evolutionary Instrumentalism

Jerome S. Bruner is an experimental psychologist become philosopher through projecting his experimental method into areas of speculative thinking. He worked on learning theory for a number of years under grants from the National Science Foundation and the United States Office of Education and then became head of the Center for Cognitive Studies at Harvard University. Under his direction, experimental studies have been conducted of the cognitive processes in problem-solving and concept-attainment, psychological studies of how people avoid learning, and educational studies of how people reach their highest achievements. Taken together, these areas constitute what Bruner calls "the growth sciences," a consortium of disciplines devoted to understanding the process by which human beings go from helplessness to control. As a member of several national panels and committees, he has become the editor of several influential books of papers and studies growing out of the work of the country's most advanced scientific educators. His own most recent publications have shown him moving toward generalizations constituting a philosophy of "the possible," consciously contrasted to philosophies based on "the achieved."

Instrumentalism

"Development of mind is dependent on ability to develop and use tools."

Bruner's primary principle in the interpretation of all growth phenomena is derived from his experimental studies. It is: All advance is based on the accomplishment of prior tasks. Applied racially, this means that the abstract functions we know as mind developed as the result of the capacity to use instruments or tools, and, in turn, that the capacity to use tools developed as the result of a nervous system that required outside devices for expressing its potential. Other animals were able to secure food or develop shelter by the use of their bodies only; man, with less physical ability, was forced to extend his reach and his strength by using other things—fulcrums and levers and rollers. The genuinely new quality introduced into evolution by tools is that it is the nature of tools to beget more advanced ones at ever-increasing speed: each new operation makes many more possible. Thus, though it took some four million years for man as a primate to

Jerome S. Bruner, *Toward a Theory of Instruction* (Cambridge: Harvard, 1966). See also, *The Process of Education* (Cambridge: Harvard, 1960).

develop his present brain size, only half a million was required thereafter for him to become a tool user. Then the rate of change accelerated geometrically: all other developments have come in a mere half million years, and they have all been aided by inventing extensions of muscles or senses or reasoning powers. Reading this history in round figures, Bruner proposes that 500,000 years ago man in his present form emerged; 50,000 years ago came the glacial migrations, man's survival made possible by fleeing southward from the encroaching cold and by the discovery of the lever and the wheel; 5,000 years ago man invented writing and the accumulation of history; 500 years ago he developed printing with moveable type and mass reading; 50 years ago he invented radio and mass education; 5 years ago he developed artificial intelligence, through automated problem-solving machines.

Growth

Individual growth, also, is based on the achievement of prior tasks. "Readiness," Bruner summarizes, "consists of the mastery of simpler skills that permit one to reach higher skills." The first and basic level of thinking skill Bruner calls "enactive." It consists of knowing through doing, learning through the stimulus-response bond with the environment. No imagery or words are necessary, as, for example, in learning to ride a bicycle. Growth of enactive learning is indicated by an increasing independence of response from the immediate nature of the stimulus. Mastery of this level permits an individual to move into "iconic" thinking. Now the individual grows by internalizing events into a "storage system" that corresponds to the world as it is. Basically this is a task of perceptual organization, then of filling in the gaps, and finally of extrapolating guesses and inferences. It is then possible

". . . the translation of experience into a model for changing the world"

to move to the third level, "symbolic" thinking. Gradually, as these skills are mastered, whole new worlds of experience and thought are unlocked. Words and symbols make it possible for one to say to himself what he has done or wishes to do. They make possible sentence structures which in effect turn reality about for a new look, for they make possible an orderly way of stating propositions that have no reality, thus releasing the mind from mere facts and data. Intellectual development is then further released by the capacity to deal with several alternatives simultaneously. But, most important, symbols make it possible for one individual to share thinking with others and to check the validity of ideas without undergoing all the developing processes for oneself. Thinking has become personal, and inter-personal. The task of thinking then becomes one of altering circumstances so that they will become more satisfactory to all involved.

Education

"*The educational system is the sole agent of evolution.*"

"If we are to do justice to our evolution," Bruner says, "we shall need, as never before, a way of transmitting the crucial ideas and skills, the acquired characteristics that express and exemplify man's powers." Education is, of course, this agency. It can keep lively society's sense of what is possible, however, only with the aid of psychology, the discipline which more than any other has "the tools for exploring the limits of man's perfectability." Education is thus to be a science, perhaps the queen of them.

"*Knowing is a process not a product.*"

The principal emphasis should be placed upon skills, always proceeding, of course, from the enactive to the symbolic through the iconic levels. Beginning with handling, the training moves to seeing and then to imagining. The goal will be the development, by pupils themselves, of new "metaskills." "Skills," says Bruner, "always lead to the mastery of still more powerful skills." Bruner's researches, especially with the teaching of the new mathematics, have shown him that there is an appropriate version of any skill or knowledge that may be imparted at whatever age one wishes to begin teaching. What is necessary is to introduce into the beginner's experience those experimentalists who are at the frontiers of learning, and the establishment of "self-reward sequences" which will help the pupil to recognize the cumulative power of learning. And beyond metaskills lies the possibility of a "metalanguage" for dealing with continuity in change. Because there is already too much history to know, there must come a shift in elementary curricula from history to the social and behavorial sciences which will enable the study of the possible rather than of the achieved—"a necessary step if we are to adapt to change"—to the end of developing a "style" capable of coping with—not defending against—the newer ways of living that are presently in development. At this level, education depends upon "the systematic and contingent interaction between a tutor and a learner." The learners must be brought to answering three questions by being asked them continuously: What is human about human beings? How did they get that way? How can they become more so? Mastering any body of knowledge, says Bruner, "is to participate in the process that makes possible the establishment of knowledge."

The goals of this education are implied in the philosophical stance. Education, says Bruner, should give pupils respect for and confidence in the powers of their own minds. It should extend that confidence and respect to their power to think about human conditions. It should provide a set of workable models that will make it simpler to analyze the nature of the social world in which they

". . . to take part in the process of knowledge-getting"

live. It should implant a sense of respect for the capacities and humanity of man as a species. It should leave the student with a sense of the unfinished business of man's evolution.

Scientific Religious Education

Ronald Goldman is an educational psychologist who has become a religious educator through projecting his experimental methods into areas of religious instruction. He has, on occasion, been presented in England as the Copernicus of religious education. The Manchester *Guardian* once referred to him as the Comenius of religious education, a somewhat more accurate accolade, and perhaps no less complementary, for it was Comenius who was brought to England from Europe in the seventeenth century to guide in the setting up of a then new and now still definitive national educational program. Goldman is English, and was Senior Lecturer in Education at Reading University when he conducted the studies for which he is best known. His primary source for categories of developmental psychology is a French scholar whom American developmentalists have largely ignored, and Goldman has taught at the University of Minnesota and many of his educational principles echo those of an American scholar whom English educators have largely ignored. His studies of the development of religious thinking in children and adolescents came at the time when English school people were girding for a full-scale review of the Education Act of 1944, which had introduced required religious instruction in the curriculum of English publicly supported schools. At the same time, some American religious educators were beginning to talk about ways of integrating the teaching of religion into American public schools.

Goldman's method involved finding out what children actually thought about religion, as a first step toward finding out what religious thinking is in children. As the result of an extensive series of experiments and trial runs, he chose three pictures which encouraged the child to project his own religious thinking into words, and three biblical stories which evoke thematic religious responses from the children. The pictures were of a child entering the church with adults, a child praying alone, and a child looking at a mutilated Bible; the concepts revealed were of the church (its nature, purpose, and the motivation of attenders), of prayer (its content and purpose, failure, or success), and of the Bible (its uniqueness, nature, and origins). The stories were of Moses and the Burning Bush, the Crossing of the Red Sea, and the Temptations of Jesus; the themes evoked were divine communication, divine justice and the meaning of Jesus. These materials were used with a carefully worked out and extensive random sampling of children in a clinical interview method administered by trained workers who freely used a set of key questions in their conversations. The results were tabulated and cross-referenced.

The results were startling to those who were fondly assuming that English children were thoroughly literate in religion because it was taught at school. A six-year-old was recorded as praying: "Thy deliberately faith I full. Faith against almighty worship to God. And faith all unto you. Faith against thy holy prayer." A seven-year-old explained the burning bush by saying "God threw a fag or match down." A six-year-old said, "Moses was telling a

"There is still very little known about children's religious thinking."

"Harold be thy name."

Ronald Goldman, *Religious Thinking* (London: Routledge-Kegan Paul, 1964).

lie." An eight-year-old helpfully responded, "Green can't burn very easily." A child a year older explained, "The spirit was there. It's a kind of watery stuff like water and paste and other things." Another youngster said, "It was just bits of red paper stuck on a bush." An eleven-year-old student surmised, "When God's feet went off the ground, the flames went off." A twelve-year-old said simply, "It was a vision." A teenager replied, "It was an experiment." And a fourteen-year-old theorized, "It was light like in a light bulb."

Thinking

"The raw material of thinking is sensation which is selected then perceptualized."

Jean Piaget, a pioneering French researcher in the field of developmental psychology, checked and refined by English and American psychologists in recent studies, furnishes the basic structure for Goldman's understanding of the growth of thinking in childhood. Thinking appears to be fashioned from a sequence of sensation, perceptualizing, and finally the forming of concepts. Then concepts tend to change with age, becoming more numerous, complex, and logical. This sequence is found to occur in four more or less distinct stages. First is the *sensory motor* level, usually characterizing the first two years of life, and defined by perceptive and motor functions in dealing with objects; language is used for retaining direct experience. Next comes the level of *preoperational* (or intuitive) thought, usually taking about five years, which is characteristically egocentric (internalized), single-focus (dealing with isolated features of the environment) and irreversible (because it works only in a forward logical direction from cause to effect). The third period is called *concrete-operational* thought, ordinarily in ages seven to eleven, and evidences both inductive and deductive logic but limited to concrete situations, visual and sensory data used directly and relied upon, and reversible logic (because it also works from consequences to effects), but little generalization. The fourth period is *formal-operational* (or abstract) thought and characterizes thought from twelve onward; it is defined by the ability to think hypothetically, situations being seen in terms of propositions rather than of data and tested in thought rather than in actuality, and reasoning by inference and implication.

Religious Thinking

Religious thinking, says Goldman, does not differ in mode and method from thinking directed toward other phenomena. It is to be assumed, therefore, that Piaget's outline can be used to understand the development of religious thought. There is, of course, one major distinction: religious percepts and concepts are not based upon direct sensory data. The sensory-motor period of infancy may therefore be assumed to be non-religious. The investigation then begins with the level of pre-operational thought (ages 2-7). It is characterized by a lack of connection between the test pictures and religion and by literalism in the children's responses to the biblical stories. Goldman's conclusion is that religious thinking is impossible at this stage and that it is dangerous to demand it. The studies showed, further, that concret-operational thinking did not begin in reference to religion until age eight. It then consisted of physical or "animistic" explanations of the pictures and stories and exhibited no extension or generalization patterns. The level of abstract-operational thought, in turn, did not begin until thirteen or fourteen years of age, when internalization, generalization, and consistency of thinking about religion began to appear.

". . . thinking directed toward religion"

Several conclusions about the transitions between stages of thinking have made themselves evident to Goldman. There is an extended and less clear movement to the next stage of religious thinking than in nonreligious thought,

Religious thinking is secondary.

and there is a consequent delayed development in religious thought. Thus concrete thought begins at age seven, but in religious thinking not until eight; abstract thought begins at about twelve but in religious subjects not until thirteen or fourteen. The result is confusion for the child who is thinking securely about objects at a level he has not yet reached when thinking about religion. The philosophical implication for the researcher is that religious thinking is a secondary and dependent form of ordinary thinking.

Religious Education

"What we have is too old for the young, too young for the old, and little real learning takes place."

Goldman's proposals for religious education are suggested by these conclusions and have stirred up considerable controversy in England. Religion is ordinary experience with an added depth, he argues, quoting Paul Tillich. Religion and life are one, he proposes, not quoting John Dewey. There are no specifically religious needs. Religion is the need for fulfillment, and as we grow as persons we grow toward God. If children are to be helped in that growth, they must be helped to see religious truth as true to their own experience. Thus, teaching large areas of the biblical material, which is specifically the reflection of adult experience and thought about religion, may do more damage than good to a child's religious development. The answer lies in the needs of the children themselves, and he suggests "a move from a Bible-centered content of religious education to a content which more closely approximates to the real world of children, using their experiences and their natural development rather than imposing an adult form of religious ideas and language upon them."

Religious education in English schools would cease to

Ronald Goldman, *Readiness for Religion* (London: Routledge-Kegan Paul, 1965).

A Visual Model of a Programme of Developmental Religious Education throughout Schools

PRE-RELIGIOUS THOUGHT	Infant School (Early Childhood) 5-7 years.	Enriching General Experience and Artistic Expression. Spontaneous worship in classroom and use of Children's Spontaneous Questions. Themes based upon these.
SUB RELIGIOUS THOUGHT	Early Junior School (Middle Childhood) 7-9 years.	Continuation of General Enrichment by Across-subject teaching. Begin elementary Life-themes, some leading to Festivals.
	Late Junior School (Late Childhood) 9-11 years.	More advanced Life-themes in across-subject projects and activities. / Religious Themes: Simple Life of Jesus. Bible background facts 'What is the Bible?'
PERSONAL	Early Secondary School (Pre-adolescence) 11-13 years.	Religious Themes; 'What is the Bible?' More advanced Life of Jesus. Some Acts. / Some Life-themes for less able pupils.
RELIGIOUS	Late Secondary School (Adolescents) 13 years plus.	Life-themes and problem-centred exploration for less academic pupils. / Religious Themes: A Bible chronology— N.T. forward into Spread of Christianity to modern Britain; Back into O.T. 'Where it began.' Or Bible themes—developing ideas from primitive religion O.T. to N.T.
THOUGHT	School-Leavers (Adolescents)	Sex education in terms of relationships and personal values. Adolescent problem-centered discussion 'What do Christians Believe?' Some comparison of world religions.

From *Readiness for Religion* by Ronald Goldman; used by permission of Routledge & Kegan Paul and Seabury Press.

be textbook Bible study. There would be a centering on experiencing life first and then only on interpreting life. "Life Themes" would comprise the religious curriculum through the levels of both prereligious and subreligious thought. At ages six and seven children would conduct conversations about themselves, adults, life and death, experience some spontaneous worship at Christmas and harvest times. The aim would be to provide for their needs for security, fantasy, and enjoyment. The eight- and nine-year-olds would deal with life themes such as friends, clothes, homes, and could study sheep, Palestinian farms, the Good Shepherd. Worship would consist of programs of "giving and sharing." In the next two years, when personal thought becomes possible, life themes would include light, growth, law and order, names, and stories; study of "The Life of Jesus" and "What is the Bible?" could be added. From eleven to thirteen there may be more Bible and Jesus for the able students, life themes for the less able. With adolescence and the capacity for religious-abstract thought, the thirteen-plus group may do Bible chronology, the history of Christianity from the New Testament to modern Britain and Old Testament beginnings; school-leavers do sex education and discuss "What Do Christians Believe?"

"The major reform required," writes Goldman, "is a new orientation so that the needs of twentieth-century children are the starting point, and that educational insights now applied to other subjects can be seen as relevant to the teaching of religion."

EXPERIMENTALISM

Theology	Empirical, "process theology"
God	Cosmic force, principle of order
Jesus	The great example
Man	Rising primate
Salvation	Process of reconstruction
Knowledge of God	Experimental method
Religious Experience	Discovery
Bible	A source of historical data
Philosophy	Pragmatism
Epistemology	"Truth is power"
Education	Progressive
Symbol	The laboratory
Curriculum	Experience-centered
Method of knowing	Discovery or experimentation
Teacher skill	The project, exploration
Method of learning	Doing
Goal of learning	Problem-solving
Evaluation of learning	Testing of practical results
Christian Education	Experiments with the hypothesis of God
Content	Moral and spiritual values
Purpose	Christian character
Goal	Reconstruction of life

The fifties was a decade of accounting for education in the United States.

The new school had been around long enough to begin to seem a bit old hat. Public education during the war years had suffered greatly in quality, and the atomic competition of the succeeding cold war years demanded sophisticated skills of young adults for which the nation's school seemed not to have prepared them. When, in 1954, the Supreme Court required the schools to deal with the children of Negro citizens as equals, and in 1957 the Russians were first off the launching pad with a man-made earth satellite, it appeared that American progressive education had not progressed rapidly enough.

Further, the climate of piety had changed. Veterans coming back from the foxholes of combat, in which popular legend asserted that there were no atheists, helped put Americans as a whole on the path of the return to religion. The religious liberalism of the thirties, in which a humanism without traditional theistic overtones had flourished, was gone, and in its place reigned an openly supernaturalistic and Christian new orthodoxy. It appeared that pragmatic philosophy had not dealt experimentally enough with the tragedies of which a scientific culture was capable.

Experimentalism was asked to account for itself on two fronts, educational and philosophical. Critics challenged. Defenders rallied. Studies were conducted. Controversy flourished and was productive of perspective.

In Education

". . . a radical transformation in American education"

In fifty years the American public school had come a long way. The notion of free, universal schooling had moved from hope to near realization. It had developed from a curriculum of studies based primarily upon traditional and adult requirements to a series of learning activities based primarily upon the natural interests and needs of the child. Its emphasis had shifted from training wholly for the future to training that values the present life of the child as the springboard into his life of the future. It had changed from an education focusing on intellectual development to one concerned for the development of the entire personality. It had moved from the goal of verbal knowledge acquired by memory to the goal of scientific insight acquired by activities in controlled environments. A science of education had developed, grounded in experimental studies of learning and culminating in the scientific training of teachers for the classroom. It had become, indeed, one of the wonders of the modern world, and a constant stream of visiting educational specialists from abroad repeatedly reported their amazement—and sometimes bafflement—at the widespread education of adults in the United States, the extent of academic freedom, the forms of student life, the training of teachers, the extent and variety of research, the relation between teachers and students. The American conception of education in general and of educational institutions in particular is far removed from that which is characteristic of Europe, England, or Asia.

If an institution is the lengthened shadow of a man, the American public school may be said to be John Dewey's shadow. During the ninth and last decade of his life, he was often praised and blamed for the entire development. Though in many a college of education half of the faculty had studied at Columbia and others had done their graduate work under professors who had studied with Dewey and his disciples, either position is, of course,

". . . holding Dewey responsible for everything that has happened in American education"

Oscar Handlin, *John Dewey's Challenge to Education* (New York: Harper, 1959).

an oversimplification—a "trap," one Dewey interpreter calls it. There are at least two complicating factors in evaluating Dewey's contribution. The first concerns his philosophy and the second its interpretation.

Dewey's own philosophical foundation lay in his epistemology. It was intellectually rigorous and a radical departure from traditional philosophy. Further, there is the mobility of Dewey's own thought, which kept developing throughout his life and may be characterized by his discard of the name "Pragmatism" as too easily subject to misinterpretation and the substitution in later life of the word "Instrumentalism" as more representative of both the difficulty and radicality of his philosophy.

. . . a ritual practice of half-truths and cliches among unsuspecting children

Many a teacher of the philosophy of education never grasped the content, the intent, or the portent of all this when he lectured to eager young teacher trainees, forming the understandings and purposes with which they went out to their own schoolrooms. One of the results was that Dewey's educational philosophy has been applied mostly to the education of children. Dewey knew that intellectual activity is as real as physical activity when the pupil had learned the skills to sustain it, but little attention was given to the projection of this principle into secondary education. The recent revolts of university students at widely separated American campuses reveal that one of their common demands is that appropriate forms of action-learning be given a try even in higher education.

Another result was that some of Dewey's principles have been turned into half-truths by simplification and repetition. For example, Dewey said that "we learn by doing,"

Compare, for example, Robert Hill Lane, ed., *The Progressive Elementary School* (Boston: Houghton-Mifflin, 1938) and Bernard Iddings Bell, *Crisis in Education* (New York: McGraw-Hill, 1949).

which often turned out to mean that in the classroom children did more moving than reading, while Dewey meant that a pupil learns most effectively by what he does in response to what he reads or discovers in whatever way. Dewey said that "education is growth," which was often taken to mean that learning tasks were no longer important, while Dewey meant that education is the process of arriving at maturity. Dewey said that "education is a social process," which was often thought to mean that all learning must be done in public and every learner should become extroverted, whereas Dewey was combatting the excessive individualism of the nineteenth century. Dewey had said that "education is not preparation but life," and some took it to mean that schools need not worry about preparing children for further education, and Dewey probably meant only that learning should not be distasteful. And a third result of inadequate interpretation was the tendency to doctrinalize the understood half of principles like these into a kind of authoritarian jargon and ritual-talk. Parents began to recognize it at conferences with teachers and to reproduce it themselves in PTA meetings.

This last result, built on the others, was clearly the antithesis of Dewey's own principles and could be taken, experimentally, to demonstrate the impending failure, no matter what the proximate results, of his educational reformation. In the year of Dewey's birth, the incoming president of Harvard had said in his inaugural address that "the very word education is a standing protest against dogmatic teaching," and Dewey's lifelong goal had been freedom of inquiry in the learning process at all levels. But now, in some colleges of education the open debate of experimental philosophy is beginning again, and Dewey

Paul Woodring, *Let's Talk Sense About Our Schools* (New York: McGraw-Hill, 1953).

is sometimes being recalled as a primary source. The new questions run deep. Are children more than socio-biological phenomena undergoing an everchanging flow of sensory experience? Have the instrumental epistemology and experimental method been applied too generally in education? Must each individual learn everything for himself? Have the importance of tradition and accumulated human wisdom been underestimated? How much can children be helped and guided to adjustments without interfering with the child's integrity? Should the objectives of education include more than social efficiency? Can education aim at social responsibility as well? As questions like these are dealt with, education may once again move toward first principles and Experimentalism may become more rigorous again. In that case, both the educational practice and the philosophical position will be enriched.

In Religion

From the theological point of view, the fatal difficulty with Experimentalism in general and Dewey in particular was precisely what Dewey claimed to be its greatest strength—the absence of reference outside human experience.

"Definitions of education evade the real questions."

George Buttrick, an influential preacher and theologian in the tradition of Geneva, was explicit about that. One by one he challenged the experimentalist philosophers with the issue. Conant says that education is "preparation for the good life," but, Buttrick pointed out, neither the word "good" nor the word "life" is given any content. Brubacher says that education is "pupil growth," but what kind of growth? "A cancer grows," Buttrick objected. Kil-

George Buttrick, *Faith and Education* (New York and Nashville: Abingdon-Cokesbury, 1952).

patrick says that education projects "ideas of social change," but Buttrick wants to know what kind of change and in what direction. Counts says that it is the responsibility of education "to prepare the young of America to discharge wisely and well their political obligations," but what is his understanding of wisdom and to whom are the young obligated? Dewey says that "education proceeds by the participation of the individual in the social consciousness of the race," but what kind of participation and what kind of consciousness? In short, Buttrick wants to know what is the criterion for experimentalist education and from whence it comes. Failing to find one, he concludes, "surely teachers will soon turn from this hocus-pocus to the depth and clarity of the Christian creeds."

Henry P. Van Dusen, president of Union Theological Seminary in New York, traced the history of the shift from the medieval God-centered world to the modern man-centered world and pointed out that though there was no longer a recognition of religion in the curricula of American colleges and universities, there were, however, the assumptions that truth was an organic whole and that knowledge was coherent. It is in asking the questions, How does truth come to be whole? and Whence comes the coherence of knowledge? that the question of God arises for Van Dusen. It is impossible to set forth the whole truth without acknowledging the divine mind, which gives truth its unity and knowledge its coherence. Religion, affirms Van Dusen, cannot be an incidental subject in the scheme of education, but is the queen of the subjects, "not because the churches say so, but because of the nature of Reality." The issue of truth is, for Van Dusen, the

". . . a recognition of God in education"

Henry P. Van Dusen, *God in Education* (New York: Scribner's, 1951).

issue of "fidelity to the Sovereign which all learning acknowledges as liege Lord."

At times it seemed that Dewey had been right in insisting that Pragmatism and Christianity were on opposite sides of a great divide. Though controversy did not produce conversion of either side or much actual conversation between them, the combat did light up the common sky occasionally. To those who were neutral enough to be observers, it began to appear that one of the greatest weaknesses of Experimentalism as a philosophy was that when the common sense on which it was based was universalized it suffered a loss of wisdom. The experimental method which worked so well in solving practical problems leaves many of the knottier problems of life unsolved. Are all situations in which man finds himself really indeterminate? Is every situation radically new? Is human life just one thing after another? Are there not some situations in which ancient solutions are the best? Are not solutions sometimes delivered to us from outside the situation itself? Can all indeterminate situations be rendered determinate by the action of man? Are all meanings strictly operational in character? Is there not some meaning which has its own independent rightness quite apart from whether it solves immediate problems? Is there not truth which exists quite apart from my use of it? Is not the mind a container for these meanings as well as an instrument? Is there not a sense in which a man exists even if he does not act? Are there not times when it is more important to be than to be busy? In plunging into the immediate problems of living without dealing with questions like these, Experimentalism had simply, but significantly, short-changed life itself. It was a method of following the ways of wisdom without troubling about the existence of wisdom, a way of having all the advantages of religion without any of its responsibilities. Robert E. Fitch said that

. . . Protestant
thought
completely
secularized

Pragmatism was "an excellent example of what happens to Protestantism when it forgets its deep-thrusting roots and goes all to foliage and to fruits," John Dewey, a satisfied prodigal son "who has no desire to return to his father, and has finally developed the argument that he never had such a father, anyway."

But Dewey and the experimentalists had also raised some significant questions for the traditional supernaturalists. Was it not true that popular Christianity had lost the rigorous monism that had characterized Paul, Augustine, and Calvin? Was not Dewey right in insisting that a simple dualism was fatal to both religion and science? Was it not true, also, that religion had become otherworldly, and that religion ought to be expected to have a functional significance by actually making a difference in life? And did not this mean that salvation for man is not simply some far-off transaction by God arranging for the justification of man's sins but something that has to do with man's acts in present-day experience? Was it not true that the insistence on the instrumental nature of meaning challenged the built-in tendency of theology, with its spiritual reference, to become authoritarian about non-spiritual matters? As far as Christianity was concerned, Dewey was always more corrosive than constructive, and it may well be that Experimentalism's chief contribution to religion—on the whole and in the long run, naturally—may be more in the line of challenge than of cooperation.

. . . the merit of asking disturbing questions

Christian Education

In the nineteenth century, Horace Bushnell had identified the key issues which came to characterize Christian edu-

Robert E. Fitch, "John Dewey—the 'Last Protestant.' " *The Pacific Spectator*, VII, Spring, 1953.

cation in the twentieth century: *historical change, religious experience and knowledge,* the *god-man relation,* and *personal growth.* Without taking up a specifically Christian and directly useable position on any one of them, John Dewey had brought them all into focus for the Christian educator. He had made change the central plank of his philosophical platform. Never again would Christian educators be able to talk as if the purpose of Christian education were merely to enforce past mores or reinforce ancient creeds. He had put the issue of the experiential nature of knowledge at the center of the educational enterprise. Never again could Christian educators treat religious knowledge merely as items of technical or theoretical information. He had insisted that the relationships of man determine both his nature and his learning. From now on Christian educators must be aware of the learner in his total situation. He had defined life as growth. Christian educators will now always find it necessary to think of Christian experience as developmental rather than as a single event. For Dewey, of course, *change* was nonhistorical, *experience and knowledge* nonreligious, *man's relations* nontheistic, *personal growth* nonspiritual, and the philosophy that embodied all these issues was, on his own definition, religious without religion. He had raised, for the first time, the alternative for Christianity of an education that was religious in its claims and aims but secular in concept. Though subtle, the challenge seemed unmistakable. An education for Christianity would have to make these same emphases. It would also have to define itself.

PERSONALISM

"... the self is the datum"

... Idealism

"... truth is more than it appears to be"

... child-centered education

... learning-by-becoming-a-person

... person-oriented religion

... liberal theology

George Albert Coe, 1862-1951

The silence lengthened, but there was no slack in it.

"Yes," said George Coe slowly, seriousness lining his lean face, "I can understand. The rest of the book can be taken without that last chapter on 'Education Revealing God.' But I was constrained to add it. God means something personal to me." The lines remained serious, but the eyes crinkled. "You admit that I was not dogmatic," he added. "I'm grateful for that. Let it rest there."

The constraint to include God and the determination to keep an open mind produced in George Albert Coe a significant combination of theology and science in education. It set Coe apart from the secular educators and helped Christian educators define their position and clarify their purposes.

When a group of leading American educators met in Chicago in 1903 to organize a professional association, there were those who hoped it would become an agency for enriching secular education. They were led by a youngish professor of education from the University of Chicago named John Dewey. There were also those there who wished it to become an agency for the development of a distinctively religious education. Their spokesman was a youngish professor of the philosophy of religion at Northwestern University named George Coe. His address, "Salvation by Education," stated the position that won the conference. It became the Religious Education Association, and John Dewey dropped out.

"Salvation by Education"

For nearly twenty years they taught across the street from each other in New York City, Dewey at Columbia University and Coe at Union Theological Seminary, and for five more they were together at Teachers' College. Dewey never acknowledged the existence of a liberal Christian faith such as Coe represented. There were many traditional theologians, on the other hand, some of them at Union, who found it difficult to acknowledge that Coe was Christian. But Coe was the independent sort, a Christian committed by early experience and choice to a personal God and to a continuing reformation of the church and society, a radical whose faith in the Kingdom of God was not shaken even when, in later years, his faith in the American dream was.

The Radical Christian

"It seems to me, as I survey my experience," said Coe at a dinner celebrating his sixty-fifth birthday on the eve of his retirement, "that I have been most nearly right when I have leaned toward the radical side of any question, and most nearly wrong when I have leaned toward the conservative side." Coe was the sort of man who leaned toward the radical side of questions, but his feet seemed to be placed near the middle of both life and the philosophical spectrum.

Commitments

"Fortunately I was kept out of school until I was nine years old."

George Albert Coe was born, grew up, and went to college in western New York State. His father was a Methodist preacher, home life was simple, and religion was warmhearted; the public schools were poor, and there was a good library in his father's study. By what he later described as "an easy and painless process," he learned "the rudiments," as he called them, at home—to read and write, of course, and to attend worship and to believe. He also learned, as country boys do, to think for himself, and when he reached adolescence he knew that though he intended to be a Christian he had committed no great sins and could not therefore expect to undergo a great conversion experience. He had, in Horace Bushnell's words, grown up a Christian and never known himself to be otherwise.

It was as a college student at the University of Rochester that his definitive intellectual choices were made. It was a step-by-step process. The tension about his relation to Christianity had been growing for some time. The resolution came through a deliberate decision following a period of intensified study of the matter. He committed himself to the Christian way of life, acknowledged that conversion was not his affair, and concluded that he would not seek it. But something else happened that he had not expected and turned out to be immensely important. He had begun to look for the core of religious experience in the ethical will. The decision made it possible for him to plunge into the study of biology in his senior year with an open mind. The professor was a vigorous exponent of Charles Darwin as a resource and of independent thought by students as a method. Coe was ready. He caught the excitement of the scientific method of data and testing. He saw clearly how contrary this was to the revealed truth he had learned as a child. He settled the matter on a Sunday morning, "by solemnly espousing the scientific method, including it within my religion and resolving to follow it wherever it should lead." Little did he know how far this commitment to the scientific method within religion would eventually lead him.

"I cut the knot by a rational and ethical act."

It lead him, next, to the School of Theology at Boston University. The commitment to religion convinced him to major in systematic theology, and he ran full tilt into Borden Parker Bowne. Bowne approached theology as a philosopher in the Idealist tradition, assuming that the world was a unified cosmos and rational in nature, originated and held together by the mind of God. This appealed to Coe. But Bowne also functioned as an apologist,

"The religious enterprise is to me the most important undertaking in life."

George Albert Coe, "My Own Little Theatre," in *Religion in Transition*, ed. Virgilius Ferm (New York: Macmillan, 1937).

assuming that there is an authority in theological propositions before investigation of their content and meaning began. This distressed Coe. But he found the scientific method freely applied at Boston by the professor of Old Testament studies, who was deeply involved in tracing the historical development of the biblical concepts that antedated the assumptions of Christian theology. This excited Coe. Coe put them all together by rejecting theological orthodoxy and settling on the religious experience as the crucial matter for theological development as furnishing empirical data to be examined by analytical processes. It was Bowne, however, who recommended that Coe abandon his plans to enter the parish ministry and prepare to teach.

Exposure

". . . to work side by side in our respective professions"

It was the custom in the 1880s for seniors of the School of Theology to deliver a graduation sermon in the vast old Tremont Temple in Boston. Just before George Albert Coe preached, Sarah Knowland said that she would marry him. "It was for me," he said, "a word of destiny." Coe had done his seminary field work in downtown Boston and had organized the Boston Northend Band. Sarah was a music major at the University and had stayed on after helping with the band to play the organ at the worship services when he preached. She even agreed to go to China with him as a missionary, but he accepted an invitation to join the faculty at the brand new University of Southern California in Los Angeles, and on September 3, 1888, they were married at the Knowland home in Alameda, California. Sarah became an instructor of piano in the music department, and they lived for a year in a boarding house near the campus. But they both yearned for more study, and when Boston University offered Coe a fellowship to study theology for a year in Europe, they began to make plans. Coe decided to go to the University of Berlin, Sarah selected the *Königliche Hochschule für Musik* in Berlin.

For the next five years they commuted between Los Angeles and Berlin, and were much apart. In spite of the fact that USC was "mostly raw edges" and "the financial management was wretched," they returned to California for the academic year of 1890, Sarah was made director of the piano department, and, pooling their salaries, they built a small home. In 1891, Boston University awarded Coe the Doctorate in Philosophy. During the summer, however, Coe insisted that Sarah return to Berlin for two full years of musical study, and he taught in Los Angeles in the winters and studied in Germany in the summers. Coe was exhilarated. He found Wilhelm Wundt at work in "physiological psychology." He found Wilhelm Herrmann establishing an ethical ideal of spiritual personality through a study of Jesus' "inner life." He discovered Albrecht Ritschl's teaching that fact and value constitute a single whole and that what works in religion is revealed truth.

". . . destiny, duty and highest happiness"

In 1893, while Sarah was still in Berlin, Coe accepted an invitation to become Professor of Philosophy at Northwestern University, Sarah was invited to teach in the piano department, and on the way to Germany for the summer, Coe moved their State-side belongings into a faculty house in Evanston. The next year they built a house which had a studio for her, a large living room for his gatherings of students, and a huge debt. But they were supremely happy there. "Our home never ceased to seem to her a gift in trust for others," said Coe, and students remembered the *conversazione* they conducted there on Sunday afternoons. They would all sing some hymns which Coe had selected for their theological acceptability

". . . such self-giving and self-forgetting as makes credible the love of God"

and Mrs. Coe would accompany. Then he would open up some religious topic and call for questions and discussion. These sessions fed Coe's restless mind. Meanwhile, Sarah's piano teaching was becoming popular, and she soon became Professor of Piano and Musical History in the university School of Music. She was a good teacher, instinctively combining demands for technical accomplishment with genuine fondness for young life and a dedication to the fruit of music in the growth of personality. Coe watched her and learned. In their discussions, she would frequently remark that, "after all, this or that principle that Jesus taught is the only one that really works." Coe listened and learned. And then, suddenly, she became very ill, and after surgery and suffering died of cancer in August of 1905. Coe went immediately into seclusion in the north woods. His mother quickly wrote, "I hope you will not worry about the future, just live one day at a time and let God take care of the rest." And later, "None but the All-Knowing and All-Merciful One could have ordered the whole case so wisely and lovingly. We cannot for a moment doubt this wisdom and love, and we shall see it more as time passes." Coe himself wrote, "Time and death and eternity have found their meaning, and that meaning is good." He never remarried.

Solidification

Coe was literally bursting his intellectual seams. His articles on the psychology of religion appeared often in scholarly journals. In 1899, Edwin Starbuck published a study of religious experience based on the questionnaire method of gathering data and concluding that the psychological phenomenon of conversion was directly related to the physiological phenomena of adolescence. Coe was doing questionnaires, too, but Starbuck's work convinced him of the necessity of adding interviews, personality profiles, and other checks on the data. He published his findings in *The Spiritual Life* in 1900. His study of the childhood preceding conversion provided a brand new dimension in religious psychology, and from it he concluded that the child is but "a candidate for humanity" and that religion was related to social functions of which the child was as yet incapable. He showed that in adolescence the awakening of religious consciousness is related to personality development more than to physiological conditions. With this as a base, in 1902 he published *The Religion of a Mature Mind*, projecting the implications of the psychology of religion into constructive theology for adulthood, urging an experimental rather than inferential awareness of God's presence, and affirming the passion for truth as common to both religion and science. In Methodist circles it was common to refer to the book as "the irreligion of an immature mind," and Coe was regarded locally as "the most dangerous man in all Methodism." An invitation from Union Theological Seminary in New York seemed to offer an opportunity to leave the site of his recent personal tragedy and a newly developing professional one, and he accepted. Shortly before he left for New York in 1909, he made an address at a Methodist conference which was reported in the Chicago papers as theologically radical. Rumors that he was leaving Northwestern because of his theological views spread so rapidly that the administration was embarrassed enough to request Coe's permission to retain his name as honorary professor of philosophy and religion. Coe agreed, and his name so appeared in the faculty rolls until his death in 1951.

The move to Union was the beginning of a new life for Coe. His chair was Practical Theology. It gave him an opportunity to develop theology as it grows out of life. It

"Orthodoxy cannot take the place of righteousness."

also gave him the opportunity to apply psychology to the development of religion. The result was to be religious education. His inaugural address was titled, "Can Religion Be Taught?" and the principle he used for answering the question affirmatively was "We learn by doing that which we wish to do when we have learned it." Religious education, he asserted, is a way of living which unites ideas and action by drawing upon the learner's own experience and projecting the resultant convictions into actual social regeneration. He had set his course. Theology, psychology, and education combine practically in the "growing realization of the divine side of life." The two books he wrote while at Union were his best known, *A Social Theory of Religious Education* and *What Is Christian Education?*

At forty-seven years of age, Coe put the pieces together and began again. For twenty years he gave every appearance of enormously enjoying New York, his classes, and his students.

He would take a student to the theater downtown, during the intermissions slipping in enough comments about Shaw and Ibsen to keep the student reading all night to catch up, and meeting him in the morning on the way to class say, "By the way, what did you think of Watson's remarks in this morning's *Times* on the mind?"

A student once submitted a report of a laboratory school class condemning the teachers for neglecting a certain child. When the report came back with Coe's scrawl across the top, "Nothing here but a string of guesses," he marched into the professor's office. "Are you asking me to doubt the evidence of my own eyes?" he demanded. "Certainly I am," replied Coe and reached for the telephone to call the teacher, who said that the child had failed to respond to every approach and was being left alone while

Religion "seeks life in the sense of completion, unification and consumation of values."

"Teaching is a ministry."

the staff waited for some sign of spontaneous response. The student had forgotten to trust persons.

Coe often reversed the severest grades administered by his graduate assistants, though agreeing that student performance frequently left much to be desired. One reader reminded Coe of some of the things the Professor had done to him. "Oh, that's different," said Coe, "I'll slap you down every chance I get: you bounce." "So I learned," the student said later, "that teaching is not just experience in handling subject matter and rating student performance."

In class, the charm and friendliness of his personal relations with students slipped away, and he became vigorous and convincing. He frequently began a session with a challenging statement, and then he would spend the hour defending it philosophically and psychologically, driving home his points with illustrations and contrasts, his index finger leading the attack like a rapier His classes were always interesting and became very popular. But his majors were sometimes troubled that he taught in a traditional manner rather than in the social-project method he recommended for others. "I'm too old to change now," he said when one of them asked him about it. "You younger men can do what I can only talk about doing."

Those who knew George Coe personally spoke of an intellectual and spiritual receptivity bordering on the mystical. They were certain that in his own untraditional way he walked with God. Though he was sixty years of age when he resigned his post at Union in 1922, the action came as a surprise to most of his colleagues. It was in protest against an action taken in a faculty meeting and was consummated on the spot. Some of them were even more surprised when he promptly moved across the street to Teachers' College of Columbia University. After five years there, Coe retired in 1927.

For twenty-four more years George Albert Coe leaned toward the radical side of questions.

His life revolved around two widely separated and very different places. One of them was new, a little house in a retirement colony of ministers and missionaries called Pilgrim Place in a village then called Glendora in southern California. The climate and the sun reminded him of the early days at USC, the fellowship was envigorating, and his old students came to see him. The other was a camp at Lonely Lake east of Sault Ste Marie, which he had begun to build almost immediately after Sarah Knowland's death and to which he had gone every summer thereafter, fishing, cooking, building, and conducting informal evening seminars with the students who accompanied him. During the years at Union he had owned a small motor cruiser in which he had made the round trip several times, but now he accomplished the annual journey to Evanston and Lonely Lake in a blue Chevy convertible. There he could choose his company by invitation and spend long hours alone.

But two things troubled his restless mind, the resurgence of reformation theology in the neoorthodox movement of the thirties and the interruption of democratic development in the United States during the forties.

He was not invited to the Oxford Life and Work Conference of 1937, but he participated in it by correspondence. Emil Brunner prepared the paper on "The Christian Understanding of Man," and Coe submitted a critique. Brunner reaffirmed the classical formula of original sin and human depravity as the basis of Christian unity; Coe warned of the danger of dividing Christen-

George Albert Coe, *What Is Religion Doing to Our Consciences?* (New York: Scribner's, 1943).

dom by absolutizing dogma, of confusing the demand for submission to God with the demand for submission to what some men think about God. This was, for Coe, an anti-ethical and therefore anti-Christian act more significant in its negativity than any positive results to be derived from doctrinal solidarity. In response to the urging of friends, Coe made this the subject of his last book, stating even more radically than ever the principle that God and man are inseparable, that God works through man and is, indeed, the sum of human social personality in its ideal state.

It was the trend of public education during the forties that inclined Coe to lean toward the radical side of social and economic questions. Under the pressure of wartime patriotism, he saw secular schools adopting authoritarian attitudes and dividing society rather than unifying it. The schools, to which he had pinned his faith as the source of democratic social revolution, had fallen under the economic subsidization and political control of the government. The wartime economy, he felt, was producing a kind of competitive capitalism to which Christian ethical principles could not be accommodated. The Christian faith, on which he had relied as the chief moral critic of capitalism through its principles of love and personality, was being used by capitalism as the means of furthering its personality-defeating goals. During the last two winters, his correspondence, especially with Harry Ward, a sociologist and old friend, explored the "fundamental ethical question" raised by Marx, "whether it is humane or just that man's sustenance should depend upon his contributing by his labor to the private profit of another." This ethical core is being ignored, Coe said, by

". . . a claim to speak a divine word unmodified by the experience or reason of those who communicate it"

"We are not done with Marxism."

George Albert Coe, "My Search for What Is Most Worthwhile," *Religious Education*, XLVII (1952), 170-76.

both the political and ecclesiastical thought that is most characteristic of the United States. "May I quote you?" Ward asked, for it was a time when leftists were under great suspicion in the United States. "Quote me as much as you like," replied Coe.

Religious Education

"We shall never do justice to the young," wrote Coe as a young professor of philosophy in 1902, "until we look down through our Sunday School methods, young peoples' societies, junior societies, and every mere device, to the ultimate relation in which the three parties concerned —God, the child or youth, and the adult—stand to one another." Coe began with a search of "the ultimate relation" in religious experience, mixed in his commitments to a personality-creating God, and in his efforts to do justice to the young built a person-oriented religious education that became definitive among liberal Protestants and influential even among conservatives.

The Revaluation of Values

"Religion is interested in all values."

The psychology of religion was an infant science—a mere branch of philosophy—when Coe began to study religious experience as the source of theology. There were some psychologists, following Hegel's philosophical lead, who identified religious experience as primarily an intellectual matter and concerned with a knowledge of eternal truth, in brief, a reasoned belief having for its object an intelligent being. Others, following Schleiermacher's theological lead, identified religious experience as an emotional

George Albert Coe, *The Psychology of Religion* (University of Chicago Press, 1916).

state, "neither thinking nor acting, but intuition and feeling," in short, "the feeling of dependence" every man experiences with respect to universal being. Both these approaches came from early nineteenth-century sources and were largely speculative. The growing edge in the early twentieth century, however, lay with those who identified religion as a conative or end-seeking experience, that is, a part of the struggle for life to be observed and studied empirically. With his commitment to scientific method, Coe naturally belonged among these researchers. He also felt that "end-seeking" was an activity of the whole personality, not merely of the mind or emotions. Some defined the religious experience as value-seeking activity concentrating on the achievement of values more inclusive or enduring than individual values could be, namely, social values. Coe took his cue from them, but not his answer. He identified religion with the constant process of judging or testing values, which, in turn, produces a functioning integration of all discrete and competing values into a whole operational method of living. This process, not any specific value in itself, is precisely what gives meaning and worth to life. He called it the "revaluation of values." It is to religion exactly what inquiry is to science, but it is not the same thing.

Thus religion does not introduce a new value into experience, to be rated in the hierarchy of values. The revaluation of values is an operation simultaneously lying at the base of all values and capping them all. It arises in the tension between old and emergent desires and involves the reconciliation of old and new. It achieves the unification of all values in a constant process of completion and conservation. It culminates at the point at which all values are fused into total meaning.

"Religion is an operation upon or within all values."

Therefore, religion is not a system of ideas for application, but an operation of experience requiring continuous

"Religion
aims at life
and its
greatest
possible
fullness."

participation. Coe believed that Christian principles and practices could only remain Christian by changing, and he spoke of "the divine plan of human development" in the slow discriminating growth of meanings and values in human experience, both individually and socially. Man is not only a self-identifying being, he is also a self-valuing being; more even than that, he is a self-transcending being.

The Personality Principle

Coe delighted in persons. He never forgot the laborer in Evanston who refused to use the public library because it was the product of rich men's largesse and the embodiment of rich men's attitudes. He never ceased to be amazed when instinctive judgments of value like that pricked his own highly educated conscience.

The appearance of personal judgment in organic evolution could not be exactly explained, and for Coe that added to its wonder. There must have been some "overplus" in an organism to bring preferences to birth in a being that had never before preferred anything. "Continually out of the unfree clod that is the organism there springs the flower that is the free person," he wrote. It could not have been by chance. It must have been rooted in the depths of cosmic and earthly reality. But it was equally impressive to Coe that, personal experience having emerged, the overplus continues to operate, producing "leanings" which result in the increase of moral significance as history and individual life continue. Taken together, the emergence of persons within nature and the growing moral significance of persons is all the evidence Coe needs for the existence of God. More important than

George Albert Coe, *What Is Christian Education?* (New York: Scribner's, 1935).

this, however, is the inference concerning the nature of God. He, too, must have been capable of making a moral choice and of working it out in nature—that is, God is both personal and immanent.

It is more impressive still that in each person that supra-historical overplus and these historical leanings produce something unique. It is neither ontological nor complete, however. It is flowing, "like time itself," said Coe. It binds together its own past and future in the decisions uniting old desire and new. It holds to meanings in the flux of events, but more, by redirecting its experience it creates new meanings where otherwise there would have been none. It is not only unique, it is genuinely original. Persons must therefore be called creative.

"There is something original in every person."

However, while the personality principle produces in each person something that is unique, it also leans him toward other persons. Since we all share group life, "Whatever any person prizes has some value for me," Coe said, enough to make it possible for me to enter into fellowship with him. "I never become a mere individual," Coe wrote. The permanence that all human beings experience in the flux of growth is directly related to the fact that personality is inherently interpersonal. My thoughts, my desires, even my willfulness, are expressions in me of the groups—domestic, political, economic, and religious—within or among which I have lived. The name for this sharing relation is love. "Only on the basis of out-going good-will can we really get acquainted with each other," he wrote. But it is not the sort of love, he warned, that makes man "dependent, crowd-minded, institutionalized." It is a radically religious matter because it has to do with growing values, a radically scientific matter because it is not self-centered, and a radically ethical matter because it guides action by regard for personality. "If discoveries are

". . . the stern as well as friendly love that can create a just society"

not made," Coe wrote, "this is a sign that our love is languid."

The Creative Principle

The principle of the worth of persons is not a new thing, of course. Some of the prophets of Israel approximated it. Jesus appears explicitly to have ascribed worth to the humblest of persons and to have ascribed the attitude to his Heavenly Father as his source. It would appear to be a prime essential of the Christian faith. Thus, if there be a God, the Great Valuer of Persons, "he will be most manifest where we take risks on behalf of persons." But the fact is that the principle is still in an undeveloped condition in the Christianity that professes it. "Our slips and our evasions are a disgrace to us," said Coe. Even more significant, however, is that "we have not done the thinking and the planning that alone can give effect to what we think we believe." If this be the case, Christian education must not consist of transmitting to the young what Christianity presently is. Because transmission of known facts and assumptions looks to be an easy task, this is what education has generally amounted to in Christianity. What is required, rather, is an education as creative of original meaning and value as the personality principle itself. This will never even have the appearance of being easy. Indeed, it would be an education actually participating in the creation of new values. If "to be Christian is to embark on voyages of exploration, with all the uncertainties, dangers and frequent failures," as Coe once wrote that it was, Christian education would need to be an exploratory enterprise, too.

The Educational Principle

"The art in Christian Education," wrote Coe, "must consist in inducing pupils to make experiments that, being real at the learner's stage of experience, will show where the truth lies, and at the same time leave the personality fresh for further experimentation." He intended it to be a radical concept.

The principle is that persons will discover and practice the worth of persons as they discover the differences that exist here and now between relations that are governed by active love and those that are not. Persons do not do that by being told and commanded. They learn through first pleasurably experiencing what Coe called the "living epistles" of family, church, and school that make Christian fellowship a reality to him. Then, in order to lift the learner above mere imitation, or "good-natured drift," he must be exposed to situations in which regard for personality is difficult, so that he may learn to discriminate differences, recognize problems, see causal relations. It is then that the Bible may come alive for him, not as a part of "the dead past," "a thing per se," to be learned apart from experience "on a dead level," but with all its own "sparkle of highlights" and "gloom of shadows" and "demonstrations of the meaning and power of love." The word that gives life, Coe insisted, is "always that which is made flesh and dwells among men": "the systematic, critical examination and reconstruction of relations between persons, guided by Jesus' assumption that persons are of infinite worth, and by the hypothesis of the existence of God, the Great Valuer of Persons."

Christian education is involvement, under the judgment of love, in present relations and interactions between persons: "We love God only when we take his point of view, and we can take his point of view only through some experience of our own in which we actually exercise Godlike interest in another." For Coe, "indwelling love" becomes the basic principle in education.

". . . experiments with the hypothesis of a Christlike God"

"The first thing in Christian Education," wrote Coe, "is a personal fellowship." Thus, it will consist of providing for children "conditions in which love is experienced, wrought into steady and deliberate living by the help of both intellectual analysis and habit formation, and developed into a faith that illumines the crises and mysteries of life." Expanded and applied, this is the social theory of religious education that exerted influence and precipitated controversy among American Protestants between the two World Wars. He wrote *The Social Theory of Religious Education* during the First War, with "the wail of children in the lands at war in my ears." It was a cry, he felt, for "the sort of education that faces, and understands, the great madness that is abroad, and not only understands, but also knows, the resources of human nature and religion." The future of society, he believed, depended on a social education created and guided by Christian principles. He was specific about that ten years later in *What Is Christian Education?*

The first step was to make pupils acquainted with persons who really love them and others also. The process begins in the home. In the school, the teacher of the new class of preschoolers makes it her primary task to make the little children happily acquainted with her and with one another. The love that the teacher has for the individual pupil is a disciplined, adult capacity, and it becomes the support and catalyst for the children's love for each other. The class is freed to learn to become a sharing group, a little beloved-community, by virtue of its own interpersonal relations. Rules and regulations and schedules are discarded as obstructions to this learning process.

George Albert Coe, *The Social Theory of Religious Education* (New York: Scribner's, 1917).

Once this introductory experience is under way, the second and more difficult phase begins: the enlargement of this primary level of learning to larger and more diffuse groups. What begins as family loyalty must be merged into human interests of the widest scope. The experience is channeled to flow out toward the whole needy world in steps as large and as fast as the individuals and groups can take—church, community, races and classes, world government. Education is an expanding series of social activities; repeated social acts become social habits; enlarged social consciousness is developed in a series of actual social undertakings. The "law of love" becomes "the law of instruction." A great deal of specific factual learning and experimental discovery is necessarily involved, but it comes as the result of discovering negative relationships that are not understood or not adequate and of turning them into positive relationships that instructively increase to more inclusive application.

". . . to awaken personality and to help it to rich self-activity in a society of persons"

Finally, in this loving, the learner discovers the love of God. This education in the art of brotherhood contains within itself the most vital of all possible methods of evoking faith in a fatherly God and in a unified human destiny. Insofar as any pupil finds satisfaction or what seems to him to be a real life in this sharing, he experiences the divine purpose, and that is a Christian experience. "If it be possible, thus, to fuse love and faith," Coe said, "so that even in childhood the voice of God and the voice of human need shall be one voice, this is the path that religious education should by all means choose." Then he added, "It is possible."

"Where love is God is."

One student enjoyed repeating the statement of a child in one of the Coe-dominated schools: "In that Sunday School they teach you all about God. In this one they teach you to help God."

Though his theology is technically implicit, Coe is explicit enough about it. Theology is implicit for Coe because it is projected from the religious experience of men. It is not speculative because it arises directly from data. It is not systematic because it does not deal with the spectrum of classical Christian doctrines. It is not orthodox because Coe makes no effort to correlate his assertions with tradition. It is explicit, however, because Coe states clearly the theological implications of his psychology of religion, specifically denies any effort to construct a theological system, and makes no apology for the unorthodox nature of his theological conclusions.

A Personal God

Liberal Christian theology had entered the twentieth century generally committed to the doctrine of the immanence of God. On the basis of the classic insistence of the absolute separation of the natural and the supernatural, theologians had found it almost impossible to deal meaningfully with the theory of evolution. John Dewey, of course, had solved the problem by rejecting the supernatural outright. Liberal theologians had suggested that if God could be thought to be actively related to the physical world, evolution could be his way of working in nature. The discovery of oriental philosophy by such men as James Bissett Pratt, who taught philosophy at Boston University, gave an unexpected boost to the principle of immanence. The theological Darwinists talked about "resident divine forces within nature." In comparison, it seemed a rather modest claim when theologians like Borden Parker Bowne at Boston University School of Theology asserted that God was at work within man.

But all this was far too speculative for Coe. He began with man and worked out into both God and nature.

The basic datum for Coe is personality. That it appeared from the ground of nonpersonal nature is a fact to be both appreciated and projected. Naturalism, such as Dewey's, is precisely the result of failing to deal as seriously with the phenomena of personality as with the phenomena of the subpersonal. There must be some explanation for the fact that there is a being dominated by purposes rather than by impulses. "The human type of living," Coe says, "has come into existence through persistent selection of hard lines of action rather than easy ones." The answer, for Coe, is that man has been "called" to choosing the difficult and the creative. Every man experiences this sort of choosing as a self-assertive "yielding," a "surrender in which I nevertheless achieve freedom." The immanent force in this creative choice is God. And since the result for man is personality, the force itself is that of a personal being, "in that he realizes himself by promoting our self-realization."

The fact that the appearance of man does not represent a break in evolutionary development indicates to Coe that the whole of evolution is a process of realizing moral purpose. This means for Coe that "the laws of nature are simply the orderly methods of his rational will," that "in all the things that our hands handle we deal with him," that "in whatever our eyes look upon or our ears listen to we have to do with God," and that "the correlation of mind and brain is just the phenomenal aspect of the real correlation of our mind with the divine power which sustains us." God is, for Coe, "the deepest fact of man's mind."

The implication is clear and Coe does not dodge it. The development, both physiological and moral, that man receives through nature is part of God's intent for the whole universe. "In all our faculties of intellect, of will, of conscience, of emotion, we are with and in God." When we, in turn, consciously work as educators, helping children to achieve their own personality through choosing and experiencing, God is working through our reason and will to carry forward the universal plan.

A Creative God

There is, of course, more ahead. The emergence of personality is a milestone in evolution, but not the end of the journey, for God's creative work continues. God is the indwelling germ-principle in the creation of human beings. He is also the indwelling germ-principle in the creation of an ideal society of persons.

". . . a
divine-human
democracy
as a
final
social ideal"

The development of personality is a tender thing, easily distorted and blighted. It must have fellowship in order to flourish. "Only in and through some human godlikeness," said Coe, "does any of us know the Father." The real drive of God's work within man, now, is to the achievement of a society in which brotherly, ethical love operates, in which "there is no separation between human society and divine." Jesus' own fusion of divine love with human love "leads on with the inevitableness of fate to the ideal of a democratic organization of society." If the Father wishes loving will to be the rule in all human relations, "How can the Father himself," Coe demanded, "be willing to be an autocrat, an aristocrat, or a plutocrat?" It is a rhetorical question: "Divine love cannot realize itself anywhere but in a genuine industrial democracy." Christians must learn to think of God as a co-creator "within human society in the democratic manner of working, helping, sacrificing, persuading, cooperating, achieving." The end is a "Democracy of God," which Coe substitutes for the regal concept of a Kingdom of

God. It is a progressive ideal, for "in and through his growing participation in the creation of an ideal society, (man) will realize his fellowship with the Father," and the growing life of brotherly love will produce "a massing of human energy" that will eventually make impossible greed, licentiousness and the lust of power.

Christianity is a part of this grand creative enterprise, not because of its doctrines or its special persons, but because of Jesus' ascription of the principle of worth to persons. Because Jesus perceived and demonstrated it, he will always be a source of inspiration and guidance. But if Jesus had not happened to grasp that principle, it would be of ultimate worth anyway, for it is not secondary to any thing or any body. "The loyalty of the Christian, accordingly," Coe once wrote, "is loyalty not to one person, even Jesus, but to persons."

Sources of Idealistic Concepts

Taken in the widest possible sense, Idealism is the main road of European philosophical development from ancient to modern times. Beginning in the Golden Age of Greece when man was discovering the wonders of the human mind, and running through to nineteenth-century Germany when abstract speculation reached its highest pinnacle of fascination, it leads from Athens to Berlin. The road is not always straight or distinct: sometimes it wanders, and sometimes it is almost completely overgrown; during one period it seems to be the only road there is, and in another it seems straight and level with many side roads leading in; in the last hundred years, most of the side roads seem to be leading out.

Idealism holds that the apparent self-sufficiency of nature is illusory and that nature depends on mind. It says that if we are looking for the reality of things—nature or anything else—we shall find it to be mental: "the thinker and his thought, the will and its doings, the self and its self-expression." If nature appears to be different, philosophical analysis will show that, sooner or later, it is dependent on mind for its being and behavior. Idealism had its first sources in very ancient intuitions about the meaning of life and may be described as an attempt to make human hunches intellectually respectable. Since these hunches were originally religious in nature, Idealism has often appeared to be a philosophical outgrowth of religion, and since Christianity came into a world dominated by Greek philosophy, it has traditionally been closely associated with Idealism.

William Ernest Hocking, *Types of Philosophy* (New York: Scribner's, 1929).

Plato, 427-347 B.C.

Looking back, especially a long way back, it is easy to give exaggerated credit to the first man in any movement of whom history provides a fairly complete account. As the first fully documented philosopher of Western history, Plato is often accorded either praise or blame for being the first idealist. In any case, he lived at one of the most exciting times of world history, a period in which the human mind was becoming conscious of itself and its relation to the universe. Greek architects and sculptors had achieved buildings of grandeur and grace. The politicians had developed the city-state and its ordered and peaceful way of life. Only a generation before, Sophocles and Euripides had been annually contributing new plays to the Athenian festivals, working out through the control of poetic form and dramatic action the relation between men and gods in classic tragedy. Socrates was using the imaginative narrative and the question-and-answer dialogue as a medium of philosophical discussion.

At the age of twenty, the handsome, graceful, and intelligent son of a noble family, Plato became the pupil of Socrates and for sixty years devoted himself to "the search for truth." Truth can be achieved, he believed, through the application of man's most exciting resource, the mind, and the best thinking was in the form of dialogue. When a man thinks, he sets the stage in his own mind and becomes all the actors in the speculative drama. Playing one against another in his own mental theater, he asks questions and answers them, evaluates the answers and tries others. But the total control of each of the actors,

Man is a thinker.

See especially **Republic** and **Phaedo**, and also **Symposium** and **Phaedrus**, in whole or parts in collections and anthologies.

though an intellectually fascinating discipline, is artificial because the living individual is not an isolated thinker, and the live give-and-take of ideas in actual dialogue is the best method of thinking. Both the goal and the method for reaching it illustrate the assumption of the primacy of mind and reason in the experience of man. In Plato's Greece it was an assumption almost unchallenged.

Physical reality is a temporary embodiment of idea.

There are ideas, Plato found, that continue to crop up in these dialogues, and when they do they seem so real and enduring that objects of sense are found to be fleeting and insubstantial when compared to them. Indeed, it seemed that when he and his pupils through the years talked about physical objects, they could be dealt with best as imperfect embodiments of mental concepts. Each actual thing is somewhat less than pure representation in time and space of a permanent and complete mental quality. Of course, there are also concepts which do not have physical form, such as absolute goodness, pure beauty, and essence in general. Moreover, these are precisely the greatest and most important realities. Appropriately, we know them only abstractly, that is, in pure thought as never actually embodied in physical objects.

Ultimate reality is of the same substance as ideas.

And since there are no sense-clues to their abstract conceptual existence, as with cabbages, kings, and many other things, it must have been that we ourselves knew them in some purely conceptual existence of our own before we were embodied in physical form. Indeed, ultimate reality is conceptual in quality, exhibiting the form and order of abstract thinking. Before the present world existed, it must have been a capacity for thought which imposed a sufficient degree of form and order on shapeless matter to produce the physical things with which we now deal in this life.

The prologue to the Fourth Gospel is a prose poem, and it begins, "In the beginning was the *logos*." In the Mediterranean world, the word *logos* was capable of double meaning: "idea," or the principle of conceptual meaning, if one were Greek; "word," or the embodied speech-act of God addressed to men, if one were Hebrew. Though it is something of an oversimplification, idealist theologians have translated it to read, "In the beginning was the Idea, and the Idea was with God and the Idea was God. . . . And Idea entered flesh and dwelt among us."

In the beginning was the Idea.

This translation, however, should not obscure the more subtle fact that both Platonic metaphysics and Hebrew theology understood ultimate reality to be non-physical: to the Greek it was mental, to the Hebrew spiritual. The Hebrew was never certain as to how rational it might be without ceasing to be spiritual, the Greek as to how spiritual it might be without ceasing to be rational. The Greek tended to think that it was essentially different from physical reality, the Hebrew that it was directly related to physical reality. But for both, this metaphysical reality could not be something solitary, it was something to be expressed. The *idea* is embodied in physical things, the *word* is spoken and is heard. For both the ultimate reality is in relation to this world, and this is achieved through a creative process which is the outworking of its own nature.

It was this common ground that was emphasized by John, for what purposes or to what extent it is no longer possible to know. That emphasis was carried on by the Apologists, Christians of the second century who desired to commend the Christian faith to a world dominated by Greek thought. It became the intellectual foundation for

Descartes, *Discourse on Method* (in many editions and anthologies).

Augustine, a theologian of the fourth century who wished to unify Christian thought as the sole claimant to Roman allegiance. It was the thread for early medieval thinkers, Christians who felt the need of establishing the permanence of the church in a world of short individual life and social disunity.

René Descartes, 1596-1650

In his celebrated Gifford Lectures of 1932-33, Archbishop William Temple blamed Descartes for personally imposing on modern philosophy the Idealist assumption of the distinction between thought and things. He labeled it "the Cartesian *faux pas*" and called the arrival at that conclusion "the most disastrous moment in the history of Europe." Descartes, himself, gave Temple the right to name a moment, and subsequent philosophy has tended to agree with Temple's judgment.

The moment came, to the never ending amusement of contemporary philosophers, "in a stove." Descartes spent the whole day there. He had been discharged from his service with French mercenary soldiers in Flanders and was waiting to go home. It was wintertime and cold, and the only place he could find to be warm was in a kitchen with one of those traditional Dutch ovens that occupied an entire corner of the room. The intensity of his thought turned the whole room into an oven. He was twenty-three, "delighted with Mathematics because of the certainty of its demonstrations and the evidence of its reasoning," and ravaged, as the saying goes, "with so many doubts and errors that it seemed to me that the effort to instruct myself had no effect other than the increasing

"I think: therefore I am."

William Temple, *Nature, Man and God* (London: Macmillan, 1934), and other editions.

discovery of my ignorance." He determined to spend the day exploring his selfhood by putting the doubts to work. He would systematically and meticulously examine every idea or proposition his mind contained, and if he could doubt it he would discard it. At last he found himself with one idea he could neither doubt nor discard: it was the idea of himself, and what he found to characterize it was that it was thinking. It was an original hunch. "From that I was a substance the whole essence or nature of which is to think," and "this me is entirely distinct from my body."

He had distinguished sharply between thought and matter. As between the two, it was thought that was the more original and real, and selfhood is the nature of thinking. Descartes then finds God on the thinking side of the distinction. Descartes is not a perfect being because he has doubts. But he is able to conceive of a kind of knowledge which is perfect because in it there are no doubts. Since he was imperfect, he could not be the source of the idea of a perfect being: the less perfect could not be the cause of the more perfect. On the other hand, he could not receive it from nothing: nothing cannot be the cause of something. The only alternative is that such a perfect being exists to cause the idea to occur to an imperfect being: God therefore exists. He has been proved to exist by the same mental operations that demonstrated that I exist: we are both thinkers. From these two basic certainties—himself and God—he moved on to assume the reality of his own body and of nature, but it is of a different kind: they, too, exist because I think, but they are not thinkers.

"Whence did I learn to think of something more perfect than myself?"

Descartes' immediate successors tried to minimize the chasm between mind and body but fixed it as the primary problem of modern philosophy. Baruch Spinoza (1632-1677), son of a Dutch family of Jewish refugees from

. . . Substance, Thought and Extension

the Spanish inquisition, who learned his Latin in a Jesuit school, attempted to deal with the issue by proposing an absolutely infinite and indefinable necessarily existing substance with two attributes, thought and extension. God is thus both the body and the mind of the world, and man is a unique mode (or "modification") of God in which both thought and extension are present, "a little island of God's essence" surrounded by the modes of God's Extension. Gottfried Wilhelm von Leibnitz (1646-1716), a diplomat, jurist, historian, mathematician, and theologian, met a disciple of Descartes in Paris and knew Spinoza at the Hague. He tried to solve the Cartesian problem and to avoid the pantheism of Spinoza, and he strengthened the hold of idealistic rationalism on European philosophy. From a speculative analysis he proposed a theory of monads or "living units" of which the world is made: simple monads, which constitute all material things; soul monads, which possess the perceptivity and awareness of animal consciousness; and spirit monads, which are characterized by the power of reason. All these monads are absolutely independent of each other in both kind and number—"windowless," Leibnitz called them—but each functions so perfectly that an organic and intellectual harmony results, something like that of a multitude of clocks in a shopwindow, all their different kinds of wheels and levers working separately to tell precisely the same time. The source of all this intricate development and intermeshing of monads is an all-inclusive Macro-Monad, limitless and rational.

. . . Body, Soul and Mind

George Berkeley, 1685-1753

"Idealism," says a contemporary authority, "starts with Berkeley." Berkeley was English, and English philosophers have been at the center of what has sometimes been called "the idealist controversy," both because some of them had the courage to state Idealism with clarity and without compromise and because some others took issue in the same manner. However, being an Irishman who arrived in English philosophy by way of an unsuccessful attempt to establish a college in Bermuda and three years of school-teaching in Rhode Island to earn his passage back, Berkeley is not parochially English. "Westward," he said, "the course of empire takes its way." And the central arguments on which Berkeley based his attack on the independent existence of matter had been used separately in some form by previous philosophers who have often been called idealists. Nonetheless, it was Berkeley who put them together so unequivocally that it has been necessary for philosophers since to be either for or against. Indeed, he made it so easy to be against that his positions have often been caricatured.

Berkeley argued that the specific qualities we ascribe to physical objects are such that they could not exist apart from being perceived by an experiencing being. Particular things like trees or tables or the spokes in the wheels of railway cars are given their existence by sentient beings who see and touch them. They exist, that is, as ideas. Matter, "qua matter" as Aristotle would say, does not exist for it is an ideal speculative substance and cannot be seen or touched. What one can experience directly, without the

"To be is to be perceived."

A. C. Ewing, *The Idealist Tradition* (Glencoe, Illinois: Free Press, 1957); Berkeley, *Treatise on the Principles of Human Knowledge* (1710).

help of the senses, is the reality of self, an existent more
important and real than physical objects. By comparison,
the existence of objects is inferred from the data provided
by the self. When all that is not taken seriously for
exactly what it says philosophically, it is easy to make fun
of it. If a tree falls in the forest and there is no one to see
or hear it, the tree neither existed nor fell. Or even more
amusing, the railway wheels have spokes only when the
train is standing in the station because when it is passing
through the country no one can see them. But Berkeley's
answer is that there is one personal self who always per-

ceives everything. Because of his continuous perception,
things have the continuous existence our common sense
supposes. By perceiving, God is constantly creating. Thus
reality is precisely what we experience it to be in ourselves,
a meaningful world of idea. All this Berkeley worked out
as a young man. Later he became an Anglican bishop and
abandoned philosophy for the church and tar-water, the
latter of which he described as providing the cups that
cheer but do not inebriate.

Immanuel Kant, 1724-1804

Contemporary philosophers are still working with the material Kant provided. Some call him "the founder of German Idealism." He was on Berkeley's side of the issues,
though on the other side of the Channel, and the Channel
is much wider philosophically than geographically. Kant
was a professional philosopher, prodigiously gifted and
informed, whose chief life events are the publication dates
of his books and whose daily life was so disciplined that
the people of Koenigsberg set their watches by his morning walks.

It is the unity of our own conscious experience that

gives the world its apparent unity, he reasoned. From the world we receive a multitude of chaotic impressions. Our perception organizes them. Kant claimed to have examined all the possibilities and to have discovered that, reason being what it is, there are just twelve kinds of perception —three each of quantity, quality, relation, modality. Physical objects are actually there, of course, but are known to us only through this filter of purely rational categories. What I know is therefore the product of my own mind. I never know the things themselves. The self contributes unity to the things because it is unified.

. . . rational apriori categories

Antecedent to this purely rational set of categories, there is a practical set. There are universal moral laws, and they may be stated by pure reason, for example, "an individual cannot morally engage in some act if he sees that such an act cannot be universally practiced by all men." However, as a matter of prerational experience, man feels an obligation or imperative to act in accordance with these universal moral laws. This sense of duty is not the result of experience, though: it is rooted in a priori practical reason as are the categories of perception in pure reason. Duty gives us, in practical terms, the same sort of assurance about behavior as do the categories of perception in rational terms about objects. The moral imperative is categorical.

. . . categorical moral imperatives

However, when it comes to practical behavior, man has a real freedom: he may choose to act morally for rational rather than practical reasons, that is, to perform the good act solely for the sake of good and not for the sake of reward. Now, the ultimate good for man, as implied by the categorical moral imperative, is that man shall live in harmony with the moral law, and the freedom of man

. . . freedom

Immanuel Kant, *The Critique of Pure Reason* (1st edition, 1781; 2nd edition, 1787).

implies that he will take a long time to learn to do so: an infinite progress—immortality of the soul—is necessary in order to attain perfect moral holiness.

Not only the existence, a priori, of the purely rational categories through which man knows physical objects, but far more significantly, the existence of the categorical

moral imperative and the lack of moral guarantees in the natural world, make a Supreme Moral Being morally necessary to guarantee contentment as a result of moral acts.

In agreement with the idealist tradition, Kant read everything from physical objects to God in terms of self-hood and its given qualities. His great contribution was the addition of moral to rational characteristics of human and divine selfhood.

Georg Wilhelm Friedrich Hegel, 1770-1831

Two realities fascinated Hegel, the incongruities of daily life and the capacity of the mind to produce meaning from them. A story, probably apocryphal, tells that when he was a student on one of those long walking tours through the country German students traditionally take as part of their education, he was offered a great bowl of cherries for breakfast. He had never seen such bounty. Over-whelmed by the prospect of all that physical enjoyment, he was unable to eat them and fell to pondering the significance of balance in life and logic as contributing to the positive meaning of the whole experience. In his mature philosophy he was passionately concerned about "whole-ness" and logically concerned about the way in which parts contributed to wholeness.

The world, for Hegel, was not a collection of self-sub-

Immanuel Kant, *The Critique of Practical Reason* (1788).

sistent units, but a whole. Separateness, no matter how it might appear at first glance, is unreal, and nothing is ultimately and completely real except the whole. The Whole is "The Absolute." Each unit has reality only as it is related to the whole.

. . . The Whole

The Whole is also rational. The logic, however, does not proceed from major premise to minor premise to conclusion in a straight line; it is both complex and dynamic, for it proceeds from the interaction of opposites through the production of a new unity to a synthesis. For example: the thesis is that "The Absolute is Pure Being" without qualities; but Pure Being without qualities is Nothing; therefore we are led to the antithesis that "The Absolute is Nothing." It follows that "The Union of Being and Not-Being" is neither, but rather "A Becoming" which results from the interaction of both. The synthesis is that "The Absolute is Becoming." This, also, won't do, of course, because there has to be something that becomes. In this dynamic way our views of reality develop. The process is what is important: each stage contains all the earlier stages, still at work. Knowledge is developed in this way. History works this way. At the base lies the paradox between *idea* and *nature* which produces the synthesis *mind* or *spirit*. By participation in the dialectical process we enter into reality.

. . . Parts

. . . Dialectic

The *absolute idea*, toward which the process leads, is God. "The Absolute Idea, as unity of the Subjective and Objective Idea, is the notion of the Idea," says Hegel, "a notion whose object is Idea as such, and for which the ob-

. . . Absolute Idea

Hegel, *Phenomenology* (1807) and two volumes of *Logic* (1812, 1816). An introduction to Hegel (and others) is supplied by Bertrand Russell in *History of Western Philosophy* (New York: Simon and Schuster, 1945), though he does not agree with Hegel (and others).

jective is Idea—an Objective which embraces all characteristics in its unity."

During his last thirteen years, Hegel lectured at Berlin, enjoying an almost total preeminence in the philosophical world. At the end of the nineteenth century, most of the leading philosophers of America and England as well as of Germany were Hegelians. Many Protestant theologians were influenced by him. Karl Marx was a disciple and wove many of Hegel's dialectical principles into his dialectical materialism.

Idealism is any philosophical view emphasizing the mind, or what is characteristic of persons, as fundamental to understanding the world and of more permanence and significance than the physical things of the world. Briefly, *idea* is ultimately real, and *idea* is held in mind, ultimately the *Mind*. In theistic ages the inevitable implication is that God is mindlike. I have a mind; because I am able to possess real ideas, I am real. By this mind of mine I am related to the *Mind*. Knowledge comes through mind, from inside out as well as in response to what is *out there*. The universe and I cohere in the process of logical operations. Walt Whitman, the nineteenth-century balladeer of the American dream, celebrated the divine-human cohesion in "Song of Myself." "I celebrate myself and sing myself. / I believe in you my soul," he wrote. "And I know that the hand of God is the promise of my own, / And I know that the Spirit of God is the brother of my own."

Idealists have been system-builders, teachers and writers, and they have left a traceable line of development from ancient to modern times. Their influence on modern thinkers has been vast, though sometimes by way of opposition and correction rather than by way of agreement and refinement.

The Idealistic Nature of Personalism

The great discovery of the nineteenth century was the I. Psychologists described it, and psychoanalysts accounted for it. Frontiersmen applied it, and industrialists exploited it. Philosophers absolutized it. "Idealism," said one of them, "models the universe on consciousness."

Personal Idealism

By the beginning of the twentieth century, especially in the United States, Idealism had become Personalism. It was a subtle but significant shift, for though it had its precedents it went beyond them. Protagoras had emphasized the personalistic character of knowledge in the famous dictum, "Man is the measure of all things." Socrates had recognized the soul of self as the center from which sprang all man's actions and had counseled, "Know thyself." Plato had recognized the person in his doctrine of the soul, but turned philosophy toward the abstract idea. Aristotle had contributed by insisting that only the concrete and individual could be real. Augustine asserted that thought, and therefore the thinker, was the most certain of all things. During the century of Roman collapse, Boethius said the word that proved to be definitive for the Middle Ages, "A person is the individual substance of a rational nature." During the scientific revolution, Personalism offered the main opposition to Naturalism and Positivism. Step by step, Idealism had become the affirmation of reality in the person, the distinguishing characteristic of which was the capacity to reason, and of the personal nature of the universe.

The Reality of the Self

"Personality," modern personalists like to say, "is the key to reality." They begin metaphysics with the facts of human experience, and one of them boasts that personalism is the only position that is really empirical. Experience begins with self-experience: I find myself; I do not invent myself; I am experience. It is a first datum.

Self-experience is characterized by a conscious unity of many parts. We are aware first of unity, only thereafter of the parts. Psychological and philosophical analyses help uncover the complexity, but experience shows it to be there. Every person is thus a system, not a substance or an essence. Personality is thus also, from the start, active and interactive; each person is a process of constant interaction with brain, nervous system, the subsconscious, the physical and social environments. This self-activity is regarded by personalists as being free to choose among given possibilities for action, to shape the direction of his life without supposing that the self is the creator of his own being and capacities. Personality is also purposive, aware of ends, ideals, conceptions of a possible future, and able to apply freedom to produce achievement. Personality is rational, which means the ability to relate parts to wholes in systems and to relate the present to the future in purpose. Personality is social, which means the capacity to communicate feeling, purpose, and thought between persons.

Some such profile comprises Personalism's "first principle"—a postulate which enables one to interpret and organize the facts and implications of his experience.

The Self and Knowledge

Awareness of the self is, however, not knowledge. It is, rather, a kind of immediate experience, unchallengeable but also undemonstrable. Immediate experience has to do

Edgar Sheffield Brightman, *An Introduction to Philosophy* (New York: Henry Holt, 1925).

with the actual presence of feelings, qualities, relations within the given. But one also experiences references beyond immediacy into memory, to other persons and things, and relations beyond the given. Knowledge relates the data of immediacy and reference into a coherent whole. This is, of course, a subjective knowledge of the self. But the self is always in interaction with something not itself. When we observe what acts on the self from outside, we can know the self objectively through its interaction with its environment. But more, the behavior of a self provides a great deal of knowledge about the physical world. The same is true of the social environment. Communication with other persons is a form of adding to knowledge about persons.

Knowing is ultimately personal. The self-experience relates itself to a complex set of facts beyond and outside direct experience. Knowledge consists of relating, interpreting, and understanding these facts in the only way I can, namely, in terms given by self-experience. To be knowledge, it must be adequate and coherent, that is, it must take into account all the relevant facts and organize them into a consistent whole. I know reality not only because I encounter it but also because its very nature is such that my personality can deal with it on the terms provided by my selfhood. In short, that which is known must be personal in order to be known.

The World and the Self

Personality is thus asserted to be a principle in me giving unity and meaning to the outside world as persons experience it. The world out there must therefore be sufficiently like me to permit this interpretation. Because I encounter reality, I assert its existence; because I can deal with it personally, I assert its personal qualities. "The personalist," says one, "matches belief in the self with the belief that the entire universe is personal in nature."

Anthropomorphism, the insistence that the cosmos is like man, is an ancient practice, of course, and has long been considered somewhat primitive. Modern personalists would rather think that theirs is a cosmomorphic principle, that man is like the cosmos. The universe, they argue, is such as to include and explain you and me, with all our characteristic qualities. Just as my personality is a clue to the understanding of other persons very different from myself yet possessing certain powers in common with me, so too it may be a clue to the nature of all energy or power or being or whatever. This is the hypothesis of Personalism, that what man knows about himself is true about the cosmos. As a small but indigenous and representative part of it, the self is the first datum for dealing with the whole.

Some personalists posit the absolute Self. They hold that they are required by the implications of their own experience to infer the existence of such an absolute. The absolute contains and includes all finite selves. It is thus not unlimited but self-limiting. It is an all-experiencer, experiencing what every finite self experiences. It thus knows all the yearning, struggling, and fulfillment of finitude while being absolute. It both shares and transcends, a characteristic of personality, and relates parts and wholes, a characteristic of rationality, and is conscious, meaning "essentially what I mean when I describe myself as conscious." This absolute, however, is the object of finite reason, not the subject of finite experience, and is therefore thought not to be the same as God.

Mary Whiton Calkins, *The Persistent Problems of Philosophy* (New York: Macmillan, first edition 1907).

One personalist has based a long and persuasive book on the principle that "the philosophy called Personalism is on the whole the most coherent and inclusive account of our world that he knows of." Coherence is the principle that everything is a connected, "sticking-together" whole. Any judgment is true if it is both self-consistent and coherently connected with our system of judgments as a whole. The coherence principle implies that, as truth is one coherent system to the mind, so reality must be one coherent system in the cosmos. My experience is fragmentary, my personality is incomplete, but truth is one organic whole. Fragmentariness and incompleteness do not impair the whole, but rather suggest the existence of a whole which includes and transcends them. Only a mind, it is argued, could be such an individual whole as our logical idea requires that reality shall be. What we call nature is not a miscellaneous assemblage of unrelated facts and events. It can only be understood as being a whole and therefore having some kind of mental life at its core that resembles in its working the ways in which our own minds work, comprising a logically coherent whole because its own nature as exhibited in us requires it. It provides us with a continuous, interrelated set of problems and answers that simultaneously makes thinking necessary and successful.

The world is rational.

Theistic Personalism

Borden Parker Bowne of Boston University is usually credited with giving Personalism its systematic form in America. It was only after calling his own system "objective idealism" for a long time, however, that he adopted the name "personalism." William James told his students at Harvard that Bowne had crawled into a hole and pulled the hole in after him. Bowne called God the "World Ground"—often in German—and said that it was personal in nature. The World Ground is the source of both thought and thing, knowledge is mediated through personality, personal life as known to both man and God is the test of form in logic and of value in ethics.

However, theism had been personalistic ever since the ancient Hebrews spoke of God in human terms and Jesus called him a Heavenly Father. It has always been a conviction of religious people that God is personal.

The Ontological Assertion

"A finite being cannot invent an infinite being."

Anselm, said to be of Canterbury because he spent his last sixteen years there as Archbishop though he did the writing for which history knows him as an Abbott in Normandy, originated the philosophical argument from man to God in the late eleventh century. He began from the universal human experience of the Middle Ages: I have an idea of a perfect Being. However, I am myself an imperfect and finite being, and since the imperfect cannot produce the infinite, it must be that I am able to think of it only because it does exist. Further, this idea I have is of a Being than which nothing greater can be conceived; now, an idea which exists in reality is greater than one which exists only in conception; therefore, if my idea is the greatest it must exist in reality; accordingly the perfect idea does exist and it is God.

Ideas are the result of realities.

It has been pointed out repeatedly that this is not a logical demonstration at all, but an assertion. Hocking says that "the God-Idea is the leap of the mind when confronted with the actualities of empirical existence." The

Anselm of Canterbury, *Cur Deus Homo* (in various editions and anthologies).

modern form of the argument is that when man thinks about his relation to the cosmos the idea of God arises as naturally as the idea of color arises in response to light waves. It is as reasonable to assume that there is an actual something which gives rise to the God-Idea in me as it is to assume that there is an actual color which gives rise to the color-idea in me. This God-Idea is not merely a subjective work of the imagination. And once in mind, Hocking goes to some length to point out, we find that it works as a tool with which to discover God in thought and in worship.

Man Is Personal

Personality is the master category: "The self is *the* datum," says E. S. Brightman repeatedly, and his teacher Bowne wrote, "Reality is what the rational, aesthetic, moral and religious nature of personality requires." What we find in our own personalities affords a basis for interpreting everything in terms of personality.

"The self is the datum."

The self is a genuine, organic whole and more than the sum of its parts. Gestalt psychology, especially, is helpful in making this clear. Yet, the self is not merely individualistic. As selves we are very much aware of dynamic interaction between individuals, and the social sciences reveal the presence within all individuals of common laws and common meanings. Political theory helps fill out the picture with its concept of the free cooperation of different and distinct individual persons in the attainment of common purposes.

Thus personality is not merely an idea, though it has ideas. It is, rather, a dynamic and conscious combination of thought, will, feeling, purpose. And this is the way the

William Ernest Hocking, *The Meaning of God in Human Experience* (New Haven: Yale, 1918).

world is. There is no power, no causality, no activity except in personality, and even matter is a kind of willed organization of consciousness. The aim of the universe, at all levels of physical things, universals, values, and consciousness, is a free and moral cooperation in support of personal worth. The essence of religion, then, is cooperation with this personal universe.

God Is Personal

For most Christians among American personalists, God is neither absolute nor idea, but person. He is complete, total, universal, infinite personality. Men are incomplete, partial, local, and finite personalities. It is true that I project on the universe what I discover to be most characteristic of myself. My own limited intelligence seeks total coherence, my need for individual companions suggests cosmic companionship, the organization of my partial personality suggests complete wholeness. It is also true that in the moment I become aware of these projections, I find myself to be a part of a greater whole. The qualities of my own experience, the harmony of nature and reason, the certainty of my own reality, seem also to come from beyond. God is experienced in this intersection, at what Hocking calls "the frontiers" of human experience.

". . . the divine companion"

What I discover there on the frontier is a dynamic combination of qualities, the pull and tension of which I recognize in my own personality. There is the subject-object tension in me which man has recognized in his tendency to regard some things and places as holy, and in his tendency to address God as "Thou" and not only as "It" or "He." There is the truth-error tension in me which man has found God dealing with in man. There is the one-and-the-many tension in me, which man has found and expressed in polytheistic, henotheistic, and monotheistic religions and which Christians have explained as the Trinity, "a procession out of the infinite reserve of life of the universe and men, without abandoning its absolute selfhood." There is the near-and-the-remote tension in me which men have found working in the transcendence and immanence of God. "The soul finds at length," says Hocking, "its divine companion."

But the word *person* must not be used referring to God too easily or romantically. "I do not love the word personality," Hocking wrote, and Brightman was determined to use it the hard way or not at all. If God is, like man, Person, and if man as Person is related to all other Persons, God must be related also. Now, being related means being relative. Brightman has the courage to print the implication: God is "finite-infinite." He is limited in a number of ways, for example, by physical creation including time and space. But most personally, and therefore most significantly, he is limited in will: there is a *given* element which is not part of the will of God. The *given* is "eternal within the will of God," a combination of the uncreated laws of reason and of all the equally uncreated disorderliness, pain, and suffering that may be called "surd." The *given* is in man, too, and he uses it freely not only to rebel but to do things genuinely original and unpredictable to God. However, God is not finally defeated, and the will of God "finds new avenues of advance and forever moves on in the cosmic creation of new values." God and man are both personal in that they are both in a continuous state of becoming. "God is the Cosmic Person," Brightman concluded, "whose will is governed by creative, patient will." And, he added, "the

". . . building into new creative advances every possible value"

Edgar Sheffield Brightman, *The Problem of God* (New York: Abingdon, 1930) and *Person and Reality* (New York: Ronald Press, 1958) edited posthumously by Bertocci, Newhall, and R. S. Brightman.

personalist insists that no process in nature or man is ever adequately understood, unless it is seen in relation to the possible cooperative, creative growth of persons."

The Liberal Lean

"That the personality of God and the sacredness of human personality express the true genius of the Christian religion, whatever may be said of its theology," wrote an American theologian, "is hardly open to question." It was precisely what liberal American churchmen were ready to hear.

Those eggheads who cared could find complete philosophical justification in personalist and idealistic metaphysics. Most preachers and laymen, however, shared an anti-intellectual inclination. The average theologian, said one of their critics in the fifties, is nothing but "a nervous, verbal word-magician"; he supposes that the life-process can be "neatly labelled, pigeon-holed, or cast into paradoxical form." Life is not that way. "Experience comes from within," and all that is real about me is the result of my personal understanding of it. Each person comes to his own understanding of experience at his own tempo. The infant learns to walk when he is ready. Persons build a ladder by which they rise from one experience to another. "Nobody," therefore, "needs to be told what Paul or Luther said about redemption before he can experience relationships that are redemptive." My religious experience comes to me as a person of final, infinite worth related directly to God. It must happen to me, individually, and "it can just as well happen before I know about anyone else's experience." Jesus said that the Great Commandments were, "Thou shalt love God, thy neighbor and

"The God of idea is the God of living ideas."

"Growth takes place in the present."

William C. Knudson, *The Philosophy of Personalism* (New York: Abingdon Press, 1927).

thyself." The experiential order runs from known to unknown: we begin by loving (with the aid of depth psychology and psychoanalysis) ourselves, move to loving (with the aid of group dynamics and group therapy) our neighbors, whom we cannot love if we cannot love ourselves, and finally are able to love God (whom we have not seen, with the aid of loving our neighbor whom we have seen).

At the beginning of the twentieth century, Bowne and others battled for the right to teach theistic Idealism, and in the twenties philosophical Idealism came under the attack of pragmatists and realists. But in the thirties, theistic personalism was the reigning theology in American seminaries and pulpits, in the forties it probably dominated the thinking of Christian education more than any other kind of theology, and in the fifties a popularized Personalism was the typical theology of the Protestant layman.

Idealism and Education

A recent educational textbook for teachers opens with a summary: "Thousands and thousands of pages, millions of words, and one conclusion: children grow; and a discovery: it is their own idea." The Greeks invented the word for education, *educatio*, and it means "to lead out" *from within*. Socrates said that virtue is knowledge, knowledge is teachable, and the knowledge a man most needs is knowledge of himself. Plato taught that the good life is the just life, the just life is the life ordered by wisdom, life is ordered by wisdom in the ideal state, the ideal Republic is established and maintained by education, and education is "a continuous discourse with oneself." For the idealist, educative experiences are personal in character, and the development of the mind is from within out, not from without in. However, this is but one side of the idealist educator's tradition: the other side is that man is not alone. Man exists in groups, and education takes place in an *Academia* in Athens, a *familia* in Rome, and in a Brotherhood in medieval Europe.

Johann Heinrich Pestalozzi, 1746-1827

Pestalozzi has been called "the champion of successful failures." His tombstone carries the motto, "All for others, nothing for himself." He said of himself that he was "everybody's plaything." His widowed mother brought him up "in complete self-abnegation" and with "tact and delicacy." His schoolmates called him "Harry Oddity of Foolbourough," and he apparently did not learn very much in school. He trained for the ministry but broke down in his trial sermon, shifted to law but became involved in anarchistic political movements, bought a farm near his native Zurich and failed miserably. Left with only the house and his own family, he turned it into an orphanage. Gradually he turned the orphanage into a school. In 1782 he published *Leonard and Gertrude,* a novel portraying a Swiss village with its poverty, drunkenness, and autocracy, contrasted to the sweetness and efficiency of Gertrude who trained children in her home. To Pestalozzi's disappointment, it was never viewed as an educational work. "To my grave," he acknowledged, "I shall remain in a kind of fog about most of my own views." As a result of writing it, however, he decided, "I want to be a schoolmaster," and took charge of an orphanage in Stanz. It closed soon, but historians say that it was "the cradle of the modern elementary school." During his last twenty years he was head of a boarding school at Yverdun. A peasant who came there to visit his son exclaimed, "Why this is not a school but a family!" Pestalozzi replied, "That is the greatest praise you can give me." Yet, he was visited by philosophers and educators, one of whom wrote, "Never have I been so filled with a sense of the sacredness of my vocation and the dignity of human nature." They spread his reforms throughout Europe.

"This work was founded by love."

His combination of eccentricity and love did much to change education from rote-input to self-development. Education was for Pestalozzi the way of leading a man from youth to destiny, but at the base of the conviction lay an impassioned concern for unprivileged children: "I lived like a beggar," he said, "in order to learn how to make beggars live like men." He democratized education by demonstrating that it is the right of every child to have his God-given powers fully developed. He became the first educator to make systematic observations of the growth of children, and learned to call it "organic," an inter-relating development of "head, hand and heart." It

". . . Not the head or the reason but the heart and the mother"

Heinrich Pestalozzi, *Leonard and Gertrude* and *Recollections,* parts of both appearing in many educational anthologies.

begins with concrete, individual experiences, and teaching consists of assisting the gradual unfolding of powers. Teaching depended upon the mutual sympathy of child and adult. No teacher was ever permitted to punish a child. He excluded all textbooks. He grouped children so that they could help each other. He discontinued the use of the catechism for religious teaching, insisting that religion was an inner emotion that expressed itself in its own ways and that they be developed in personal relationships. His principle always was that "Life Teaches," and he likened the teacher to a gardener. "The powers of our nature must, as it were, spring out of themselves," he said.

Friedrich Froebel, 1782-1852

Froebel has been much praised but little understood. The praise has been for his establishment of the *Kindergarten*, but popular understanding has not grasped his philosophy. He grew up in southern Germany with a father who was too busy preaching and teaching to take much notice of his son, and with a stepmother who was convinced that he was stupid and assigned him to the class of girls his father taught. Later he studied philosophy with a panentheist who taught that everything participates in God and is a product of his immanent will. At one time he spent three years with Pestalozzi at Yverdun, who, he said, "set one's soul on fire for a higher, nobler life, although he had not made clear or sure the exact way towards it." It was not until 1837 that he opened his first kindergarten in an old mill in the mountain village of Blankenburg. Those who were enthusiastic said that he was the most perfect man since Jesus. In Germany it was generally said by scholars that he had nothing which was not to be found in Pestalozzi. Froebel once declared that only in America would his ideas have complete success. He was right about the kindergarten.

Froebel looked upon man as "the human plant" and God as the original organism, from which the entire universe has evolved by virtue of his creative self-expression. Man is the last and most perfect product of this cosmic evolution. Until he appeared, the development was largely unconscious, but man "feels, understands and knows his own powers." There are two implications. First, this development will continue, "from one stage of culture to another, toward its aim, which partakes of the infinite and eternal." Second, man relives the whole development in himself. "Every human being who is attentive to his own development may recognize and study in himself the history of the development of the race." Individual life thus proceeds, naturally, by stages, and the successful development of each stage "depends upon the vigorous complete and characteristic development of each and all preceding stages of life." A boy does not become a youth, that is, by achieving a certain age but "by having lived through childhood." Thus a boy who loves to play at cave-life is not imitating someone else so much as expressing the inner craving of his own and racial development. "Play is the germinal leaf of all later life," Froebel said. The playing child is also making the next step possible. Because God is in this whole process, it is the "special destiny of man" to become fully conscious of "the divine effluence" in him. A child's self-expression is therefore God's expression, and if it should be evil it is due to distortion. "The purpose of teaching," wrote Froebel, "is to bring ever more and more *out* of man rather than to put more and more *into* man." Education is, therefore,

"God created man in his own image; man should create and bring forth like God."

"Play is the purest activity of man."

Friedrich Froebel, *The Education of Man* (New York: Appleton, 1892).

skill at noninterference. The American kindergarten is an exhibit of his educational thinking and has made his techniques familiar to everyone.

Herman Harrell Horne, 1874-1946

During all the years that John Dewey was at Columbia University in Morningside Heights, Horne was 120 blocks away at New York University in Washington Square, teaching at the other end of Manhattan and of the philosophical spectrum. Idealism, said Horne, "finds ideas and purposes to be the realities of existence; and personality, which is the union of ideas and purposes, to be the ultimate reality." Pragmatism is the belief that "the theories that work are true." "Ideas," said Horne, "work because they are true." Dewey defined education as "the reconstruction of experience," and Horne as "the perfection of humanity in the image of divinity." Dewey defined educational method as "intelligence in operation," and Horne said that "the transmissive function of education is slighted." Dewey rejected theism, Horne said that "God is the great educator," and was instrumental in establishing the department of religious education at NYU.

Dewey came from New England and received his graduate education in the near South. Horne was born in Clayton, North Carolina, and he received his graduate education in New England. In 1900, at the age of twenty-six, he began teaching at Dartmouth College. He spent a year's leave studying in Berlin and in 1909 moved to New York. Later he reviewed these life-stages in terms of ideals: the ideal of Christianity which he received from his mother, the ideal of the Southern gentleman which he learned in the honor system as an undergraduate at the University of North Carolina, the ideal of the scholar which he discovered while a student of James, Royce, and Hocking at Harvard, the ideal of manhood which came from the students at Dartmouth, and the ideal of cosmopolitanism which dawned while at NYU.

When he retired in 1942 he had published twenty-one books, one of which was a direct answer to Dewey's *Democracy and Education*. Though he was "openly hostile to Dewey" and "dedicated to Christ," as one of his students recalls, Horne was neither acrimonious nor evangelistic. "Freedom of thought and speech characterized the nature of his classes." His method of teaching was Socratic, except that "he gave out written questions beforehand." He taught by interrogation, "strolling around the classroom," leading students to their own conclusions which were in turn evaluated by the whole class. He was, by all accounts, "a born teacher."

The Philosophy

Mind, according to Horne, is the last gift of evolution to man, and is still "realizing itself by stages and degrees." All evolution, he said, occurs as process in the being of God, "the infinite Person in the unity of whose consciousness all things exist." Matter is God's objective thought, and everything is the direct result of his intention. "God is the including consciousness; the world is a part of the included content." Mind is the highest type of temporal reality, and man comes into being as he is known by God. As man experiences the "felt indisputable values of life" —love, beauty, truth, goodness, and personality—he becomes conscious of the presence of God. This awareness not only proves the existence of "the self-existent Intel-

"I know; therefore I am known."

Herman Harrell Horne, *The Democratic Philosophy of Education* (New York: Macmillan, 1932).

ligence," but moves man along toward the spiritual fulfillment of his own physical and mental evolution. "Man's progress," Horne says, "is his increasing participation in the abundant life of God." This growth is always toward the Ideal or Absolute Person, "the unity of all the perfect characteristics one knows." In the case of Jesus, this perfect person may have been actually concreted once in human history, and the process of growth is made easier with a specific and real example. God is also drawing man onward, rewarding confirmity to natural law with health, rewarding thinking his thoughts after him with science, rewarding expressing him perfection with art. "Progress in time," says Horne, becomes "perfection in eternity." Education is "the increasing realization of the temporal and eternal values of life," "the eternal process of superior adjustment of a free, conscious human being to God."

The Pupil

"The individual is a whole and also a part of a larger whole."

When Horne says that the pupil is a person, he means to imply everything Idealism intends to say about the identity of personality and cosmos. Beneath all the growing body and its physical behavior, the enlarging mind and its intellectual adjustments, lies a spiritual reality. "The body is the home of the mind," says Horne, making reference to the New Testament phrase, "the temple of the Holy Spirit." The learner is a finite person growing into the image of an infinite person; his real origin is deity, his nature is freedom, and his destiny is immortality. A teacher will, of course, approach this person with respect.

The pupil is also in the process of becoming, and the teacher does not pamper his pupils just because he knows

Herman Harrell Horne, *The Philosophy of Education* (New York: Macmillan, 1927).

they are spirits. "The Absolute is, the finite becomes," Horne says, and the hiatus between a person's present and ultimate existence is moral in quality, a period of "the decisive realization of values." Thus a child is neither good nor bad but potential, and education is one great thrust toward personhood. "Bad characters," Horne says, "are not born, they are made."

". . . a finite
person
growing into
the image
of an infinite
person"

The Objectives

Education is centered in ideals and in their realization because ideals are the foundation of all things and their realization is the cosmic intention. The objective of education is "that our pupils should act rightly, think rightly and feel rightly," or "adjustment of the child to Goodness, Truth and Beauty,"—"these essential realities that the history of the race has disclosed." Right acting is conformity to the mind of the race and the will of God. From right acting it is easier for right thinking to follow, says Horne, and from right acting and thinking is bound to come right feeling. At one point Horne lists thirty-three parts of the whole objective, beginning with physical fitness and running through knowledge, goodwill, wisdom, and loyalty in various forms to sensing "kinship with all men and with the Reality of which they are an express part." In another place he arranges the objectives of education in a hierarchy with "worship" at the top, "character in individual and justice in society as expressing his (own) will," and "production and enjoyment of the beautiful" in the middle, and at the bottom of the pyramid "knowledge of the universe." Individually, says Horne, education aims at "culture, knowledge and development," socially at "efficiency, character and citizenship," and adds, "individual aims are also secondarily social, and the social aims are also secondarily individual."

". . . Truth,
Beauty,
Goodness"

". . . efficiency,
character,
citizenship"

*". . . the
universe
made
personal"*

The teacher is the key to the educational process for two reasons. He is the embodiment of personal reality for the child, and he determines what the child's opportunity for growing shall be. It is his purpose to "make men and women who can idealize." Horne lists his functions. He specializes in the knowledge of pupils. "As it is impossible to teach a subject without a thorough knowledge of it, it is impossible to teach a student without a thorough knowledge of him." He should be a person who commands the respect of the pupil. "He does not demand respect, he wins it." He is a personal friend of the student. "To be a good friend is to be a good teacher." He awakens in the pupil the desire to learn. "He is a life-sharer who enters into and takes upon himself the lives of his pupils that they may become one with him." He is a master of the art of living. "The result of his greater maturity and experience." He is a co-worker with God in perfecting man. "His is the task of perfecting persons, the highest form of existence in the cosmos." He capably communicates his subject matter. "He becomes the medium of communication between the pupil's mind and the subject matter." He learns at the same time that he teaches. "He actively gives himself in each new teaching situation." He is a maker of democracies. "By his own self-less sharing in the group he creates group climate." He is a study in self-elimination. "He loses himself in helping pupils to give birth to what it is in them to become." Teaching is more than "the scientific and impersonal manipulation of a situation securing desirable responses," Horne says. "It is a tactful and artistic contagion of personality."

Herman Harrell Horne, *This New Education* (New York: Abingdon Press, 1931).

Learning proceeds primarily by imitation and by self-activity. "All educative experiences are personal in character," writes Horne, and by that he means both experience aimed at another person and experience initiated by oneself. "The principle of imitation has its highest educational service," he says, "in the realm of personality and its influence." Because imitation is natural, the teacher must cope with it in someway in any case, and the best way is to give direction to it as a method. Growth always goes much better when the ideal toward which one is moving is personal.

"Children become like their ideals."

But even more significant is the fact that all education begins with the person of the learner. "The development of the child mind is from within out, not from without in," Horne says. Education actually takes place within the self of the pupil, not only as a social or physical organism, but as a soul, capable of genuine initiative. The teacher not only regards his relationship with the learner with something akin to awe, but regards the pupil himself in the same manner. It is the action of the child in response to what the teacher does that constitutes the actual education. And children have an innate capacity to do one's duty when one doesn't want to, to listen to the still small voice of conscience instead of the whirlwinds of passion, to pay voluntary attention to unattractive tasks because drawn on by an ideal. Interest, effort, and discipline are the heart of educative accomplishment, but they will come from the child himself if he is presented with ideals that challenge and nourish.

"All education is self-education."

The Content

"The experimental method," wrote Horne in criticism of Pragmatism, "is a very expensive method of transmitting funded knowledge." Children have the right to benefit by the best the race has to offer. Home says that to construct a curriculum one must perceive clearly "the ideal character of man and the characteristics of an ideal society." Then he must "select those experiences, activities, life-situations, and studies that, according to one's best judgment, best contribute to these ideal ends." The curriculum will thus not be limited to "instruction," but will include content. Subjects are "a means to the great end of living completely through understanding life," and books are "earthen vessels in which the treasures of truth are kept." Thinking is the heart of the curriculum and you cannot make a pupil think by thinking for him; we learn to think by thinking, to think by doing and to do by thinking. Instead of confronting pupils with specific items of information or directions for problem-solving, Home prefers that there always be alternatives laid before them so that they will be challenged by selection and decision. In the classroom, therefore, the content is shaped in a dialectic in which the primary subject matter is persons and their interrelationships and ideas. "True education," Home wrote, "is the process of becoming ever better adjusted inwardly and outwardly, that is today, in our relations with ourselves, with our fellows, with nature, with God."

The Method

Home once estimated that about fifty percent of his method was in agreement with experimental education, but his emphasis was on the development of thinking, and difference of opinion was for Home the most appropriate method of teaching thinking. The assumption is that the truth is not to be found in one view, whether a lecturer or a textbook, but in many different forms, based on experi-

Herman Harrell Horne, *Idealism in Education* (New York: Macmillan, 1910).

ence, observation, study, and experiment, as they confront each other and finally harmonize. "Truth is found," Horne said, "in the total view of truth of the group mind." And the process by which it is discovered is personal interaction.

There is a legitimate place for the lecture in teaching thinking. It may in itself be "a work of art," evoking personal response. And all freer methods of teaching presuppose information, which may best be set before the pupil in lecture form.

. . . a *formal dialectic*

Questions-and-answers is a basic method of teaching thinking, especially as a thought-starter. It does not use questions so much to find out what the student knows as to precipitate choices. It can open the student to alternatives that might not otherwise occur to him. It can expose him to the breadth of ideas and opinions he may face when he meets the world. It can confront the students with alternatives evoking decision. It can lend meaning and significance to the content being studied. And it is the student's own thinking that the teacher is interested in.

. . . a *precipitated dialectic*

In discussion, students create their own dialectic, in which their various backgrounds and unique personalities confront each other. The teacher makes the most of the free conflict, never substituting his own ideas, coming in himself as an interlocutor to keep the fire going. However, not everything has to be learned by hard experience, and the teacher must find tactful ways of making the wisdom of maturer experience available in guiding the experience of the immature. He may propose study, observation, experience, and knowledge. But it is to be remembered that the purpose of education is not primarily the development of information but of personality.

. . . an *informal dialectic*

Horne counseled the use of the project method, but warned that the purpose of a project in education was not to solve a knowledge problem but to develop personal poise and maturity. The emphasis on projects was to be more on the student's personal interaction with social and physical environments and less on the experimental testing of a hypothesis—more on creative student production in poetry, painting, and interpretation and less on solutions —more on creative responding and less on practical doing.

As Horne's friend Hocking said, the first thing in education is to bring the person into existence, and the second is to conduct him to the farthest point in our own horizon.

Defining Christian Education

Perhaps the most decisively Christian definition of education along personalist lines was achieved by a man who was a student of neither Coe nor Idealism. His concept of personality rested on biblical rather than Greek foundations. His understanding of the singular unseen reality beyond and sustaining the physical realities of this world was derived from Calvin's theistic monism rather than from Plato's doctrine of ideas. His principle of wholeness depended more on the integration concepts of psychology than on the logical concepts of Hegel. His concern for education arose originally from his experience as the pastor of a church and his teaching from his concern to prepare men for the pastorate. "Christian Education," he says, "is the attempt, ordinarily by members of the Christian community, to participate in and to guide the changes which take place in their relationships with God, with the church, with other persons, with the physical world, and with oneself." It occurs within the Christian community; its process is interaction between persons; its dynamic arises in one's relation to himself and others; its concern is that human persons may enter into the high destiny for which they were created.

Lewis Joseph Sherrill, 1892-1957

By those who knew him, Sherrill was often described as a southern gentleman and sometimes as a saint. The latter title was most often accorded by those who knew him late in life. During his last seven years he was Professor of Practical Theology at Union Theological Seminary in New York, where he became a favorite counselor of students, faculty vice president and confidant, and, as the last volunteer executive of the American

Association of Theological Schools, the man who welded
it into a national organization with professional authority
and leadership. By this time his peripheral vision had
failed so that it was almost impossible for him to read,
but in this period he published his most influential books.
His southern characteristics came earlier. He was born
and went through college in Texas, did his seminary work
at Louisville Presbyterian Seminary, held a pastorate in
Tennessee, and was a faculty member and dean at Louisville for twenty-five years. His graduate education appears
to have been almost incidental to his teaching and was
accomplished at Northwestern and Yale during leaves
of absence. His doctoral dissertation was a study of
Presbyterian parochial schools during a thirty-six-year
period of the nineteenth century; in the introduction he
stated an understanding of both Christianity and education which was his own principle as well as that of the
schools he studied—"integrating human lives."

In his first book Sherrill indicated his pastoral orientation and commitment: "The fundamental principles of
the present-day program of Christian Religious Education," he wrote at the end of the preface, "can be
better carried out in a small church than in a large
one." The twenties were, of course, peak times for the
small church in the rural middle south, but Sherrill's
thesis was taken on principle: Christian education is essentially a face-to-face matter, and this is the distinctive
life-style of the small church. "Real fellowship is found
when the spirit of Christ is so prominant in the association that people of all ages are found, not only believing,
but doing the things he bade."

Changes take place in persons who are in fellowship,

Lewis J. Sherrill, *Religious Education in the Small Church* (Philadelphia: Westminster, 1932).

and education means the guiding of these changes; the educational strategy is to provide persons who can educate others, and the pivotal point in the test of the church is the pastor's work with adults. The emphasis is not on organization, but "on what is happening in persons." Succeeding books laid emphasis on "the inner world of children's experience of God." One was directed to parents, and urged them, "in living together with their children," to help them experience security, fellowship, and righteousness; if this can happen, and their freedom be respected, then "we have at least paved the way for a journey of discovery on their part which may take them farther than we have gone in quest of the kingdom of God and in the experience of fellowship with its Lord." Another book was directed to the teachers of children. Teaching is "guiding the changes that take place in children," and the teaching of Christianity has two central purposes: to lead children into awareness of God and to lead children into awareness of the neighbor. These purposes are accomplished through "a geniune sharing with others in experiences which have meaning and worth, both for the teacher and for those who are taught."

The sabbatical leave following the one in which he completed his doctoral dissertation provided the opportunity to work on a project that had fascinated him for a long time, the history of Christain education. Beginning with education among the Hebrews, he reached only the end of the Middle Ages, but the book remains the major volume on the subject. Clues from history sprinkle the book: the family as the channel through which the will of God is first made known to the child in Hebrew culture, the thorough literal acquaintance with the Torah

"Education is an inherent necessity in Christianity."

Lewis J. Sherrill, *The Rise of Christian Education* (New York: Macmillan, 1944).

taught by the Jews in Diaspora, Jesus' dealing with the relationship between men from the standpoint of man's relationship with God, the combination of inspiration and stable tradition in the early Christian community, the emergence of the church as the carrier of Christian life in the early medieval period, the substitution of sign for reality in the Middle Ages—and throughout, the emergence of faith as a personal trust in a Person. The book marked a watershed in Sherrill's development, providing not only background and perspective for his definitive work, but also both freedom with which to move on and the conviction that authentic Christian education must be relevant to its immediate historical world.

Thus, he arrived at Union in 1950 talking a theology comprised of the worldwide experience of violence, hostility, and defeat, widespread individual conflict, anxiety, and guilt, and the metaphysical promise of hope, healing, and redemption. It was a combination of psychology and psychiatry with Bible and theology which he had first proposed publicly in lectures at Union Seminary in Richmond five years earlier. Man's highest right in the universe, said Sherrill, is sonship to the Father in the Kingdom of God, and its absence is the final root of all his hostility, anxiety, and guilt. Because all his malignant relationships are caused by a malignant relationship with God, his ills cannot be remedied by tinkering with social arrangements or increasing religionistic busyness. Only a radical cure in line with causes will do: acceptance of himself for what he is to match the acceptance given him by God and accorded him in the society of Christian believers. Self-acceptance is self-judgment of guiltiness before God, who makes the same accepting judgment, establishing between

"The Christianity of a given time governs the nature of the education."

"The Spirit of God is now a Person, able everywhere to produce the same effects as Christ did in human personality."

Lewis J. Sherrill, *Guilt and Redemption* (Richmond: John Knox, 1945).

man and God a "co-consciousness" like that experienced by Jesus Christ, through which a man is freed "to be on God's side in the lifelong, agelong, conflict between the flesh and the Spirit."

A Theology of Wholth

The word "wholth" is a sophisticated pun. By it Sherrill means to refer to both the biblical and philosophical meanings of "whole." He uses it to refer as well to the psychological and biological concepts of "health." It may even be made to include the personalist principle of individual "worth." In addition, it has the advantage of sounding as if it had been used by the King James translators.

In his inaugural address at Union in New York, Sherrill referred to the unity achieved by the medieval world and its breakdown in the modern world culturally, politically, socially, and academically into divergent streams, states, classes, and departments. The ancient unity of self has also broken down, and the word to describe the condition of contemporary man is isolation. In deepest contrast to this debilitating situation of cultural and individual disintegration stands the possibility of "wholth"—health of the entire self, body and soul; the human counterpart of what is called "holiness" in God: in short, what the biblical and theological writers have usually called "salvation." Because wholth is there, so to speak, in reality and over against man, man is called to strive for it. Indeed, God himself is seeking this same wholeness for man: "in the end of the story," Sherrill concluded, "that which God has willed for man is what man under God is seeking in the church."

"God himself is seeking wholeness for man."

The power to become whole is the *dunamis* of God. It is within man. It is the right to become whole that makes

man the unique being that he is. It is the capacity to
empower wholeness in man that identifies God. Thus
Sherrill establishes the unity of theology and experience.
Wholeness is the outcome of positive relationships. There
are negatvie relationships, of course, and Sherrill calls
them demonic. Left alone, man's relationships both within himself and with others, tend to be destructive, deform-
ing the self. The other side of the equation is Sherrill's

"Belief in God
must be
constantly
validated
by one's
experience
with the people
closest
to him."
conviction that the self may also be re-formed or transformed in its relationships. "The relationship which
heals," he says, "is one in which two or more selves open
themselves honestly to one another at deeper and deeper
levels in an atmosphere of safety." Wholeness may not
be achieved by oneself: "It is the relationships which make
the man, break the man or remake the man." It is in
relationships that God makes himself and his power
known.

God is never known apart from relationships with
persons, says Sherrill, and in the Bible God relates himself
to us in a person. Thus Sherrill identifies the unity of the
Bible and theology-and-experience. The Bible is precisely
not a book of doctrines or a content to be learned, but the
record of God's relationship to man through nature,
human nature, the events of history, and above all,
through the life, death, and resurrection of Jesus Christ,
the incarnate Word. Making himself known in relationships, God is thus revealed in the Bible not as a proposition or as truth, but as a personal being. The biblical
record shows the involvement of God as immediate in the
specific events of history and at the same time as prolonged
throughout history: the sort of relationship that God
sustains to a man is thus special and may be called "encounter."

Lewis J. Sherrill, *The Gift of Power* (New York: Macmillan, 1955).

The Bible shows how God relates to man in a series of immediate and profound "human predicaments." Because they occur again and again throughout the long story, a special perspective on them is encouraged and they are seen as gathering into transcending "themes" such as God in creation, in lordship, in vocation, in judgment, in redemption, in re-creation, in providence, and in the life of faith. Each of these themes comes to its fulfillment in the drama of Jesus Christ. There is a "correspondence" between "theme" and "predicament" that is universal and revelatory, that is to say, in our own predicaments today the matching themes of God's biblical revelation show us how God's personal nature works to bring wholeness out of threatened disintegration. Thus the Bible in general and Jesus Christ in particular are relevant to every dilemma of man. The disclosure of God is to man-in-situation, and every situation of man may be illustrated in the Bible. Since there is a correspondence between them, it is possible to begin Christian education with either the situation or the revelation.

The sense of predicament, Sherrill says, arises out of the profound anxiety which we carry as human creatures in an existence where every form of security tends to be threatened sooner or later. Thus Sherrill identifies the unity of psychology and theology-and-the-Bible. The self is threatened by an intricate mixture of opposites and contradictions struggling within. From without, security is threatened by cultural attacks on traditional values, undermined by a competitive society, and challenged by the inability to escape death. Anxiety is the inevitable result, and in the attempt to escape anxiety one submits to others, dominates, or retreats. Such behavior not only distorts one's relationships, it distorts one's self-understanding. So long as one's knowledge of self is distorted, Sherrill continues, his knowledge of God and his rela tionship with God will be distorted. But "when man as a personal being knows himself as 'I,'" says Sherrill, "he is then able to enter consciously into a relationship with infinite Personal Being who is God, who knows himself as 'I am.'" To the extent that a man truly knows himself, he truly knows God. Of course, he is not identical with God, and does not know all of God by knowing himself. Conversely, knowing God throws light upon his own selfhood. The correspondence is like that of the biblical correspondence between theme and predicament.

God is the personal being who is within man and yet is infinitely beyond man. He confronts us from within as Person, and from without as persons. The ordinary relationships between man and man, however, tend to produce more predicament than salvation. For there to be "wholth" among men there needs to be a community of persons in which both God and man participate. That community God has supplied in the *koinonia*, "that innumerable company of persons in all times and places who, in being found by God who is altogether worthy of supreme devotion, have begun to find themselves." It is in the church that "living persons are indwelt by the Holy Spirit," and are constantly being "confronted by the biblical record of God's revelation of himself in corrective and redemptive power." It is in the church that men turn to each other by turning to God. It is there that God meets persons and that relationships are nurtured into creativity. Thus Sherrill identifies the unity of the church and psychology-and-theology-and-the-Bible.

"He must know God if he is to know himself."

"The Christian community is the scene where God is constantly confronting man, where men participate with one another and influence one another."

A Psychology of Struggle

When Sherrill talks theology he tends to talk of the self as a being (related by nature to God in Christ and to fellowmen in *koinonia*) both dynamic (constantly being formed and reformed) and ambivalent (constantly mingling creative and destructive interaction). It is a mixture of Paul-talk and Freud-talk. When he talks psychology he tends to talk of the self as a becoming, existing in the midst of relationships and forces to which he must make some kind of response and in which he becomes involved as a participant.

There is "an inward propulsion to grow." Sherrill classifies the inevitable growth into five stages: *childhood*, in which the task is becoming an individual; *adolescence*, in which the change is being weaned away from one's parents; *young adulthood*, in which one establishes his basic identities and becomes a self-directed person; *middle life*, in which one achieves a mature view of one's own life and meaning in general; and *old age*, which involves the achievement of simplification. This inward propulsion toward becoming is induced, of course, by the presence of the Person.

> "God takes the initiative in confronting man."

One may meet the crises precipitated by growth by shrinking back from them through compromise or rejection. In this case life may seem to be a *treadmill* consisting of continuous problems to be dealt with in as unadventuresome a way as possible. Or, one may plunge into the crises with enthusiasm, determined to meet and beat them on his own strength as a human being. In this case, his life becomes a sort of *saga* consisting of problems to be dealt with in as adventuresome a way as possible. But, because the propulsion onward is God-induced, one may respond to the crises as a confrontation with God in a person-producing process with an attitude of ongoing faith. In this case, his life becomes a *pilgrimage*, in spite of the anxieties and insecurities moving on in

> "In hours of crisis the soul is under divine judgment."

Lewis J. Sherrill, *The Struggle of the Soul* (New York: Macmillan, 1951).

hope and trust. All three of these responses are religious. Both shrinking back from God and unawareness of God are sin; acknowledgment of God and moving forward is faith.

"The garments which God wears when confronting man are the circumstances which require him to grow."

Thus, at each level of life—indeed, at each moment—the becoming person is exposed to "the reality of the living God." The spiritual crises of childhood have to do with the kind of parental love, the nature of the parental view of life, and the kind of formal religious training the child experiences. They incline him to move forward in openness to God or to seal him off from God. Adolescents confront the opposite sex, the secular view of history, and the claims of the kingdom of God. A new self is called into being by love, and the crisis is what sort of love it shall be. Young adults are faced with the problem of achieving responsibility. It is forced on them by marriage, parenthood, vocation, and citizenship. They are peculiarly exposed to the moral demands of a holy God, and the crisis is what the nature of their response may be, for on it is based their whole lives. Adults in middle life face the necessity of finding a philosophy of life. Crisis is precipitated by the conflict between the acquired philosophy one has been taught, the spontaneous philosophy by which one lives, the formulated philosophy by which one explains himself to others, and the formulas by which one copes with problems. They are exposed to God as they attempt to integrate their materials with the realities of life. The elderly must begin to deal with the results of life and with diminishing capacies to cope with new problems. They are exposed to the possibility of discover-

"Through struggle the soul becomes whole."

ing God as the single integrating core of life. At every stage, Sherrill makes his basic claims: God constantly confronts man in diturbances of the spiritual status quo; the manner of dealing with the God-possibilities at each stage depends on "the deposit of growth" left by the preceding stage; the church as a fellowship of pilgrims is the community that gives evidence at every stage to the reality of God and support to its individual discovery.

Guiding Struggle Wholthward

"In Christian Education," Sherrill writes, "we are given the opportunity to participate with one another in that encounter wherein God goes forth to meet the soul struggling for its own existence." In its broadest sense, education means that society participates in the striving of its members to achieve selfhood and attempts to guide it toward those ends which society regards as most worthy. It occurs in the scene of human interaction. In secular education the state determines the forms, the participants are human being interacting in natural processes, and the goals are well-being as an individual, worthy membership in society, and worthy citizenship in the state. Christian education, however, is to be differentiated. The Christian community with revelation as its guide determines the forms; God joins the human participants by grace turning natural processes of interaction into redemptive encounter, and added to the goals of secular education is entrance through Jesus Christ into the kingdom of God. The scene is the *koinonia* in which men and God participate in an intricate web of relationships. The end is wholth.

". . . attempting to guide the changes which take place in persons."

At the base of all education is interaction. It may be called demonic when the changes it produces in persons are such as to weaken or damage the self in which the changes occur. It may be called spiritual when the changes are such as to lead the self into a deepening fellowship with God. In spiritual interaction, relationships become confrontation. God is imparting himself, seeking to interpenetrate spiritually into the human selves and their interaction by means of self-disclosure. This divine-human

"The goal of Christian education is self-knowledge not knowledge-about-self, knowledge of God not knowledge-about-God."

interaction becomes the specific content of Christian education. The biblical themes show how truth presents itself to man. The method is not to search after truth but to accept its participation in life. This is achieved in a specifically appropriate method, namely, by participating oneself in the interaction. Students learn to stand inside the Bible, participating in its encounter, becoming personally involved with its people and events. Thus they learn to know themselves and God directly.

"It is the perception of reality that matters."

Perception is the process of acknowledging the meaning in that which confronts the self. The self, Sherrill says, always recognizes meaning in what is presented from the outer world in light of the meaning which life already has for that self in the innerworld. Personal motifs, as Sherrill calls "the highly individualistic character structure of each person," affect basically the nature of both interaction and perceptions. We tend, in other words, to see things not as they are but as we are, and we interact on the basis of how we see things to be. Blind men perceive the elephant differently, disciples understood Jesus differently, biblical people met God differently. Christian education has too often assumed that a logical or historical or biblical order determines the order in which materials should be presented to children. The principle of perception should make it clear that the psychological, or interactional, order of the student's experience determines the effectiveness of outside material. More important, however, is the fact that when a change in this deeply personal and individual perception of reality occurs, the meaning in life has to that degree been changed. Christian education thus becomes a project in changing perceptions. But Sherrill reminds his readers that this kind of change is wrought only in interaction, especially the kind of inter-human interaction in which God participates and is called encounter. Indeed, much that is recorded in the

Bible deals with just such transformation of meaning, and participation in its life becomes a means of guiding changes of perception.

The whole process in which meaning comes forth out of the deeper reaches of the self, passes back and forth in self-disclosure, and results in transformation of meaning, is interactional. Sherrill calls it "two-way communication." It is a giving and a taking. It permits doubt as well as faith, *no* as well as *yes*. There is no way, he continues, of communication of the gospel without this kind of communication between persons. It involves the further opening of the selves of teacher and pupil to each other and to interaction with God and changes in perception. It is thus not merely a technique; it is the necessary human condition in which God confronts the person. The use of biblical symbols is a technique by which this divine-human intercommunication may be readied. Symbols point to a reality beyond themselves by participation in or relation to the reality itself. Biblical symbols arose out of the divine-human confrontation and effectively point to it. They are therefore evocative on principle of curiosity, wonder, surprise, incredulity, and all these responses are the beginnings of two-way communication. In the Biblical material, says Sherrill, the reader encounters "something so different from common life" that "he has to come to a decision about it."

The Christian community is both the scene and symbol of this sort of two-way communication. It is, by virtue of its own nature, says Sherrill, "in the unique position of being a true community of living persons, but of being able also at the same time to stand above itself and view itself under the light of revelation and eternity." In such an association the ordinary interaction of common life is transformed into encounter, the search for meaning is met by revelation, changes are guided into the spiritual

"The community where such communication goes on is itself the word of God."

dimension. Here wholth occurs. "The Christian community as a whole," Sherrill says, "is meant to be the scene of a redemptive ministry to the human self as a whole." In that case, the church's task is the establishment of wholth in itself. Preaching, worship, counseling, administration, evangelism, missionary work, social outreach, and education become "a total ministry to a total self." Distinctions grow dim in the interest of "wholeness in the ministry to the self" and "a ministry to the wholeness of the self."

Christian education thus links man and God. "It can reach down into the depths of the human predicament, and can reach up to eternal life." In the closing paragraph of his inaugural address at Union in 1950, Sherrill likened it to "a new heaven and a new earth," which is "coming *to* man *from* God and entered by faith."

PERSONALISM

Theology	Personalist
God	The Person (Father)
Jesus	The ideal person
Man	Finite person (child of God)
Salvation	Love between man and God
Knowledge of God	Thinking (willing)
Religious Experience	Personal growth
Bible	Record of persons relating to God
Philosophy	Idealism
Epistemology	"Truth is Understanding"
Education	Social
Symbol	The Conference
Curriculum	Person-centered (or ideal-centered)
Method of Knowing	Sharing
Teacher skill	Discussion, group-dynamics
Method of learning	Sharing and thinking
Goal of learning	Positive relationship
Evaluation of learning	Evidence of growth or maturity
Christian Education	Nurture through personal relations
	of relationship with God
Content	Interpersonal relations
Purpose	Christian maturity
Goal	Creative love

Because the influence of Personalism in religious education is personal in nature it is difficult to trace. Respect for
personal worth implies freedom, and if teaching it has
been successful the pupil will differ somewhat from his
teacher. For a third of a century, George Albert Coe's
pupils occupied almost all the significant teaching posts
of religious education in the colleges and seminaries of
the United States; they were deeply influenced by their
major professor as a person, both echoing and developing
aspects of his philosophy, but no "Coean School" developed. Coe spoke of "cooperating" with them. "To be
in fellowship with them is to feel that great things have
been accomplished," he mused in 1938. Because one of
Coe's religious "new schools" sometimes looked very
much like one of Dewey's "progressive schools," it was
difficult to tell from which came the inspiration for
methods and curriculum. The difference, of course, was
that one of them met on Sunday in a church and explicitly related personal development to God. The difference between them was theology. But because there
was very little difference between religious liberalism and
religious education in the United States during the
twenties and thirties, it was difficult to tell whether liberal
theology or educational philosophy more influenced the
church schools. However, in the forties differences in
theology became an issue within Protestantism. Two men,
one of them a pupil and the other a student of Coe, personally spearheaded the debate in regard to religious education. One said that religious education would be Christian if Christianity were right-headed, the other that
religious education would be right-headed only if it were
Christian.

Religious Education Can Be Christian

The theological debate concerning religious education began at Union Theological Seminary in New York. It boiled beneath the surface for a while, and then in the late thirties erupted spectacularly, as student legend tells it, in the open air. Harrison S. Elliott was Coe's own choice to be his successor when he retired, and Elliott gallantly carried on the Coe tradition in his classrooms at the end of the long hall on the top floor. However, new theological voices were being heard at Union, and one of them was that of Reinhold Niebuhr who vigorously and brilliantly expounded the judgmental action of God's righteousness constantly invading man's immoral society. Down on the second floor, as his classes and fame grew, Niebuhr often attacked theories of progress and pointed to Elliott as the personification of the personalists' faith in man. One day they met crossing the quadrangle, as the story goes, and spent the rest of the afternoon slugging out the issue chin to chin as the entire student body gathered and listened.

Elliott's book came out in 1940. "There has been an increasing tendency," he reported, "to repudiate the adjustments which have been made in Protestant theology under the influence of modern science and social developments." Religious education, as a leader of those adjustments, was once regarded as the practical savior of the churches, but is now being attacked as a theological menace. Elliott's reply is partly defensive but mostly aggressive in spirit.

Defensively he argues that religious education is not in conflict with the historic nature of the Christian religion.

Harrison S. Elliott, *Can Religious Education Be Christian?* (New York: Scribner's, 1940).

Neither in early Christianity nor in the Reformation period was there a single authoritative interpretation of the faith, and in all periods religion reinterprets past truth as part of the living experience of the time. The problem arises in regard to how these variant interpretations are to be treated. The traditionally minded say that variation is due to misunderstanding or modification of an absolutely authoritative revelation. With this, religious education is in direct conflict, according to Elliott, insisting that the variety has been evidence of religious vitality. Religious education "is in no sense a method for bringing saving truth to children," but is rather "a process through which growth in Christian life and experience take place and in which the Christian goals and beliefs are determined."

From this point on, Elliott argues aggressively. He reviews Emil Brunner on the human predicament, Karl Barth on the authority of the Bible, Reinhold Niebuhr on the Kingdom of God, and concludes that their positions are authoritarian and therefore in basic conflict with religious education, indeed, that the principles of religious education developed independently of theology and are distinctly educational in their emphasis. What education offers to Christianity is a method for making the past relevant and real in present experience. In Christianity education implies that the past will be left behind as God is directly active in present events. "In an educational process," wrote Elliott, "there is an assumption that human beings have the capacity for choice and that growth takes place through making choices, through acting upon these decisions and through evaluating the consequences of action." Domination of children and young people by the authoritarian attitudes of an elder generation or a sacred history only prevents them from having a vital Christian experience of their own. The essential Christian belief is in "the limitless resources of God made available to individuals and groups who meet the conditions for their release." In short, the only way that Christian faith and experience can continue to be Christian is "by being integrally related to an educational process."

Religious Education Must Be Christian

The debate was joined most directly and publicly by H. Shelton Smith in 1941. Then Professor of American Religious Thought at Duke University, he had been a professor of education at Columbia and active in the International Council of Religious Education and the Religious Education Association. "It seems to me," he wrote, "that the thought-patterns of modern liberal religious nurture have largely exhausted their vitality." The reason was a preoccupation with educational method and social experimentation. The result was an ignoring of certain basic aspects of the Christian faith. In this situation, Smith believed that the need was "less for construction than for unsparing criticism." George Albert Coe was one of his primary targets.

"The immediate task of the Christian Educator is penetrating and persistent criticism."

The principle that human personality is of final worth, Smith claimed, subtly deifies man, denying the historic Christian doctrine that man is a theonomous and not an autonomous being, deriving his meaning and value from God. The principle that personality arises in social interaction tends to replace the kingdom of God with the kingdom of Man, and to substitute the process of discovery for revelation. The dangers are subjectivity (substituting myself for God) and activism (substituting human striving for divine initiative) and democracy (substituting divine immanence for divine transcendence). Education is a practice of "nurture," expecting a gradual

"Modern liberalism needs nothing so much as a realistic and credible doctrine of man."

and natural unfolding through moral persuasion and and personal example. The coming era, however, calls for change on a revolutionary scale in which force will be used increasingly as an instrument of social control. In such a situation humanistic psychology and romantic philosophy will not be an adequate source, Smith affirms. It can only come, he says, from a Christian view of man, emphasizing man's origin in the creative action of God. It is this transcendent source that enhances human value. Man's value comes through his relation to God who is alone supremely wonderful, and only therefore is he worthful before his fellowmen. He comes to personal fulfillment in a community which is held together by something more than human life, and in which alone he is able to cope with sin. Sin is a fundamentally theological tragedy, not to be outgrown by healthy social experiences, but to be conquered by the redemptive act of God in Jesus Christ. Only through this forgiving love can one commit himself to ethical righteousness and the transcendental demands of the kingdom of God. It is not by education, but by grace that man is saved.

"Men are saved by Christ."

The problem comes into practical focus for Smith in the relation between public and religious education. The religion of the public schools is Dewey's "positive creed of life implicit in democracy and science." Dewey considers progressive education to be essentially religious. Unfortunately, Smith believes, the liberal religious educators have joined Dewey in this assumption by relinquishing basic Christian concepts. However, Smith is convinced that only the historic and revealed Christian faith supplies the basis for either religion or democracy. The crucial question then becomes, "What kind of religion shall the public school teach—the religion of the

"The religion of experimental democracy is anthropocentric."

H. Shelton Smith, *Faith and Nurture* (New York: Scribner's, 1941).

churches or the religion of humanistic experimentalism?" This question will turn out to be the battleground. And it can be won for a truly democratic culture, Smith affirms, only if religious education becomes specifically and theologically Christian.

The Theological Dimension

In the forties Smith offered his unsparing criticism as the first step toward "positive reconstruction." In the fifties Sherrill went a long way toward strengthening "the elements of weakness" Smith had exposed. It may be significant that neither of them was a Coe man. The theological problem, however, had been named: the vertical dimension. It was not merely a matter of technical doctrine and theoretical orthodoxy: it was the practical and personal matter of how to deal with the relation between God and man in a Christian manner.

Theological Personalism, with philosophical Idealism at its base, had acquainted formal Christianity with life. The principle that human personality is of supreme worth because reality is personal is greatly needed in a time when personal worth is threatened by the machine age, the personality market, superstates and new levels of human inhumanity. When man is threatened by impersonal forces, it is important to be able to assert that the most personal of all forces—the immanent God—is at work within men, that from within are the real issues of life. When men are not being what they know they could be, there is significance in saying that personality is a process of becoming rather than a state of being. When men are lonely in a condition of increasing geographical proximity to other men, it becomes helpful to show that personality is formed in relationships and to be able to point out a community to which persons gather in the conviction that universal love is a creative way of life.

The issue for Christians is whether all this can be said in more than a horizontal way. Without a vertical dimension, the Cartesian *cogito* tends to become solipsism, the principle of human worth tends to become subjectivism, the principle of divine immanence tends to become pantheism, the attribution of personality to God tends to humanize God, the emphasis on relationship tends to destroy individuality, the assurance of becoming tends to destroy traditional wisdom. There is in the personalist emphasis on the horizontal axis of personality a tendency to cancel the traditional Christian emphasis on the vertical axis of creation, revelation, and salvation. The problem seems to come from philosophical Idealism with its insistence that logical coherence—total linear connection of parts in a rational whole—is the key to personal being, which is in turn the nature of reality. The rational impossibility of a horizontal axis connecting lineally with a vertical axis seems always to preclude the separate existence of the vertical. On the idealist assumption, Christian Personalism created an educational movement in the churches dedicated to a program of lineal growth: the necessity of love, the extension of human love, the discovery of God's love. In biblical experience this is neither logically nor personally so. The vertical and the horizontal both exist and they intersect.

Christian Education

Horace Bushnell has often been specifically claimed as the patron saint and immediate forerunner of the personalist religious education movement in the United States. In the nineteenth century he identified the key issues which came to characterize Christian education in the twentieth century: *historical change, religious experience and knowledge, the God-man relation, and personal growth.* Christian personalists adopted the concept of change as enthusiastically as did Dewey, but to them it meant something very different. It meant that Christianity was primarily neither doctrine nor tradition but personality-enhancing life. It meant change in accordance with the personality principle, a one-way, God-guided, continuing evolution toward a universal society of persons on this earth. They adopted the identification of knowledge and experience, and for them it meant that all knowledge begins with self-experience, and that knowledge of the world, others, and God is built on self-knowledge because all reality is sufficiently selflike to be known. They placed the God-man relation at the heart of human experience, defining it as the relation between finite and infinite personalities. It is, in fact, a relation in which the finite grows toward the infinite. Personality is thus an inevitable process of becoming, and Christian education is the effort to guide the growth toward God-likeness so that it may be as productive and personal as possible. In the process, Personalism created an educational program that was very much like experimental education in method and practice but was very much unlike humanistic Pragmatism in conviction and intention. Whether the combination is either rational or practical is still open to question.

ESSENTIALISM

"... sitting down before the facts humbly"
... Realism
"... things are essentially what they appear to be"
... content-centered education
... learning-by-knowing-about-things
... truth-oriented religion
... traditional theology

Maria Montessori, 1871-1952

D.Blank

"Closed on Thursdays."

The ambassador from Argentina sighed. He had deliberately come to see the educational wonders widely reported to occur daily in this school for children. But in Italy, foreigners are never quite in step. Today is Thursday. Of course.

"*Buon giorno,* Signor." The boy was dressed as one would expect in a tenement house in Rome, but his eyes glowed. "You have come to see the *scuola* and the *bambini, si?* The door is locked today but the porter has a key and all the children live here. *Un momento.*" Soon the door was open and the children coming. Easily and naturally they settled into learning.

"But these children are teaching themselves!" exclaimed an American teacher as she watched the Montessori class from the bleachers outside the glass enclosed schoolroom at the San Francisco World Exhibition in 1915. Only two gold medals were awarded at that fair; the Montessori children took both of them.

It was the children and their capacities that Maria Montessori had discovered. In working with them she felt that she was not a gardener "turning over clods," but an Aladdin "who had in his hand a key that would open hidden treasures." Children of four learned to write "without fatigue or forcing." On the day one little boy discovered he could write he went about telling everybody, "But nobody told me how!" A Montessori disciple once said, "It was as if a higher form of personality had been liberated, and a new child had come into being." Queen Marghuerita of Savoy prophesied that "a new philosophy of life will arise from what we are learning from these little children." The head of a religious order exclaimed, "This is a discovery which is even more important than Marconi's." A member of the educational committee of the London County Council remarked at the end of a teacher's report from Rome, "Gentlemen, this is not a report, it is a rhapsody."

The Life-Seer

"Life," Montessori was fond of saying, "consists of being obedient to events." Events had a way of crowding in on her. "Anything new," she often said about education, "must emerge by its own energies." The principle was one she seemed to have learned from experience. She never forced things to happen to others or to herself. But the secret of meaning as well as of learning was to recognize genuine newness and to move with it. That required vision, and vision is a combination of the kind of seeing that comes with disciplined observation and the kind of seeing that comes from being willing to let emergent facts gather into unexpected combinations. Montessori was a disciplined scientist. She also had a way of seeing truth in moments of mystical intuition.

". . . seeing life steadily and seeing it whole"

She was born into minor nobility near Bologna at a time when it was rather expected that nearly titled Italian girls attempt and achieve little beyond grace and motherhood. But she was both brilliant and stubborn, and one thing opened upon another. She began by siding with the underprivileged as a child and later on sided with the child against the adult. By the time Mussolini began applying governmental control to individual thought, she was both internationally famous and intellectually uncontrollable. Publicly her books were burned and her effigy hung, but the British Navy secretly slipped her out of Italy, and in 1939, when World War II broke out, she was giving a teacher's training course in Madras. Retained

"I have work to do."

E. M. Standing, *Maria Montessori, Her Life and Work* (New York: Mentor-Omega, 1962).

as an enemy alien, she spent the war years writing. A number of her most important books thus bear an Indian imprint. When she returned to Italy in 1947 it no longer seemed like home to her, and she spent the rest of her life teaching and lecturing and receiving honors in western European countries. She died unexpectedly in Holland and is buried there.

". . . the most interesting woman in Europe"

Dottoressa

"I know," she said, shaking hands with the head of the Board of Education who had just told her that it was quite impossible, "that I shall become a Doctor of Medicine." At fourteen she had horrified her parents by deciding to become an engineer. They had moved to Rome so that she could have a better education and had suggested teaching as a fitting feminine occupation. "Anything but that," she had replied, and enrolled in a technical school for boys. But her interests shifted to biology, and she entered the medical school at the University of Rome with a competition scholarship. Her classmates contemptuously emitted sounds through ther lips. "The harder you blow, the higher up I shall go," she replied. In the interests of modesty, she was required to do her dissecting alone, and that meant at night. One night when it all seemed too much to bear, she started home across an almost deserted park. There she saw the two-year-old child of a beggar playing happily on the ground with a scrap of colored paper, and she went back to medicine. Her lecture to the faculty at the end of the first year received a standing ovation, and in 1896 she became the first woman in Italy to receive the degree of Doctor of Medicine.

"Blow away, my friends."

"It just happpened like that. You will think it a very silly story."

The next ten years were years of preparation. One of her first responsibilities as a doctor at the psychiatric clinic of the university was to select patients for the clinic from the insane asylums of Rome. She was touched by the

"The preparations of life are indirect."

retarded children she saw there and the disgust with which their supervisors regarded them. "It is because, as soon as they have finished their meals, they throw themselves on the floor to search for more." But to Dr. Montessori it seemed that they were not so much interested in their bellies as in finding something physical in that barren room to handle. It occurred to her that for them the only path toward intelligence was through their hands. In 1899 she delivered a lecture, which became the first of a series, on defective children in which she argued that "defective children are not extrasocial and not only deserve education but perhaps need it more than normal children." She was placed in charge of an orthophrenic school and soon brought a class of children to an examination in reading and writing who scored as high as the children from a public school. "I became convinced," she said, "that similar methods applied to normal children would develop and set free their personality in a surprising way."

"These two years of practice are my true degree in pedagogy."

Meanwhile, she was practicing medicine privately, lecturing at the medical school, teaching hygiene at a women's college, and taking courses at the university in philosophy and psychology. In the course of all this concentration on the human being as a body and mind, she discovered the work of two French doctors on mental retardation. They proposed that the secret was "to lead the child, as it were, by the hand, from the education of the muscular system to that of the nervous system and the senses." It was the springboard for her own convictions. "The physiological method," she called it. It began with a medically oriented observation of the growing body and the physical behavior of the individual child, it moved to the insight that intelligence is supported by physical movement and the bodily senses, and it produced the educational method that learning begins with the physical

". . . the importance of the body"

manipulation of objects. Her experience had shown that this method leads the way "to a complete human regeneration." Again there was the question: What might be the results with normal children?

Casa dei Bambini

In 1905 a housing project was opened in the San Lorenzo quarter of Rome, a thousand families from the surrounding slums were moved in, and the parents put to work in the nearby factories. No one had provided for the children, however, and it soon became evident that unless they were policed they would soon ruin the new buildings. Someone remembered an article by Montessori and contacted her. She immediately recognized the opportunity to test her methods with normal children and soon events began to command the new to emerge. There was no money for furnishing a schoolroom, but there was provision in the budget for office equipment, so she ordered desks and chairs—in child sizes. No teachers were provided, so she trained the porter's daughter—she had "no preconceptions." And then the children came, sixty tearful, frightened, bewildered, uncared-for, poorly fed, ignorant little vandals from three to six years of age. "They were closed flowers," Montessori remembered, but she said to the visitors on opening day, January 6, 1906, "Here is the beginning of an undertaking of which the whole world will one day speak."

Her intuition was right again. With retarded children, she had patiently invented and provided and led. With these children, however, she merely provided the physical learning materials she had found useful before, and they worked with the things spontaneously, discovering how to learn for themselves. She observed and recorded with her doctor's insight: it was the children's own interest that kept them going, they enjoyed keeping things in order,

"Things are the best teachers."

". . . a first glimpse into the unexplored depths of the child's mind"

"Any unnecessary aid is a hindrance to learning."

"The children never chose the toys."

"The greatest reward is to pass on to a new stage."

they preferred work to play, work was its own reward, they enjoyed being quiet—and then, suddenly, they began to discover with but little help how to read and write "without a word of direction being spoken."

Visitors began to come. Other children's houses were set up, first in Italy and then abroad. But Montessori continued to be as moved as she was the first time she saw those San Lorenzo children "explode." "Where did it come from?" she asked. In time she answered, "They had found the orbit of their cycle like the stars that circle unwearying and which, without departing from their order, shine through eternity," and quoted Baruch from her Roman Bible, "The stars were called, and they said: Here we are, and with cheerfulness have shined forth to Him that made them."

The Life-Helper

Dottoressa Montessori, the trained medical observer, never ceased to wonder at the capacities of childhood. "There is no ceiling on accomplishment," she said. Directoressa Montessori, the master teacher of an educational movement, increasingly insisted that the teacher's role was to free childhood for growth. "Any work accomplished by God and nature," she said, "demands a deeper respect than what we do solely by ourselves." This is, however, not an easy thing to learn to do. The adult has reached "the norm of the species" while the child is in "a continual state of metamorphosis." The teacher must learn to respect and trust the learning child. "Teaching is not correcting," she would say; more often she put the counsel affirmatively, "Teach teaching," by which she meant that the teacher's task was to help the learner find methods of teaching himself.

Childhood, which reached to eighteen years of age according to Montessori, was a succession of births. There were two periods of transformation, from birth to six years and from twelve to eighteen years; between there was a six year period of uniform growth. In all three periods mental development is precipitated by and dependent upon physiological changes. Learning will therefore be accomplished spontaneously if it is not interfered with, and the amount is prodigious.

The first three years are both the most amazing and the most important to Montessori. It is a period of unconscious absorption. It begins at a mental content of nothing. Everything is objective, a chaotic "thatness." Out of the chaos a child laboriously catalogues a cosmos. "The head doubles in size," Montessori notes. The child achieves order in objective things not by mind, for he has none, but by exercising what he has, life. Prehension always precedes apprehension, according to Montessori. By physically establishing connection with the world through his large muscles, there is some sense to be made out of space, the sizes of things, their relations. Imagination, dreams, and fantasy must be sorted out from the reality of things. Cause and effect are discovered in the results actions cause in things. Time is to be understood and accepted. The child builds inward from the outside world, the same order the Creator is reported to have followed in creating the world and then man. "He looks in the world," says Montessori, "to find himself." During this period of unconscious absorption, the child cannot be reached by a conscious mind or helped directly in his tasks. He is "more interested in growing than in knowing."

"Life begins at a zero."

"The child creates his own mind."

Maria Montessori, *The Absorbent Mind* (Madras: Vasanta, 1964 —5th Edition).

The critical passage to conscious absorption is made "through movement which follows the path of pleasure and love." It is another birth. For three years the child adds construction to absorption, and by six years of age has produced an individual. This major miracle has been accomplished through "independent work."

". . . plateau of stability"

From six to twelve years of age there follows a period of stability. It is caused and heralded by the achievement of the vast physical growth of childhood. Now for a period of six years physical growth proceeds slowly and "without transformation." Mental development follows the same pattern: the development of fine physical skills, the expansion of the herd instinct, the exploration of reasoning facilities. Adolescence is a kind of second childhood, as Montessori sees it, another period of massive physiological changes inducing new directions of mental development.

". . . consciousness thrown outwards"

The well-established, individual consciousness of childhood is now turned outward toward the world in an aggressive exploration. Reason develops in a "radial" manner, moving from established "centers of interest" out along "rays of interest"—several of them simultaneously —until something of a vision of wholeness is established "at the periphery." It is a "preparation for going out" into adulthood, another birth-time.

The Sensitive Periods

Montessori borrowed her concept of "sensitive periods" from biology. "Conditions extremely favorable to development" often cause new organic evolution. Favorable biological conditions produce periods of readiness for mental development. It comes as "an irresistible urge," "a burning passion" to select elements from the environ-

". . . a burning intellectual love"

Maria Montessori, *The Secret of Childhood* (Notre Dame: Fides, 1966).

ment for attention. It is "the realization of a divine plan."
During the first year of life there is "a sudden mysterious
urge" to speak. An intricate physical coordination is required, and the infant can be observed practising, but it is
accomplished by simply living the infant life in response
to the environment. And when language comes, it is all
at once, "a kind of music that fills the soul." During the
second year the passion for order appears. "A child," says
Montessori, "cannot live in disorder." By putting and
keeping things in their right places, the child is constructing himself out of environmental elements. This is
followed in the third to sixth years by an indescribable
urge to refine the senses. The mastery of the small muscles
makes it possible for the child to control small objects, and
"the special epoch of sensation" dawns. Physical mastery
of small objects leads to dealing with invisible objects of
sensation, such as sounds and music, and then to even
more refined tactile sensations such as memory. The world
makes reasoning possible. During the slow-growth period
at the end of childhood, when the child has become aware
of his capacity for bodily control and of his individuality
and of the relations of persons and groups, there comes
a period of sensitivity to good manners. And in adolescence
there is the sensitivity to abstract reasoning made possible
by all the prior tasks achieved.

". . . psychic fugues"

Conditions of Learning

Development, Montessori observed, was interrupted only
when the body and the mind were separated by inhibition
of movement or by the substitution of adult will for the
will of the child. Freed to respond to a supporting environment in their own ways, the children demonstrated "the
interior laws of the formation of man." They are love
of the environment (exhibited in the desire for natural
order), a love of work (not playing, but an intense kind

". . . inner directives for growth"

of task-accomplishment), spontaneous concentration (the needs of the species acting through the individual), love of silence (though many children are working near each other), sublimation of the possessive attitude (not "to have" but "to use"), power to act from choice (not mere curiosity), obedience (a sense of mutual aid rather than of competition), self-discipline (always the fruit of liberty) and joy (a sheer satisfaction produced by obedience to the laws of one's own nature).

The famed "Montessori Method" in education was probably not so much a technique of teaching as the discovery that children learn best in these circumstances, which are of their own will.

The Method

The effect of Montessori's approach is to put the world on the side of the child as he builds a self out of the world. Teaching is placing the child in direct contact with "real things," protecting the child's right to work, and never helping him when he can help himself. A popular American magazine recently observed that "Montessori methods turn out to be a showcase of nearly every 'new' idea that U. S. education has lately discovered."

". . . the Third Factor"

"The prepared environment," Montessori calls "the new factor" in education. Education traditionally consisted of a direct relationship between teacher and children; Montessori thinks of education as a three-way relation between teacher, children, and the physical environment. It is "an expanded space" prepared by the adult in advance. The furniture is child-sized, inviting the child to carry out for himself the exercises of life. All the equipment is designed to invite the child to movement

Maria Montessori, *Spontaneous Activity in Education* (New York: Scribner's, 1965).

and to encourage his own work of discovery. In such an environment, where everything is "good," the child may be given freedom to choose, because all his choices will be good.

The "sensorial materials" embody natural orders, from large to small, dark to light, low to high, then to now, and so on. Even letters and numbers are made large enough to be lifted and with textures to be felt. The child is invited by them to find his own orders. "The prepared paths to culture" for older children work in the same way.

"Things are the best teachers."

The teacher is "the dynamic link" between the child and the prepared environment. She brings to the task a profound respect for children, introduces them to the physical materials. Her respect for children means that she will give each child "the least necessary assistance." She is there to support and protect the child's right to work for himself. For the most part, this means freeing the child; she knows that "a child who is instructing himself will always be moving." Her respect for the real things of the environment means that she will help the children keep the *casa* clean and in repair, that she will help children learn how to use the materials. But more important, she "animates the environment" by observing, listening, responding, and by never interrupting. Her chief skill is sensing "the creative moment." The most important learning goes not smoothly but by leaps, and not from known to unknown but by "saltations" from things to self. These mental mutations "come for a moment" but "last a lifetime," Montessori said. At that moment the teacher simply introduces an appropriate activity without

". . . the dynamic link"

Maria Montessori, *The Montessori Method* (New York: Stokes, 1912).

Dorothy Canfield Fisher, *The Montessori Manual for Teachers and Parents* (Cambridge: Bentley, 1964).

prodding or interference. If the child does not respond, the error is the teacher's, and she is tireless in offering objects again and again to those who have refused them, in the confidence that "the moment will come."

The World-Former

In 1938 a priest in Barcelona set up a children's house in a church. The school was a natural combination of Montessori's native Catholicism and of Catholic parish education. Montessori had apparently not thought of the formally religious possibilities of her methods. For her religion and education were not clearly distinguishable; she spoke of them both as "life itself." Still, her respect for the child was so profound that she often used biblical language in speaking of the givenness of the relation between child, the world and destiny. It was a sense of awe in the presence of children that prevented her from fondling them, of wonder at their extraordinary progress that prevented her from taking credit for it, and of intimacy that prompted her to suggest to teachers that they see them as Jesus saw them. She once proposed the possibility of a layman's apostolic order within the church devoted to teaching children. It would apply Montessori methods in hospitals and nursing homes for the very young, in homes for small children, and train teachers in the method for Catholic elementary and secondary schools. In 1916 Benedict XV had acknowledged the analogy between the mission of the church and the Montessori method, and in 1917 Montessori had written, "I believe that this method of education is the instrument God placed in my hands—for His ends."

The concept of movement as the basis of learning clearly suggested that the liturgy was the place to begin. First

". . . that the Church of Christ in a reformed humanity may triumph midst the splendors of civilization"

there would be a children's chapel, built and beautified by adults with child-sized furniture and equipment. It would be the most beautiful room in the school. The children would themselves grow the grapes and make the wine for Mass. They would learn their own parts in the ritual, and practice the actual movements of all the participants, including the priests. Movement, exercise, and real things are combined. "The sense of self" is practiced at a spiritual retreat before taking first communion, and communion itself is set in a festival of games and activities followed by an agape-feast to which each child contributes. All along the way "explosions" occur, but the most important would be "relating of unlike things" and "seeing the difference in like things"—man-and-priest, bread-and-body, wine-and-blood.

The Liturgy is "the pedagogical method" of the Church.

". . . the best for the smallest"

Montessori sometimes spoke of the twentieth century as the age of the New Child and the growing acceptance of her vision of the way God forms the adult through the child as the last revolution. Through the "full normalization" of the child, a more perfect adult may come into being. To this point in history, social evolution has always been by the wish of the adult, "never the wish of the child." But full recognition of "the two poles of humanity," beginning in every home and school, provides "the fundamental framework for harmony among mankind," the "two legs" on which man may walk into a new epoch. Throughout her life she spoke of education as "an aid to life." In her last book she described education as "the armament of peace." "Let us give the child a vision of the whole Universe," she said—an imposing reality, an answer to all questions. "We shall walk together on this path of life."

"Education is the Armament of Peace."

Maria Montessori, et. al., *The Child in the Church* (St. Paul: Catechetical Guild, 1965).

The Ground of Realistic Insights

Realism is a multi-colored, many-sided, much-starred banner. Those philosophers who gather under it have two things in common, their rejection of the singular super-sensory reality claimed by Idealism, and their pluralism in regard to what is real. The latter means, of course, that they differ among themselves, but the former means that realists share the commonsense hunch that the physical things of the world are just as lumpy and impersonal as they appear to be, especially when, say, stubbing one's toe.

Some historians have regarded Western philosophy from Plato and Aristotle on as a debate between mentalism and materialism. In every age the idealist says, "No matter," and the realist replies, "Never mind." However, one philosopher who is a realist has called Idealism an interlude. The awareness that knowledge comes to us through our five senses is indeed a more primitive explanation than Idealism's sophisticated theory about the ideal reality behind appearances. There are evidences of a basic Realism in ancient Egyptian and Hebrew religions long before Plato. Now in the twentieth century theoretical Idealism has given way to the reminder of science that in spite of the vastness and sophistication of our knowledge it still begins with the senses and their extension by sensitive instruments. In this case, the middle would appear to be longer than the ends, stretching from roughly the middle of the fourth century B.C. to the middle of the twentieth century A.D.

But both philosophy and its history are complicated. William Hocking, the idealist, says that "everybody is necessarily something of a realist," and in the systems of the most comprehensive of the idealists, including Plato and Kant, there are realistic elements. Absolute mental Idealism is a fairly recent and very sophisticated phenomenon. Furthermore, the hottest debate of the Middle Ages was the realism-and-nominalism controversy in which both parties accepted the Neo-platonic assumption that mental universals are real, "realism" taking the *idealist* position that universals exist before particulars, and "nominalism" taking the *realist* position that particulars exist before universals. However, the divergents from the mainstream during that twenty-five-century interlude all shared a conviction that reality and knowledge were far more direct and apparent than philosophers generally assumed, and though they did not agree with each other on very much, they tended to be hardheaded, clear-eyed, independent, and interesting people. Antisthenes the Cynic, whose name suggests opposition, asked Alexander the Great a single favor, "only to stand out of my light." Timon the Sceptic said, "That honey is sweet I refuse to assert; that it appears sweet, I fully grant." Averroes the Mohammedan preserved Aristotle for the Christian world. In the medieval world of Platonic thought, Albertus Magnus popularized Aristotle at the University of Paris. William of Occam insisted that things are individuals, and he is responsible for the principle that ideas ought not to be multiplied unnecessarily, a rule so sharply critical of medieval scholastics that it was called "Occam's Razor." In sixteenth-century Spain, Juan Luis Vives taught that "whatever is in the arts is in nature first." Machiavelli taught that power is for those who have the skill to use it. Erasmus praised simplicity. Loyola translated soldiering into monastic discipline and ethics. In the seventeenth century, Wolfgang Ratcke demonstrated that any foreign language could be learned better than the mother tongue in six months by beginning with things. German Pietists, Franke and Zinzendorf among them, created a series of schools teaching that religion was more a matter of love and service than of correct beliefs. In Denmark the eccentric Soren Kierkegaard opposed "existing ego" to Hegel's "knowing ego."

Aristotle, 384-322 B.C.

Bertrand Russell says that in respect to his predecessors Aristotle's merits are enormous, but with respect to his successors his demerits are equally enormous. It was two millennia before the world produced another philosopher of his stature. During that time his authority in science became so unquestioned that it proved an obstacle to further progress, but thereafter almost every serious theoretical advance began with an attack on him.

William Hocking says that the difference between Plato and Aristotle was a matter of temperament. "He [Aristotle] rests on the hard nubbles of fact with a certain relish which Plato lacks." Plato was his teacher for twenty years, but then he left the academy to become tutor to Alexander the Great and a world traveler. He was a kind of practical Plato. He was fascinated by the individuality of things. He observed and analyzed them to be instructed by their differences. He seemed to be capable of leaving himself and the mind out of account when he was dealing with things. He was not much interested in the universal generalities Plato had made the primary business of philosophy. "It is clear," he wrote, "that he who would try to demonstrate the more apparent by the less apparent shows that he cannot distinguish what is from what is not evident." He may have had Plato in mind.

Scratch Aristotle anywhere and his "yen for analysis" shows immediately. This might be expected when he is talking about mechanics, astronomy, or botany, but it is true also of his aesthetics and metaphysics. For example, when considering the problem of "soul," he begins with the most observable, "the different levels of life." At the

"Nature is the starting point for philosophizing."

"The irrational is prior to the rational."

lowest level there are plants which are characterized by the capacity to receive food and turn it into life, "vegetable soul." Next is animal life, which is characterized by locomotion and perception in addition to nutrition, "the kinetic soul." There follows human life, in which is added the capacity to think, in two ways, practically and theoretically—"rational soul." "Each higher quality of soul," he says, "continues to possess all the faculties of the lower." Now the human being must learn to live rationally. Because rationality is at the peak of a cumulative development, "the care of the body precedes that of the soul," and "the training of the appetitive part" should follow. In the same manner, since the practical reason precedes the theoretical, it is educated first. "Children are like animals," he observed, and the first seven years of their education should be in the home, where they may play with peers, imitate elders, and see and hear nothing of indecency. In boyhood's seven years, four years is devoted to military training and three to music, poetry, and rhetoric. Only after that training of the practical reason can there follow a graduate education of the theoretical reason in psychology, politics, and ethics. "Happiness," he said, "is found only in what is complete."

Perhaps Aristotle's most important, certainly his most metaphysical, analysis concerns "causes." Things are real and observable, but they are always changing or being changed into something else. Matter is, therefore, potential, and form is the realizing of potential. There are four causes working in this change: the *material* cause

". . . for the sake of the soul"

Aristotle, *Magna Moralia* for the analysis of "soul," *Politics* for the plan of education. Both are available in collections and parts in many anthologies.
Aristotle, *Physics* (Book II for the analysis of causes) and *Metaphysics* (Book XII for the argument for the existence of God).

("that which composes a thing"), the *formal* cause ("the universal type which exists in individual things"), the *efficient* cause ("the source from which movement or rest comes"), and the *final* cause ("the end and goal of a thing"). He observed these causes in everything: the process by which an egg becomes a chick, marble becomes a statue, a child becomes a man. Based on observation, he applied the analysis to nonobservable issues. Because an endless chain of causes is irrational, there must be a single first cause, and this would be God. God is also the efficient moving principle, the perfect form, and the absolute realization. He is, therefore, the one Unmoved Mover.

God is the Prime Mover who is himself Unmoved.

Thomas Aquinas, 1225?-1274

Some philosophers say that Aquinas was not so much an exponent of systematic Realism as an exponent of Aristotle. He was probably the first man in medieval Europe to know Aristotle completely. Some theologians say that he did not so much expound Aristotle as adapt him to Christian doctrine. This latter was a stunning achievement, because orthodoxy was a complex and comprehensive system of thought built over a period of eight hundred years on a neoplatonic foundation.

Every man may be wise about some things, but all men wish to be wise about the universe. Now, wisdom is knowing the means to an end, like building a house, and that is the result of natural reason, the sort that everybody has some of. Natural reason is not sufficient, however, to tell us everything we wish to know about the universe; much, like the meaning of the Trinity and the Incarnation, comes through revelation. However, natural reason can prove the existence of God, and Aristotle shows how in the argument of the Unmoved Mover. Description of God is

. . . Reason

. . . Revelation

more difficult, because that has to do with essence rather than existence, but even so, natural reason can tell us what God is not, and Aristotle shows how to go about that, too. God is eternal since he is unmoved, pure activity since he is not matter, rational because he is not irrational.

Aquinas also wants to join "The Philosopher" in affirming the primary reality of matter. The problem was not whether matter exists but the relation between God and material substance. Because the biblical tradition in Christianity asserted that God created the world "out of nothing," Aquinas had a problem Aristotle did not face. Aquinas answers that God produced matter out of nothing (this is known through revelation) and that he then created the world out of matter (this is known through reason). Primary matter has no status apart from God, but once formed, objects become quite separate and distinct from God. For all practical and scientific purposes, matter is an external substance which is different from mind and soul in quality. Even modern realists have generally been content with this view. Primary matter can be regarded as "potential," in the categories of nuclear physics as nonpersonal energy or force. Some realists would rather think of this nonmental physical force as uncaused, but some don't mind saying that God caused it.

"Matter is being in potentiality."

John Locke, 1632-1704

A pivotal figure in philosophy, education, and politics, John Locke was both gifted and lucky. Some say the latter is more responsible for his place in history than the former. Son of a Puritan attorney, educated at Oxford, tutor to royalty, and a medical doctor, he had enough in-

Thomas Aquinas, *Summa Contra Gentiles*, Book I. Available in many editions and anthologies.

telligence to make common sense sophisticated and the good fortune to do it at a time when common sense was fairly rare and much needed in many fields. His *Essay Concerning Human Understanding* is said to be the most important philosophical treatise ever written by an Englishman. The essay began with an evening discussion that reached no conclusion. "It came into my thoughts," remembered Locke, "that it was necessary to examine our own abilities and see what objects our understanding were, or were not, fitted to deal with." If ideas are innate, they

There are no innate ideas.

must be found in the minds of infants and idiots, in the minds of all people everywhere, and perceived as necessary and self-evident propositions. As a physician he testified that these ideas are not held by infants, anthropology shows that not even the idea of God is to be found in the minds of all primitive peoples, and history reveals that great civilizations do not have the same ideas of mathematics, to say nothing of justice and goodness. He concluded that "not a single idea known to the human mind can be truly said to be universal," and that men should be "more cautious in meddling with things exceeding their comprehension."

"The mind of the child at birth is like a blank sheet of paper."

The natural human mind, in its original state, would seem to be blank. Its content is built up from two sources, impressions from without and the mind working on them —"external sensible objects" and "internal operations," these are "the only originals from whence all our ideas take their beginnings." The mind is like a sheet of blank paper passively receiving impressions. "The mind can no more refuse to have them, when they are imprinted, nor blot them out, and make new ones itself, than a mirror can." As an epistemology it was, a contemporary philoso-

John Locke, *Essay Concerning Human Understanding*, 1690, and innumerable subsequent editions.

pher says, "unique and erroneous." Nevertheless, two centuries have built on these principles. The Platonic doctrine of ideas, the Puritan doctrine of depravity, the educational notion that the child is a "little adult," the Cartesian principle that mind is pure thinking substance and the body a machine, were all unseated in one fell swoop.

In politics, Locke's common sense led him to proclaim tolerance, the separation of church and state, and constitutional government at a time when the world, especially in its new hemisphere, was turning against the divine right of kings and experimenting with democratic self-government. His primary contribution to education was his scorn of forms of education left over from the Renaissance and the Middle Ages: the "ado" that is made about "a little Latin and Greek," the "many years spent on it," and "the noise and business it makes to no purpose." He would cut out both language, as well as rhetoric, logic, and the disputation—all of them the jewels of scholastic education—and make usefulness the key in determining the curriculum. Upper class education would be private and tutorial: the aims would be manners, wisdom, self-control, and religion, and the purpose would be to equip "gentlemen" to take care of their estates, serve their communities, and guide their governments. As Commissioner of the Board of Trade, he designed publicly supported "working schools" which would give children food to eat, simple handicrafts, and religion. It is the basic design of education that in England has since become both classic and characteristic.

Education is discipline for usefulness.

John Locke, *Some Thoughts Concerning Education*, 1693, and cited in many histories of education.

The Objective Nature of Realism

Realism is a constellation of philosophical principles gathering around the disposition to let objects speak for themselves. The mood of humility before the facts and forces of the physical world has never, of course, been entirely absent in history, but the twentieth century was a time ripe for the objectivity that humility always implies. In the twenties, science was making it clear that physical universes, both micro- and macroscopic, went on their own ways in a fashion and according to principles quite beyond man's influence and that among them man's existence was emphatically the most adjustable and dispensable. Science is not a philosophy, but it set problems that made the philosophic pot begin to boil, as one realist put it. There is an independent object and this external object is somehow first known through the senses as a thing "out there." The mind is not a prison-house; it is concerned with external things and must avoid purely subjective judgments untempered by external relations.

The Collapse of Ideals

There could be no question about it, Western man had entered the twentieth century romantically inclined. There was no good that seemed impossible. But events began to change attitudes. It is said that Walter Rauschenbusch, who proclaimed in 1910 that the hardest part of Christianizing the social order had been accomplished, died of a broken heart when World War I broke out. Though that is more a historical judgment than a medical diagnosis, the story has become a symbol. During the thirties, it was difficult to be romantic about breadlines and dustbowls. George Albert Coe was so discouraged about the industrial democracy of God in America during World War II that he wondered if Russia might be nearer to it. In a world in which no trouble, treason, or treachery seemed impossible, a hardheaded attitude about man and his world seemed the only realistic one to take.

The Fascists and Communists introduced the word realism into popular vocabulary. The Communists had a philosophical claim to the word in Marx's materialism; the Fascists meant practicality without principle, but both claimed to be the only true realists, dubbing all moderate or liberal programs as "unrealistic and romantic." Reinhold Niebuhr never made much use of the word "realism" but he used "unrealistic" and "romantic" frequently in describing liberal theological views. Albert North Whitehead talked about "provisional realism," which meant starting with mathematics and being unwilling to speak of any ontological reality that does not appear at the end of a process of rigorous deduction from known and observable realities. Paul Tillich's "belief-ful realism" was intentionally a self-contradictory phrase, and the paradox stands for the stubborn irrationality and objectivity of facts and events, their refusal to be what we want them to be, the disinclination of problems to go away. In literature the debunking biographers, the pessimistic poets, and the hard-edge novelists took over from Whitman and Longfellow and called themselves "realists." In music and painting there was the same impatience with sweetness and pleasantness. In theater Zola's "naturalism" was followed by the "realism" of Strindberg, Ibsen, and O'Neill, replacing backdrops with doors that slammed, poetry with prose, and romance with social analysis. In philosophy solipsism became an obscene word. In common they all shared and communicated a temper of mind which craves objectivity and fears subjectivity, which prefers objective realities however disagreeable to subjective fancies how-

"Idealism is a dead duck."

ever glorious, and which means to be guided by these realities in every form of human quest whether for truth, artistic beauty, or political stability. It was a new attitude appropriate to a world that no longer seemed altogether friendly to ideals.

The Knowledge of Objects

For idealists the question is, "How do we know that things exist?" For realists it is, "How do the things that exist affect us?" The realists' answers are many and sophisticated, but they tend to agree that when we perceive objects we find them to be just what they are when they are not perceived and that in the process of perceiving we are changed. The effect is to turn the idealists' world view inside out, and also to raise many new and knotty questions.

Things are unchanged by human experience.

To understand knowing we must use what is known.

Precisely because the questions are so speculative, some realists prefer the straightforward, commonsense kind of answers. Objects are experienced directly, as my senses tell me they are, what I perceive is precisely the object out there in my senses. I feel it, I hear it, I see it: I know it. Mind is the sensory relation between consciousness and object. It is therefore as much out there with the object as it is in here with my consciousness. Knowing is thus a relation between organism and object, and of the two it is the organism that makes adjustments and the object that is unaffected by the process. For centuries idealists had been constructing theories on the model of the sense of sight, emphasizing the distance, time lag, subjective vision, and mental categories. Realists tend to prefer epistemologies built on the sense of touch, emphasizing direct

Roy Wood Sellars, *The Philosophy of Physical Realism* (New York: Macmillan, 1932).

contact, immediacy, objective resistance, and physical sensations.

Other realists prefer more sophisticated answers of the sort necessitated when one emphasizes the inner activity of the mind in the relation between object and self. The things "out there" are outside and independent, of course, but the mind is "in here" as I sense it to be, and it is important to recognize the productive activity of the mind in the knowing process. The physical object is different in quality from the qualities of my consciousness of it. The roughness of the stone, that is to say, is not physically the same as the roughness in my consciousness. This inner experience is produced by a physical organism called the brain, which neurologically accomplishes the exchange of sensations for consciousness. Object and knowledge may be said to be "compresent." There are other answers which go even further in crediting the mind with the construction of knowledge. In general, however, it may be said that the two characteristic assertions of the realist position are these: things are unchanged by human experience of them, and knowledge of things is grounded in sensory or bodily functions.

"Begin with the actual cognitive experience."

The Nature of Objects

Realism begins with the inclination to accept things as real in their own right. Realistic epistemology adds that they are very much as we know them to be. At first impact the metaphysical result is pluralism: all things are real, and each has its own special qualities and relationships. Science, however, suggests that there are at least constellations of qualities into elements and of relationships into laws, and it is the nature of the human experience to achieve some simplification of realities by general-

Things are real.

izing and classifying. The temper of Realism is to accept both the pluralism as providing an open universe with some elbowroom for the human spirit and the tendency to simplification. Dualism is as far as most realists are willing to go in the direction of simplification, for their position by definition depends on the separable reality of mind and object. There may be other dualisms, such as good-and-evil. Some realists do suggest that there is but one reality, energy, from which everything comes. The realism in this position is imbedded in the conviction that this energy is nonpersonal, that is, "objective" in nature. The nature of things is the nature of the world.

Plural objective realities do not, however, produce chaos. We experience relations among objects as well as between ourselves and objects, and those relations are as objective as the objects themselves, relating rather than dispersing them. Force causes effects, as the objective sciences describe them, and operate even beyond scientific observation. Realists differ about whether the human individual is wholly or partly within this objective relation and to what degree he may be an original cause of new effects. There is a totality but not a unity, and it, too, is of the nature of things and of man. One realist says that the world is "a single, public, spatial, or spatio-temporal order, in which the laws of physics hold good." Another says that man lives in the world as in a macrocosm of which his being is a reflection and a part. Another says that nature as physics describes it is the outside; on the inside it is feeling or emotion. Another says the world is a kind of stage for the human drama. And still another says that the world would not be very much put out if the human race were to vanish altogether.

. . . cause and effect and order

"To me," says Roy Wood Sellars, Realism is "a fascinating completion of science." For him it means that nature is "self-sufficient" as contrasted to the interpretations of nature put forward by popularized forms of supernatural-ism. The world is defined by space, time, and causality, Sellars says, and these are the essential features of human existence also. The world is "not even a machine," be-cause new patterns occur. The ultimate mystery is that there is any universe at all. There is no concentrated con-trol of the universe, and therefore all things that appear to be real must be regarded as real in their own right and nature. Any assumptions of the primacy of mind are in-valid. The function of mind is to know; not to control. "Away with Transcendental Egos and things-in-them-selves!" he cries. "We are conscious organisms thinking the things around us in accordance with our nature and theirs." To know, as far as we are able to experience it, means "knowledge about," "facts about," and "grasping the nature of the object." The mind approaches nature "to decipher, measure, schematize." By approaching the world thus, man can "see himself as he is," a creature of the world, "a creature strangely gifted to look before and after and to follow his desires and dreams on an earth partly plastic to his power."

". . . to see ourselves as we are"

Realism and Christianity

Realists who are not Christians can be nontheistic, though they are seldom antitheistic and are often very humble about man in relation to the world. They tend to be objective about religion, taking it as one of the facts about man to be observed and studied for whatever insight about man it may provide. Some say that the fact that religion has survived many changes in belief indicates that it is independent of any kind of "innate ideas." Others suggest that religion comprises a special way of knowing some facts about our universe unavailable to the methods of science. Realists who are Christians tend to think of God as an objective reality (independent of the person experiencing it), good (source of the human experience of goodness), powerful (adequate to produce new emergents in experience), and disinterested (not necessarily personal). God is thus known as he is through direct empirical experience at the perceptual level as a reality other than self, greater than self, and even over against self. Others are more sophisticated in method, finding something otherwise inexplicable in human experience, such as "value," and, in this case, defining God as "that which produces value." Man reveals himself by his behavior to be a complex of interwoven good and evil, attempting to better his condition but unable to do so unless his vision is rooted in recognition of man and the world and God as they actually are.

A Christian Philosophy

"God is not a product of wishful thinking."

"Religion is a fact of individual and social life," begins A. Cambell Garnett of the University of Wisconsin. "The philosophy of religion is an attempt to understand it." From the analysis of their religious experience, men have demonstrated that what they call God is "a factor within themselves that they naturally distinguish from the familiar self or private desire." The history of religion is "the story of man's effort to understand and adjust himself to this element of the divine within him."

Though it is impossible to get back to "absolute beginnings," because they are "too obscure to be described and too early to be remembered," Garnett's training as an anthropologist in his native Australia, and his analytical training as an empirical philosopher at the University of London demand that he start as near the beginning as possible. Historically, religion seems to have arisen from a deeply "felt" duality in the world itself. This consciousness is carried on and developed by priests and prophets, "despite the load of trickery and magic that was thrust upon it." Psychologically, religion seems to be rooted in the experience of moral conflict. This profound inner conflict and outer duality seems to be a universal fact, unwanted, perhaps, but nonetheless there and inescapable. Garnett concludes that it is a conflict between egoism and altruism, subjectivism and objectivism. Egoism is understandable; it is altruism that is difficult to account for. It is a force or pressure or "will" within us to seek the good of others which cannot simply be identified with our own desires, and we feel it as an objective agency. Garnett says it is divine: personal because it is within us, real because it goes beyond us, religious because it precipitates a moral conflict, Godly because we did not create it ourselves. God is not a person if personality must be defined in terms of human experience alone as "an isolated order of consciousness." But if we may take the analysis itself as providing the terms of a definition of personality as "an organization

". . . a disinterested will that seeks to produce the good wherever possible"

A. Cambell Garnett, *A Realistic Philosophy of Religion* (Chicago: Willett, Clark, 1942).

of will" and if we are personal because God is personal, God is an objective energy, neutral insofar as the vested interest of any one human person is concerned, by its very neutrality precipitating the conflict with individual interest which produces human personality and awareness of God. "The disinterested will appears as part of the world order, responsive to the world order of values," says Garnett, "and it is not dependent on the psycho-physical organism, but the individual psycho-physical organism functions in rationally recognized subservience to it."

Now, Garnett is himself a Christian, in fact reared in a conservative denomination and given his first education in a College of the Bible. He is convinced that history is the result of the conflict produced in man by the force of altruistic will. God is in men, challenging egoism and enabling altruism. "The influence of God upon us is through his will as it operates within," he says, "helped by what we learn from others through the operation of God's will in them." Because this is the nature of the world and man, God is in all men. There is, therefore, no specific or special revelation, and none can claim for his own thought the whole truth. History, however, has produced Jesus Christ, "in whom we find the culmination of the historic revelation of God's will as a will to the good of all," to be "pursued without exception and without limit." Others had talked about love, of course, but "he made it central, essential, and dominant." The goal of the will of God within men "has been clarified once and for all by the life and teaching of Jesus Christ." Thus Christianity may claim that faith in Christ gives to man "a unique aid in his struggle with sin." It may not, however, claim that

"God is in us."

Jesus is "unique in history."

He provides "a unique aid" to man.

A. Cambell Garnett, *God in Us* (Chicago: Willett, Clark, 1945).

there is no salvation for any one except by believing in Christian doctrine.

Sin is failure to produce altruistic good when, by some omission or action, it was possible to act in accordance with egoistic will. There is no need talking about "demonic tendencies" or "positive love of evil" in man. The selfish drives of the infantile ego "have a long start over the altruistic tendencies" in the development of man. Inertia is the problem. Jesus made it clear that man may walk "at one" with God—"may be divine." He also made it clear that is necessary to strive to overcome egoism, taking on all the built-in help of the divine altruistic will. Sin is not breaking rules. God's problem, and man's, is "to keep the human race spiritually active, growing in grace and in the knowledge of God." *"Sin is failure." "Sin is spiritual stagnation."*

Faith is the disciplined maintenance of "an active system of volitional tendencies" aiming at universally objective love-for-all. Salvation is thus by faith, neither by belief nor by works. And Garnett feels that "the larger spiritual order of the universe" implies "an organization of the will, developed within that larger spiritual order and directed toward goals not dependent upon the existence of the physical organism." Pursuit of those goals will go on after the dissolution of the body. The beginnings of the development of "the eternal part of personality" are wrought within physical life "under the stimulus of the divine will within." It was some such thing that happened at the resurrection. What actually occurred is not entirely clear: "No form of resurrection doctrine is sufficiently well established to be put into a creed and made a test of religious fellowship," says Garnett. But "the doctrine of the risen Lord has proved its value in the life of the church." There is no doubt for Garnett that the resurrection happened in some way not yet known that would satisfy the demands *"Faith is a moral attainment." "Salvation is for eternity." "Something remarkable happened."*

of science, and that "the hope of eternity rounds out the meaning of our life and gives us courage to face its darkest phases."

Revival of Essentials

Events conspired to turn theology also toward hard realities. The spirit of idealism and special optimism continued through the fighting of World War I. It was only afterwards, when the liberal and idealistic aims for which the war was allegedly fought were rudely frustrated, that reaction set in. It was symptomatic of man's felt need for objective certainties. In theology it became a determination to start with the most stubborn, perplexing, and disheartening facts of human life, and then to push through them into the solid structure of reality until one discovers whatever ground of courage, hope, and faith is actually there, independent of human preferences and desires. The method implied a willingness to accept God as Judge as well as loving Father, and to recognize the chaotic, tragic, and even demonic forces in history. The mood was significantly unlike that of theology at home in Experimentalism or Personalism.

In the United States, the first wave was the revival of fundamentals. As a widespread movement Fundamentalism dates back to about 1910, but soon after the War the fundamentalists began to take the offensive. During the twenties, candidates for ordination in many denominations were certain to be asked whether they believed in the verbal inspiration of the Scriptures, the virgin birth and bodily resurrection of Christ, the blood atonement through the substitution of Christ for sinners on the cross, and the physical second coming of Christ to the earth in a super-

. . . the Bible, virgin birth, resurrection, substitution, second coming.

298   ALTERNATIVES

natural act of intervention establishing the Kingdom of Heaven. Many liberal preachers were attacked, some were defrocked, attempts were made to get whole denominations to subscribe to lists of fundamentals, and some denominations were split. There was among fundamentalists a militancy that appeared to many to be similar to that of the Ku Klux Klan and a prescientific obscurantism that seemed to be similar to that of the antievolutionists of the Bryan-Darrow debate at Dayton, Tennessee, but they had uncovered in American theology a defective sense of human sin and a dangerous trend to reduce all the supernatural elements of Christianity to biology and psychology. During the thirties the Depression made it clear to nonfundamentalists that the Kingdom of God was not being quickly realized on this earth. Divine sovereignty, human failure, and the scriptural revelation began to appear to be irreducible essentials of the Christian position.

In Germany, however, the Nazi philosophy and the National Socialist machinery made it clear that the church must publicly assert its primary loyalty to God as known in Jesus Christ or cease to be the Christian church in any traditionally recognizable sense. In that situation Christians were driven relentlessly back to faith essentials that had no dependence on a specific cultural situation. There were many German Christians who thought some sort of compromise could be worked out. There were scientists who demanded freedom of inquiry, lawyers who insisted on justice and law, and humanists who resisted tyranny. But in the showdown, it was the confessional church, finding new sources of strength growing out of that which is timeless amidst all the changing crises of life, that made the most effective resistence. They met and adopted what is now known as the Barmen Declaration: "The Christian faith," it said in part, "rests upon the word of Jesus

"When Christ stands before Pilate, the Word of God is there in One Man."

Christ as that word is testified to in the Bible, and it rests on nothing else."

Among the churchmen of Germany, it was Karl Barth who took the lead. His vocabulary and passion were fashioned in crisis. His theology is a warning cry. The passing of time and that crisis has made it possible to see more clearly than in the heat and movement of struggle itself the essentials he recovered and reapplied: God's otherness, God's sovereignty, the crisis in human existence, and God's saving revelation of himself in crisis.

God is absolutely other.

There is no part of nature, no invention of reason, no human hope or ideal or value that can be identified with God. Indeed, it is blasphemous to do so. God is other than man, an abyss in experience, a mystery to reason. God stands over against anything human, especially what we might regard as achievement, as the judge and condemner of all that is human. That is so, not because man is finite or incomplete, but because he is a sinner and has set himself against God. For these reasons one cannot speak of God "simply by speaking of man in a loud voice," Barth says.

God is absolutely sovereign.

One way in which God is absolutely unlike man is that his power is without limit. Everything is subject to his might and his will. We have no reason to ask why, then, there is such a lack of goodness on this earth. God's absolute otherness means precisely that God is not good in any human sense of the term. It is impossible for man to judge God's goodness in any way. In the same manner, we have no right to reason out the matter of good and evil. God is superrational, and any attempt to remove logical inconsistencies in his relation to the world would be foolish and indicate a lack of faith. God's sovereignty is unchallengeable.

Because God is what he is, and man is what he is, man

faces in every concrete situation of his existence the crisis of deciding for or against God. The choice is not between sets of values, because God is absolutely other than man. The choice is to stand for God because he is sovereign. I decide for God when I hold every interest, value, hope, ideal, and course of action to be subject to God's will and judgment. Only then can I view the situation disinterestedly. By placing everything under his judgment, I am freed from love and fear, which are merely human qualities. Faith is the beginning of everything. The creation occurs in every moment of time. "Rightly understood," says Barth, "there are no Christians, there is only the eternal opportunity of becoming Christians."

It is as a result of making this choice that we know anything about God. Revelation does not come from reasoning or intuition. It comes in confrontation with the God who is absolutely other than man, an event that can only be marked by fear and trembling because God is holy. The feeling of "sickness unto death" prepares the way for the self-disclosure of God. "Man is in anguish," says Barth, "until the Word of God takes possession of him," and the word comes to him most easily and clearly, it comes to him only, as a matter of fact, when he is in the situation of anguish and despair. Therefore we must listen on our knees to what God has spoken and is speaking. The position of humility is the position of a man ready for God.

The truth that is revealed to man is not simply information, it is transformation. It provides the medium of grace by which man passes from the state of mortality to immortality. Truth is not knowledge about God; it is acknowledgment that the judgment of God is right. It is illumination of the sort that relates man effectively to the super-

Karl Barth, *The Word of God and the Word of Man* (Grand Rapids: Zondervan, 1935).

natural world, the source of grace. It is the confidence that leads man to extend his hand, knowing that God will take it in his own.

The sacred knowledge that comes from revelation guides man to salvation. It must therefore be guarded against distortion through reason and philosophy. But that is not easy. Because all forms of rational discourse are incompetent to deal with God, Barth resorts to paradox. Anything that one can say about God is true and yet is not true; its contradictory must also be true. In this way, logical form may participate in the form of personal confrontation. "We know," says Barth, "that we are unable to comprehend except by means of dialectical dualism in which one must become two in order that it may veritably be one." Or again, "Men can grasp their unredeemed condition only because already they stand within the redemption. They know themselves to be sinners only because they are already righteous." And a disciple of Barth adds, "A religious faith which can be proved does not deserve to be believed, ceases indeed to be religious faith at all."

Revelation is unrepeatable and unique.

Revelation is, further, once and for all, irrevocable and unrepeatable. Had it not been for God's free compassion and condescension to man, the eternal word would have been hidden eternally from us. Therefore the life of Jesus of Nazareth, who as the Christ is the incarnation of the eternal word, is of supreme importance. Barth says, "Only the man who knows about Jesus Christ knows anything at all about revelation." So, he continues, "it becomes inevitable that Jesus Christ alone is the revelation. All other revelations are revelations only in a perverted, invalid and loose sense." In the Bible that revelation is preserved and there it is to be found again. "It is not the right human

Karl Barth, *Epistle to the Romans* (London: Oxford, 1933).

thoughts about God which form the content of the Bible, but the right divine thoughts about man," says Barth. "The Bible tells us not how we should talk to God but what he says to us. Not how we find the way to him but how he has sought and found the way to us."

Armed with timeless and extrahuman essentials such as these, men on both sides of the Atlantic plunged with new objectivity and realism into the problems and difficulties of the high twentieth century. The world would not soon forget the toughness and heroism their theology made possible.

Theological Realism

When the theological news began to seep through from Germany, American liberals tended to think that neo-orthodoxy was too orthodox and fundamentalists that it was too new. Both complained during the thirties that the only thing America seemed to be importing from Europe was theology. Then theologians began to come to America, too, and many American seminaries hastily provided chairs for them. A mutual adjustment followed. Paul Tillich came expecting to be able to continue lecturing in German, but found that American linguistic limitations forced him to learn English; later he said that learning English taught him how to think. American students challenged and even debated with their professors. Compared to German students they were both untheological and very practical. But the students also listened and absorbed. They began to acknowledge the shallowness that had come to characterize American Christianity in the absence of political crisis and pagan confrontation. Christian heroism and Barthian thunder struck their consciences. The result was not so much a series of American Barths as a new seriousness in American theology.

The European theologian who seemed in himself to approximate most closely the new American theological temper was neither German nor Barthian. Emil Brunner was Swiss and vigorously differed with Barth. At first it seemed to many Americans that both the geographical and theological differences were obscure, and Brunner possessed neither the heroic character nor the dramatic impact of Barth, but in time it began to appear that Switzerland was somewhere between Germany and America and Brunner between Barth and Brightman.

"Christian theology can never be required to make faith rational by giving it scientific form."

Brunner is, of course, a theologian: for him the ground, content and standard of thought "alike are to be found not in any consciousness of man's but in God's self-disclosure." Even beginning with real things as "given facts," philosophy, or human thought in any form, can take us only to "a very powerful being," not to God, "never the Creator but only a demiurge." Science is to be taken seriously in its investigation of the given realities of the physical world. That is its business. It is also helpful in holding down the romanticism with which German idealism tended to view history and the biblical tradition. In general science is right in insisting that reality is primary and the knowing process secondary. In a similar fashion, the primary function of the believer in knowing God is receptivity. The attitude of theology is faith, and "faith possesses no theory of the world" because it has to do with God. God reveals himself—it is the nature of a creator to create. The believer believes—it is the nature of a believer to believe. Thus, in religion knowledge is not the result of a perceptual meeting between knower and object, but a faith encounter between knower and known.

Speculation about God is not to be trusted because it intellectually builds a concept of God from the sensory data of physical things, and then acts as if that concept were God. The concept has thus become an idol. Revelation is the reverse of speculation: it moves from God to man and relates man to God as He actually is. "Revelation," says Brunner, "is opposed to all idols." So in revelation God appears not as an idea or an object, but as a self-revealing activity. To say that self-disclosure is the essence of personality, as Brunner does, is not to say however that God is like us. In fact, he is so much unlike us in his subject-hood that were it not for the biblical presentation of God's activity, we should never have recognized either him or ourselves as subjects. "Christian faith," Brunner cries, "is biblical faith." What is shown to us in that record is a Creator. God created because he was absolutely supreme. He is therefore wholly other, because man is always dependent on this world which is in turn dependent on God. Otherness means precisely that God is incomprehensible and unfathomable. But, lest we think we can begin to understand that, God reveals himself as love, "because he loves," and love is to human speculation the antithesis of otherness: "in Christ the Eternal Word became flesh, and the word of reconciliation was spoken by God Himself." God is always in relation to man but the relation is always in terms of God's nature. Thus God is both "the basis of the creation of the world and of its redemption." He is always related to man, forever identified with man in a divine rule of redeeming love, in the incarnation, and in the unity between God and man effected by love. He is thus revealed to be Father, Son, and Holy Spirit. "He creates (man) because he loves him, and he reveals his love to him, which he has from all eternity, as he himself from all eternity is love."

God made man in his own image, as the Genesis ac-

. . . Subject

. . . Creator

. . . Wholly Other

. . . Love

. . . United

Emil Brunner, *The Philosophy of Religion from the Standpoint of Protestant Theology* (London: James Clarke, 1937).

count has it. Because God is the sort of subject who must disclose himself, man is the sort of subject who can receive self-disclosure. "The fact that God reveals himself through his Word," Brunner says, "presupposes that man is a being who has been created for this kind of communication." To this man owes what Paschal called his "grandeur." However, man is a sinner. He has revolted against the "original revelation" implicit in him by virtue of his creaturehood. He has created all kinds of speculative substitutes—idols—to keep him from facing the wrath and judgment God must necessarily visit upon rebellion. More serious than being pleasure-loving, domineering, and selfish, man is "in contradiction to his origin" as Brunner puts it. He has not ceased to be "in the sight of God," but he is in the sight of God a perverted being. We remain creatures who can only live in community, but in fact we persist in refusing community for isolation or collectivism. We are torn within ourselves. To this man owes what Paschal called his "misery."

But, to have been created by God means to have received the gift of life from God. Because God is sovereign, the gift is receivable and man is "the subject of salvation." Our false attitudes make his intervention in grace appear to be an interference: when God becomes real to a man his whole neat, self-centered organization is shattered. In actuality, God is acting in love, yearning to win us back to our original good. Man is saved by "allowing himself to be determined by the Word of God," by being willing to receive life again as a gift. In short, forgiveness of sins on the one hand and faith on the other restore the lost relation of love. A new life begins, that of the forgiven sinner characterized by a personal relation to God and

Emil Brunner, *Revelation and Reason* (Philadelphia: Westminster, 1946).

receptive to the guidance which is given within that relation. We move away from rules and into free trust of God's will. "The Good," says Brunner, "is simply what God wills that we should do, not that which we would do on the basis of a principle of love." God's command is always personal and concrete: "He does not issue proclamations or set up any kind of program." So the kingdom of God is at work in the world. Christian faith is entrance into "the movement of God in Christ," and it proves its reality by making sure that this movement actually takes place.

. . . faith

. . . free obedience

To many in America this sort of Christianity seemed more original than Fundamentalism and newer than Liberalism. By the time the fighting ended in the forties, it had become the proven base of Protestant theology at large.

Emil Brunner, *Man in Revolt* (Philadelphia: Westminster, 1947).

"Train up a child in the way he should go," begins the biblical admonition. "As the twig is bent," is the non-biblical parallel. "I took a piece of living clay and gently formed it day by day," is the rhymed form of the sentiment, "and molded with my power and art a young child's soft and yielding heart." Ever since the Reformation, educators of the realistic temperament have made the same point. The Scriptures should be "the chief and most common lesson" in schools of all kinds, declared Martin Luther, and "historians are the best teachers." "The special duty of the teacher," commands the 1599 *Ratio Studiorum* of the Jesuits, "shall be to move his hearers to a reverence and love of God." An early English Pietist summed up the essence of education, "First I command thee God to serve, and then to thy Parent duty yield." By the seventeenth century "the method of nature" began to shift discipline to physical realities. "First the thing, afterward the explanation," wrote Peter Ratich to German teachers, "everything in the course of nature," only "one thing at a time," and "nothing must be learned by rote." "There is nothing in the understanding," wrote a Puritan schoolteacher, "which has not come through the senses." "Being thus trained up" through language and arithmetic "in the way of discipline," he continued, "they will afterward prove more easily plyable to their Master's commands." "Education is the conscious and organized effort of adults," says a modern educator, "to predict and and control through manipulation of the environment the development of children in ways and towards ends which are regarded by these adults as desirable." Another calls education "apprenticeship to experts," still another "exposure to greatness." Another writes that the task of education is to "form the mold into which one's personality is poured." Men in Old School ties nostalgically recall midwinter cold-water baths, public ridicule for minor scholarly errors, and "it doesn't matter much what one studies so long as one doesn't like it." This is education of a special, hard-nosed style, and it has produced some remarkable alumni, especially recently, who have stood firmly and courageously for principle in times of political and moral crisis.

John Amos Comenius, 1592-1670

A modern scholar has called Comenius "that incomparable Moravian." He found schools "the slaughter-house of the mind," devoted to the dreary and sometimes desperately enforced study of Latin grammar in a world no longer using Latin. "If I had a dog that I loved," a German nobleman is supposed to have said, "I would not hand him over, much less a son." Comenius left the schools of Europe a very different place. Believing that in education "things must come before words," he produced a textbook of pictures. "To exercise the senses carefully in discriminating the differences of natural objects," he wrote, "is to lay the foundation of all wisdom." His dictionary of the "Tongues and all Sciences" was translated into Russian and Arabic in addition to the European languages. "For many generations," says a historian, "the schoolboy of three continents thumbed this book." His greatest work, however, remained unpublished until 1849 when it was found in a library in Poland. He survived other losses. His father and mother died when he was very young, he regarded his Latin school education as nearly useless, he lost all his property in the Thirty Years' War, he was the last bishop of a disappearing pre-Protestant movement. But he was so highly regarded in his own lifetime that he

". . . things before words"

was invited to establish schools in England, Holland, Sweden, and Hungary, in all but the last leaving a permanent impression.

Knowledge, Comenius was convinced, comes through the senses. Its acquisition is through real and useful things, "not the shadow of things." All the senses should be used, "the sense of hearing should be conjoined with that of sight, and the tongue should be trained in combination with the hand." This meant to Comenius that the objects should be "brought sufficiently near"—that is, into the classroom, "on the walls of the classroom everything that is treated of in class, by putting up either precepts and rules or pictures and diagrams." Thus the senses are "exercised constantly" as well as "in conjunction." His clues came from nature: "to observe how the faculties develop one after another, and to base our method on the principle of succession," how nature prepares the material before giving it form, develops everything from within, always ends in particulars, makes no leaps, advances only from strength. The radical reforms of education he found proposed in nature are now generally accepted. His schools opened at a uniform date, year after year. The subjects of instruction were "so divided that each year, month, week, day, and even each hour, shall have a definite task appointed to it." All work was done under the supervision of the teacher—there was no homework. Each teacher had a separate room. The length of the day was graded. There was a recess after each class. Holidays were often and short. "A rational creature," Comenius observed, "should be led, not by shouts, imprisonment and blows, but by

"The brain, the workshop of thought, is as wax."

"Follow the lead of nature."

John Amos Comenius, *Orbius Pictus* (1653); *Janua Linguarum Reseraya Sive Seminarium Linguarium et Scientiarum Didactica Magna* (1633); *Didactica Magna* (1638) (University of Chicago Press, 1953). See anthologies of educational history.

reason." Nothing should be learned solely for its value in school, he insisted, "but for its usefulness in life." And everything is learned by practice: "let the students learn to write by writing, to talk by talking, to sing by singing, to reason by reasoning."

". . . no stuffing and flogging"

His great dream was for a *pansophia*, a universal education uniting all Europe. He dreamed of an encyclopedia to which all men of science would contribute. Nothing like it existed. And of a central college with adequate facilities for advancement and discovery in all fields. And of a programmed search for new methods of instruction which would make the benefits of all human learning available to everyone. "We wish all men to be trained in all the virtues," he wrote, and they should be "educated together that they may stimulate and urge on one another." He believed profoundly that children are not born human but become so by training in knowledge, virtue, and piety, and that from a generation of Europeans so trained a "Christian Republic" might grow.

"Charity bids us not to withhold what God has intended for the use of all."

"There is no more certain way under the sun to raise sunken humanity."

Johann Friedrich Herbart, 1776-1841

At Koenigsberg Herbart was the successor of Kant, whom he admired but did not imitate. He would have preferred to have succeeded Hegel at Berlin, but he differed from Hegel even more. Herbart was a reader of Rousseau, a peer of Pestalozzi, and more an educator than a philosopher. He was saturated in philosophy, having begun the study of logic at the age of eleven and metaphysics a year later under the tutelage of his mother who taught him at home because of a childhood accident which precluded public schooling. He studied with Fichte, the idealist, but "he taught me chiefly through his errors," said Herbart,

"because in all his inquiries he aimed at exact thought."
As a professional philosopher, Herbart founded a teacher's
training school and was the first to attempt the formulation of psychology as a science. His chief influence was on
American educators. Education is both the beginning and
the end of Herbart's philosophy.

Philosophy for Herbart is the refining and elaborating
of empirical concepts by reflection. The soul he defines as
a perfectly simple, indivisible essence without parts. It
has no innate ideas, nor is it a *tabula rasa*. Much more interesting to Herbart is the mind, a manifold of concepts
built up as a result of reproducing in the mind the real
objects in the world. These representations unite in apperceptive masses. Some fall into unconsciousness, others
rise into consciousness, and a battle for recognition is going
on all the time. Thus the mind is defined in terms of its
inner content: it is the sum total of impressions made
upon it, not an agent in changing the outside world. This
concept becomes the basis for an educational psychology
and philosophy which makes assimilation of subject matter the primary objective.

For Herbart, the end of education is the production of
"the man of culture." He is a man "who commands himself." This is accomplished through what he calls "the
circle of thought," a continuous interplay of feeling, knowing and willing set in motion by "the presentation of
ideas." Instruction is therefore crucial. The uneducated
man can be mechanically good, but he cannot be intelligently good. It is the purpose of education "to cultivate
in the youthful soul a large circle of thought, possessing
the power of overcoming what is unfavorable in the en-

Johann Friedrich Herbart, *The Science of Education* (Boston: D. C.
Heath, 1902).

vironment and of dissolving and absorbing into itself all that is favorable."

Herbart's theory of instruction unifies his interests. All instruction builds on the pupil's experience. At first experience is chaotic and haphazard; instruction brings system and fills in information. The first step is "clearness": apperceptive subliminal masses are brought into consciousness by focusing attention on single objects. Later Herbartian educators divided this responsibility of the instructor into two phases, preparation and presentation. The second step is "association": the new idea is apperceived by establishing relationships to the old. The instructor helps establish likenesses and differences. The third step is "system": each part finds its proper place in relation to the other parts and generalizations become possible. Instruction in abstraction is suited for adolescents, and is the basis of all conceptual reasoning. The fourth step is "method": investigation is carried on under the guidance of the instructor until the pupil is prepared to apply ideas for himself. The instructor is responsible for preventing the mere accumulation of dead data.

There are two kinds of presentations, those that arise from experiences of things (creating empirical, speculative, aesthetic "interests") and those that come from personal relations (creating sympathetic, social, religious "interests"). Experience begins with the perception of objects, but knowledge gained only through the senses is unrefined and therefore inaccurate. The mind is to be "lifted" through government (insuring the necessary order and aversion for evil), discipline (building up the will and forming good habits) and instruction (systematically cultivating those ideas which insure individual morality). History is the primary source of uplifting personal relations. It will lead the learner through "chronological progress from older and simpler to newer and more compli-

"The teacher is a stage manager."

"Uncultured men have passions, educated men have understanding."

cated stages and conditions," from the particular to the universal. The basis of the school curriculum is in religious and folk material, "classically presented," but the curriculum moves on to the development of the national culture, and the goal is the presentation and assimilation of "large units" of history: "Great moral energy is the effect," Herbart says, "of entire scenes and unbroken thought masses." Herbart selected Homer's *Odyssey* for adolescent boys: it is "the point of fellowship between pupil and teacher," he said. He found in the heroic characters of primitive Greece the simplicity of life and the primitive moral situations which he felt fitted the ethical level of his pupils. His followers worked out the approach in great detail, moving from fairy tales, Mother Goose stories and the Old Testament to the epic literature of the Greeks and the New Testament and finally to modern literature.

For many years Herbartian philosophy was the ground of American education, and words like "interest," "apperception," "circle of thought," "culture epochs," and "formal steps of instruction" supplied the vocabulary of American teachers.

The Modern Tradition

Modern elitist education, especially in Old and New England, is classic in two senses. Though changes have occurred in the last half-century, its content is classical—the Greek and Latin classics often in the original languages, and the more recent classics of the Renaissance and Enlightenment usually in French and English. Comenius and Herbart changed the methods of the medieval Latin School, but there is a direct connection between twentieth- and fourteenth-century schoolboys laboring on Homer and Terence. Further, the tradition itself is classic—mastery of content and self achieved under the authoritative leadership of a master who is himself a product of the tradition.

Bertrand Russell, Alfred North Whitehead, and Frederick S. Breed are protégés and protectors of this tradition. Russell is English, Breed American, and Whitehead may be said to be Anglo-American. The unconventional Lord Russell was a fellow of Trinity College, Cambridge, and later a lecturer in philosophy there. His first scholarly work was on the German idealist Leibnitz, but his contribution to philosophy lies in his own brand of Realism, applying logical analysis to the empirical data of the scientists to produce rational principles. He has tended to be antipragmatic but not antimetaphysical. Whitehead was also a fellow at Trinity College, but is known to Americans through his twelve years of teaching at Harvard, to philosophers through the three volumes of *Principia Mathematica*, which he wrote with Russell, and to theologians through his definition of religion as "what the individual does with his own solitariness" and his metaphysical concepts of "process." Breed was a student of James and Whitehead at Harvard and professor of Education at the University of Chicago during its most "realistic" period under President Hutchins. "The educational method of the future," he says, nearly summing up the position of all three, "will begin with respect for the demands of the individual, but will end with respect for

"The central task in education is the guidance of learning."

F. S. Breed, *Education and the New Realism* (New York: Macmillan, 1939).

Bertrand Russell, *Education and the Good Life* (New York: Boni and Liveright, 1926).

Alfred North Whitehead, *The Aims of Education* (New York: Macmillan, 1929).

the demands of the external world, the nature of which is reflected in the content of knowledge."

For the realist, the pupil is an organism engaged in the age-old task of effecting appropriate relationships in the space-time world. In education, "the presuppositions are philosophical in nature," says Breed.

Breed is most specific of the three in opposing Pragmatism and Idealism and espousing Realism. "Knowing," he says, "is an event in which the object merely has a place." The connection between the physical and the psychical is perception. "There is no perception without perception of *something*," he says, "and no knowledge without knowledge of *something*." Thus he defines the pupil as "a complex unity" whose reactions represent "relationships entered into with other entities constituting its environment." The psychologist may call these other entities "external stimuli." The layman thinks of them as "the objects that surround him."

The realist educator is interested in the "external source" for "the content of the mind." "I do not understand," said Whitehead, "how a common world of thought can be established in the absence of a common world of sense." Whitehead does understand intellectual activity to be diffused through the body and bodily feeling. Education is thus a process effecting "a coordination of senses and thought." Sense-feeling is always immediate and present and education must always be immediate: "the present contains all there is" and "whatever possibilities of mental life your teaching should impart, must be exhibited here and now." Therefore, "the ordered acquirement of knowledge," says Whitehead, "is the natural food for a developing intelligence." Russell talks about curiosity as the product of the interaction between mind

"Realism absorbs without conflict the constructions of modern scientific thought."

". . . a reciprocal influence between brain activity and material activity"

and world. Education is, for him, the process of satisfying curiosity and giving the pupil "the skill required in order that he may be able to satisfy his curiosity for himself."

The Objectives

The aim of training a boy, Whitehead suggests in the first paragraph of his book on the subject, is the man, and he illustrates with a comment by William Temple about a successful man who had been somewhat undistinguished as a boy at Rugby. "It is not what they are at eighteen," said the Archbishop, "it is what they become afterwards that matters." Education is important precisely because so much preparation is needed for adult living. Whitehead's concern is for the creative connection between ideas and usefulness, how to produce the adult expert without loss of the essential features of the boy-amateur. "Education," he says, "is the acquisition of the art of the utilization of knowledge." Because it is a very difficult art to impart, education must focus on the "stimulation of creative impulse." Education should give the pupil "a technique, a science, an assortment of general ideas, an aesthetic appreciation," and "each of these sides of his training should be illuminated by the others." But even more than illumination is to be hoped for, namely, the capacity for "a quick transition from ideas to practice."

". . . something he knows well and something he can do well."

Russell says that "the building up of character" is the object of childhood education, and "the training of intelligence" is the aim of boyhood education. Character is composed of "the habits that will give happiness and usefulness in later life." It is thus not improved but built. In the first year parents may build love, respect, and regularity. In the second year happiness may be established through the conquest of fears. The result Russell calls "exhuberance." In following years the child may be helped to discover that construction is more satisfying than de-

. . . character

. . . exhuberance

struction, that justice may be accepted without apprehension, that truthfulness is the ground of trust. The result Russell calls "sensitivity," and he says, "the quality I have in mind is that of being affected pleasurably or the reverse by many things and by the right things." Toward the end of the period "behaviour to equals is what most needs to be learnt," and this is best accomplished in a nursery school. The result Russell calls "courage," the capacity to take "an impersonal outlook on life," the capacity "neither to command nor to obey but to follow and lead cooperatively." The education of character, as a whole, does what is possible to liberate the springs of affection. "A truly affectionate disposition," says Russell, "justifies itself because it gives irresistable charm and creates the response which it expects."

. . . sensitivity

. . . courage

Intellectual adventure should be the theme of all subsequent education. "I do not believe that it is possible to train intelligence," Russell says, "without imparting information, or at any rate causing knowledge to be acquired." There is a great deal of knowledge which seems to Russell to be valuable on its own account, "and I should not wish to encourage the young," he continues, "to look too closely for an ulterior purpose in all knowledge." Thus, open-mindedness should be one of the primary aims of education. "It will always exist where desire for knowledge is genuine." Pupils ought to be encouraged to regard every question as open and to be able to throw over any opinion as the result of an argument. The power of concentration is seldom acquired except through education. This capacity to control attention by the will is one of the admirable achievements of old-fashioned education, says Russell. It taught a man "to endure voluntary boredom." Patience and industry ought to result from good education. Grading difficulties is a better method of stimulating ambition than external

. . . intelligence

. . . knowledge

. . . open-mindedness

. . . concentration

. . . patience

authority. The discovery that knowledge is difficult but not impossible increases the capacity for persistence. Accuracy may be built, beginning with precision in physical activities. Learning poetry by heart is a step. Mathematics is a natural vehicle. "Rules must be learnt." "The world is full of puzzling things," he says, "which can be understood by sufficient effort."

. . . exactness

The Process

Knowledge is the foundation of classical education. On it all else is built. Russell says that 'it exists," enough of it to "produce a population almost wholly free from disease, malevolence, and stupidity," but that we are helpless unless it is "wielded by love." Breed says that it checks "sentimental retreat from reality" and is "a chart for our intellectual adventure," and "a prospectus of the truth that sets us free." Whitehead says that it is transformed into wisdom by imagination. The function of education is acquisition of knowledge and to assist its transformation into usefulness. The task is "apt to be wearisome," but "it is essential to any kind of excellence" and "this fact can be made obvious by suitable methods."

. . . the transformation of knowledge

The school, says Breed, is a specialized environment "which is intended to stimulate the children to certain types of activity, so as to assure a certain type of adjustment." There are laws of health, polite intercourse, and public action. The school is the place where these "external realities" may be introduced and adjusted to. But Breed hastens to label the experimental method of surrounding the pupils with materials and then letting them respond according to their own desires "stupid" because "it attempts the impossible," and "misconceives the conditions of thinking." Immature minds must be guided. Experience must be guided, and the teacher, "who presumably has a greater background of experience," is re-

". . . a specialized environment"

". . . wise guidance"

sponsible. On the model of the master craftsman, the teacher suggests to apprentices what they are to do. Teaching is for Breed the art of disclosure. For Whitehead it is the art of imparting information. To accomplish this, the teacher's own learning must be "lighted up with imagination," and that requires freedom, scholarship, and the stimulation of other minds. It is the function of the teacher "to evoke into life wisdom and beauty which, apart from his magic, would remain lost in the past." Russell says that the ideal teacher loves his pupils, loves them indeed "better than his Church or State."

"There can be no education," says Whitehead in an often quoted aphorism, "apart from encounter with greatness." The content of education provides the greatness. Breed is precise: education provides "ideas, conceptions, that have been tried by others and have not been found wanting." The curriculum of schools represents an attempt, he says, "to select portions of 'the great tradition' most valuable for the guidance of life activities." Whitehead speaks of "the joy of classics" in the finished scholar as the result of "the pleasure and discipline of character" the developing scholar has experienced in an education based mainly on classical literature and classical philosophy. The study of Latin is "a peculiarly plain concrete case of language as a structure," and provides a direct access to the Roman Empire, "the bottleneck through which the vintage of the past has passed into modern life." The study of mathematics constitutes "a training in logical method together with the acquisition of precise ideas which lie at the base of the scientific and philosophical investigations of the universe." Russell recommends the study of geography for making it possible "in later life to *feel* that distant countries really exist," the study of history to show "mastery of ourselves and our environment through knowledge," the study of literature

". . . encounter with greatness"

"learned by heart" because it "will influence the style of thought," the study of languages "taught by speaking with those whose language it is," the study of science for the formation of "a scientific attitude to practical questions" and "the principle of living objectively rather than subjectively." Let the pupils come to understand, urges Russell, "that by knowledge the world could be transformed."

In teaching, method is the means of imparting the curriculum and its subjects. Russell makes it clear that everything possible ought to be done to make the content interesting to the learners. "Flogging on week-days and sermons on Sundays do not constitute the ideal technique," he observes. When the teacher appears as the friend of the pupil, says Russell, the child will learn faster because he is cooperating, and he repeatedly cites Montessori as a positive example. Whitehead analyzes "the stages of mental growth"—romance (the first apprehension), precision (acceptance of a given way of analyzing the facts), generalisation (disclosure of possibilities of wide significance). All education, says Whitehead, should consist in a continual repetition of these natural cycles, so that learning achieves a rhythmic character in tune with attention and interest. There should, however, be no postponement of difficulty.

. . . interest

Russell is convinced that "no really thorough education can be made always interesting." Some parts of it are sure to be dull. But "a boy or girl can be made to feel the importance of learning the dull parts, and can be got through them." Especially if they can be helped to see the importance of learning, "able boys and girls will go through endless tedium and submit willingly to severe discipline." Discipline is essential in education because it is in life. Breed points to the objectivity of discipline as a positive thing, "something external really existing which

. . . discipline

it is the duty of a man to bring his will into harmony with."

After all, says Whitehead, "in the conditions of modern life, the race which does not value trained intelligence is doomed," and in the final analysis "the essence of education is that it be religious" because it deals with human destiny. A religious education inculcates duty and reverence. Duty arises from our potential control over events: "where attainable knowledge could have changed the issue, ignorance has the guilt of vice." And reverence arises from the perception of eternity that "the present holds within itself the complete sum of existence, backward and forward." The ultimate motive power in human life is the sense of importance grounded in survival, and it disciplines life with incredible labors. "The vitality of religion," says Whitehead, "is shown by the way in which the religious spirit has survived the ordeal of religious education."

Educational Essentialism

"There is not a received tradition which does not threaten to dissolve," reported Matthew Arnold of his own time when an inherited English Puritanism was being threatened by imported French Enlightenment. Not every age is a time of crisis, but many are. In the history of cultures there are seasons, and during winters there is the tendency to dig in and shepherd stored resources. During the 1940s, the world fought for survival against demonic dictatorship. Two of the victorious military allies, however, were ideological enemies, and the winter lengthened into the fifties. In times of stress it is the tendency of education to serve its culture by concentrating on strengthening characteristics and traditions. Any educational program which selects certain essentials and seeks to communicate them has defined itself as essentialism. The fifties produced forms of educational essentialism in Russia and the United States.

Education for Communal Character

"Pedagogy," said the Russian teacher's journal, *Sovietskaya Pedagogika*, in 1946, is "the planned and purposeful preparation for future participation in social life." And a year later, "The objective of our school is to bring up youth as educated and cultured citizens capable of fighting for the final establishment of communism." Within the memory of even elementary school children in Russia, Stalingrad had been held against Nazi invasion at heroic cost and Berlin had fallen to the Red Army. In the thirties the more peaceful Five Year Plans for economic reconstruction occupied Soviet leadership. An educator contrasted that "mad country" with his own. "We have a plan. In America they work without a plan. . . . We have a seeding campaign. In America they destroy crops. . . .

"After we build socialism all will have equally healthy faces."

We increase population. In America they reduce population and increase unemployment." But after socialism is built, "men will cease to regard labor as a punishment," and there will be "a new people"—"healthy, strong giants, red-cheeked and happy." The children who went to school during the Five Year Plans fought at Stalingrad and Berlin.

Marxist Doctrine and Soviet Education

"Man is what he eats."

"Der Mensch ist was er isst." Thus Ludwig Feuerbach summarized his doctrine of realistic materialism in the early nineteenth century. "Only sensibility is truth and reality." After experiencing the German industrial strikes of the 1840s, and fleeing to England and into the British Museum, Karl Marx concluded that this sort of materialism was too simple and transformed it into a social materialism. "Does it require deep intuition," he asked rhetorically in the *Communist Manifesto*, "to comprehend that man's consciousness changes with every change in his social relations and social life?" In the 1880 preface to the *Manifesto*, Friedrich Engles summarized his friend's proposition: "That in every historical epoch the prevailing mode of economic production and exchange, and the social organization necessarily following upon it, form the basis on which is built up, and from which alone can be explained, the political and intellectual history of that epoch." History may be read as a succession of epochs embodying these "sum-totals of the relations of production," each marking a major step in man's development: primitive, slave, feudal, capitalist. The law of evolution in human history is dialectical, says Marx, borrowing

"Social existence determines consciousness."

M. Ilin, *New Russia's Primer: The Story of the Five-Year Plan* (Boston: Houghton-Mifflin, 1931). Translated by George S. Counts and Nucia P. Lodge.
Karl Marx, *The Communist Manifesto* (many editions in English).

function but not principle from Hegel, whom, he said, he inverted and "stood on his feet." In every society "the forces of production" eventually come into conflict with "the property relations" of the society. "The history of all hitherto existing society is the history of class struggle," is the opening sentence of the *Manifesto*. Social revolution resolves the antagonism between "producers" and "holders" of property, and the new epoch is established, which in turn becomes polarized and is thrown into class struggle. In the capitalist society of the nineteenth and twentieth centuries, private property and labor are the antagonists and the abolition of private property is the synthesis. The final step in evolution is the establishment of a classless society in which there is no conflict, and the dialectic at last comes to rest. Freed from the causes of conflict, a new man will come into being.

"... class struggle"

"... the classless society"

"... the new people"

Nikolai Lenin (Vladimir Ilich Ulyanov), who brought the Marxist revolution to Russia near the end of World War I and guided it through its formative stages until his death in 1924, said that education is "the general and eternally social category." Historically, education differed with the epochal stages: in primitive society it was poor and limited but classless; in slavery society its purpose was to maintain the privileges of the freeborn; in feudal society training of the knights and clergy aimed to strengthen the feudal order; in capitalist society it is a "two track system" designed to keep the moneyed classes and the laboring classes separate. In revolutionary Russia education is "a social function at all stages of youth's development."

"Education is a revolutionary function."

The period of Josef Stalin was a series of crises invoked by worldwide events: depression, World War II, capitalist encirclement. The role of education was widely recognized during those years, to "stamp in" the necessary stamina. Consequently, a great deal of attention was paid

HISTORICAL DIALECTICS IN EDUCATION

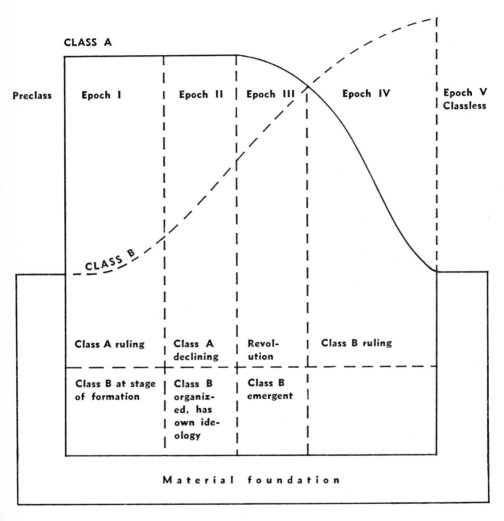

CLASS A

Preclass	Epoch I	Epoch II	Epoch III	Epoch IV	Epoch V Classless

CLASS B

Class A ruling | Class A declining | Revol-ution | Class B ruling

Class B at stage of formation | Class B organiz-ed, has own ide-ology | Class B emergent

Material foundation

Maurice Shore, *Soviet Education* (New York: Philosophical Library, 1947), p. 162.

to educational philosophy. "Although it is very difficult," said the *Sovietskaya Pedagogika*, to understand "the complicated and subtle forms of the struggle between idealist and materialist world outlooks, youth can nonetheless acquire a clear and firm picture of the essence of the difference and the superiority of materialism." In 1947 the minister of education said, "Boys and girls completing the soviet school must be in possession of the most important elements of the Communist *Weltanschauung*."

Objectives

"All Soviet education is moral education," says one Western observer. It is training in "the morality of socialist humanism," defined as an attitude which has "no personal interests opposed to collective interests." Ethical standards change, as Lenin showed, with the historical epoch. The ruling ethics in any society is the ethics of the ruling class. In a capitalist society, that means the ethics, usually said to be based on "the commandments of God," of the landlords and the capitalists. Communist ethics, by contrast, unites the working class against their exploiters, and supports whatever is necessary to serve the cause of the reconstruction of society in accordance with communist principles. "To this end," said Lenin, "we need a generation of youth transformed into responsible people by the conditions attending a disciplined and desperate struggle with the bourgoisie." And he continued, "to this end must be linked every step in the education of youth." Communist morality "presupposes action and makes struggle obligatory," says the teachers' textbook.

". . . the communist ethic"

. . . action and struggle

George S. Counts, *I Want to Be Like Stalin* (New York: John Day, 1947). Much of the source material is from B. P. Yesipov and N. K. Goncharov, *Pedagogy*, a textbook for teachers reaching its third Russian edition in 1946.

Support of the country in which this ethic is most advanced is implied. It "presupposes wrath and hatred towards enemies of the Motherland who imperil the battle-won rights of the people and all that has been created in the realm of material and cultural life by both the older and the younger generation." Positively, love of Motherland requires "devotion to the communist party and supreme readiness to serve the cause of Lenin and Stalin." It means "the recognition that labor is a matter of honor, a matter of glory, a matter of valor and heroism." It means, also, an identification with world labor, "the understanding that the interests of our people and the interests of the toiling masses of the entire world are indivisable." It means an immediate identification with the unbearbale conditions—unemployment, semistarvation, vagrancy, disease, exploitation—in which the youth of capitalist countries exist.

"To rear Soviet patriots," continues the textbook, "means to rear people of indomitable will, people of purpose." This discipline will be conscious ("founded on an inner conviction of the necessity of following definite rules and regulations"), self-initiated ("linked with the desire to fulfil in the best possible manner a given order of assignment"), firm ("unquestioned submission and obedience to the leader"), organizational ("prompting and habituating to the precise organization of individual and collective life"), comradely ("founded on the mutual respect of the members of the collective"), and resolute ("subjecting conduct to high purpose and conquering motives of low degree").

Method

"The education of the individual pupil proceeds through the collective." Children work together in what is recog-

EDUCATIONAL DIALECTICS

Society	Objectives	Relation of unorganized to organized educational processes	Relation of ideological to productive labor education	Basis of education
Preclass	Same for everyone in the social process	Unorganized education supreme organized education minor	Education presents a unity of the ideological and the productive	Empirical, traditional, and conservative. Technical education is rational
Class Society	Various objectives corresponding to the differentiation of society and its historical development.	Unorganized action of environment is foundation for education. Organized education grows with general development and formation of classes	The ideological is opposed to productive labor education	Changeable bases; from empirical to rational
Transitory Society	Objectives of the working class; state (and education) withers away	Organized education becomes foundational and enforced; unorganized education loses in importance and force	Ideological education begins to identify itself with production on the basis of socially useful labor	Rational forms of education are elastic and subject to change
Classless Society	Same for all within the social process	Unorganized education negligible; organized education is main force	United process on basis of organized socially useful labor	Precisely scientific; educational changes corresponding to changes in social needs

Maurice Shore, *Soviet Education*, p. 160.

nized to be a microcosm of socialist life. The homes, newspapers, cinemas, advertisements and literature are in harmony with the experience of the school. The pupils work in the consciousness that their society is building new towns, conquering frozen lands to the north, leading in the worldwide race into space, and creating "the socialist man." This identification is all-important: the goal is the method.

The classroom does not appear to be unusual, indeed, by American standards, a little old-fashioned. The basic method is the class lesson given by the teacher, and reading is the core of the curriculum, though film is widely used and broadcasts of music, literature, and poetry. In 1943 the Soviet of Peoples' Commissars adopted a series of twenty rules for school children which are widely posted with the notice that "for violation of these rules the pupil is subject to punishment, even to expulsion from school." They require pupils, among other things, "to obey without question the orders of school director and teachers," "to rise as the teacher enters or leaves the classroom," "to be respectful to teachers," and "to be considerate toward little children," "to be neatly washed and dressed," "to keep his desk clean and orderly," "to be diligent and punctual," "to carry always his student identification card." In general, it is agreed that Russian children are well behaved and cooperative. The teacher's textbook says "we may at times apply threats of punishments and even punishments themselves," but "we may assume that the fear of displeasing adults and the fear of disapproval on the part of the collective" will cause the pupil to refrain from such violations.

The teacher in Russia is officially admonished to be

Maurice Shore, *Soviet Education* (New York: Philosophical Library, 1947).

honest, courageous, a comrade to his pupils, direct-minded, and to be filled with love. The 1947 minister of education emphasized love as the primary teaching quality: "Love for the people, love for the toiling masses." Stalin is quoted: "People must be grown carefully and tenderly, just as a gardener grows a favorite fruit tree." However, the teacher is urged to be exact and demanding in conducting recitations. "He does not coax pupils; he demands obedience." Strictness implies that the teacher is strict with himself and has a definite system of work in mind for the class. During his teacher-training he has studied thoroughly "this broad, many-sided, and extremely significant science of society in order to work with maximum consciousness and clear purposefulness for the values of communism." He is qualified, therefore, to lead the young. Education for collectivism requires a careful approach to each individual pupil, but "through the collective and with the aid of the collective the abilities of every individual are developed." The testimony of visitors and scholars is that the method is eminently successful: "The social environment," reports an American educator, "produces a willingness and a desire to learn in the majority of school children."

"A teacher loves his work and loves children."

"Demands must be made in decisive form and carried into life with firm insistence."

Content

"The textbook," says the *Pedagogika*, "contains the knowledge which pupils are obliged to master." Teaching plans approved by the ministry of education are obligatory documents: "arbitrary changes," counsels the *Pedagogika*, "are inadmissable." "There is one branch of science whose knowledge must be compulsory," wrote Stalin, "the Marxist-Leninist science of society." The teachers are counseled to choose subjects for essays emphasizing soviet war heroes and "the extraordinary deeds of the people capable of sacrificing personal interests for the common good." Prob-

"The textbook is a weapon of communist education."

lems in mathematics "will teach pupils to save state pennies in industry and daily life." Games and exercises will develop skills "which are essential to future warriors of the Red Army." Art will foster "the beautiful feeling of love for the Motherland." All branches of science will support the science of society. Equality of races is emphasized, economic security for all, devotion to the common good, respect for the weak and aged, love of family and Motherland. Every sentence of content is aimed at "creating human beings grounded in a scientific materialist outlook, people who endeavor to make life happy in the world rather than in some world to come."

In the kindergarten, "the basic habits of socialist life are formed." The basic teaching principle is "concrete facts and examples." Thus there will be stories of how "people work in a collective," how "warriors help one another," how "the soviet government watches over every soviet person." On holidays the children play Red Soldier. At all levels history is one of the most important subjects: it possesses "exceptional significance for the education of the growing generation in communism."

Education for Democratic Responsibility

Early in 1950 the publication of an official Army Regulation by the Pentagon in Washington established a Character Guidance Program as a military command responsibility. The five years that had elapsed since the dropping of the atom bombs in Japan with the emergence of Communism as a major military threat and ideological alternative to democracy had been a time of soul-searching for

The Army Character Guidance Program (Chaplain School: Carlisle Barracks, Pennsylvania, 1950).

American military leaders. The Army Chief of Staff had said that a soldier "must know and believe in the ideals of his country, and he must be willing to protect and perpetuate them." The chairman of the Joint Chiefs of Staff had spoken of the responsibility of the military for encouraging "moral responsibility, spiritual values and strong self-discipline of the individual." On the day of military victory, MacArthur had set the tone by speaking of unsolved spiritual problems. During the war, chaplains had generally demonstrated their right to moral leadership more dramatically in personal courage than in the "Sex Morality" lectures they were required to deliver monthly to the troops. "Winning the peace" was often said to be the military problem of the fifties. As it became clear that huge numbers of young men in their formative years would continue to be in military service, it also became clear that "what the Army does with its men and women will make a tremendous difference to the future of our way of life."

"We want to make them better citizens in every way."

Definitions

Of course, the military had been in the business of education in a huge way during the War. Soldiering required training. Sophisticated equipment required specialists. The educational needs of the military had forced developments in the use of film, techniques of mass presentation, rapid learning of Oriental languages, and even elementary reading skills for the semi-literate. The education of principles was a new venture. It would be approached, however, in terms of military experience and orientation. It would be, in short, essentialist education.

Character was given a working definition: "the organization of life and behavior around a central loyalty that has moral worth and validity." It is formed by a dynamic

Character is defined by history.

clustering of personal qualities. The key to character in the American way of life is devotion to freedom. "It has created the pattern for individual life and community experience throughout the years of our national existence."

In the field of education, guidance means setting up standards and principles of conduct and behavior, filtering them through the individual, enabling the individual to grapple with problems on his own. It means establishing in the individual "the freedom to do what one ought." In military parlance, it is a course in map reading.

Guidance is defined by education.

In the military, the word *program* signifies that the project is not the private responsibility of a single person ro military agency. It is "a concerted effort by all personnel and agencies." It is a command responsibility, implying both the giving and receiving of orders from the top of the chain-of-command to the bottom.

Program is defined by military practice.

Principles

". . . the individual sense of responsibility"

The major objective of the Character Guidance Program is the development of a sense of responsibility within the individual. There are four elements: the moral fabric of the American way of life ("by destiny rather than design America has become a world power"), the moral obligations and duties of the military profession ("the soldier lives in contact with the enemies of the social order," he "seeks to push forward the social life," he "stands exposed," he "is the protector of the weak"), the consequences of attitudes and behavior ("society is held together by the intangible power of morality"), and a sense of service ("doing one's duty often requires sacrifice"). Character is developed in making choices implementing these principles. Man is a moral being in that he does not live from instinct to instinct, but from choice to choice.

"Man is a moral being."

Responsibility is defined in principle by the moral law

THE ARMY CHARACTER GUIDANCE PROGRAM

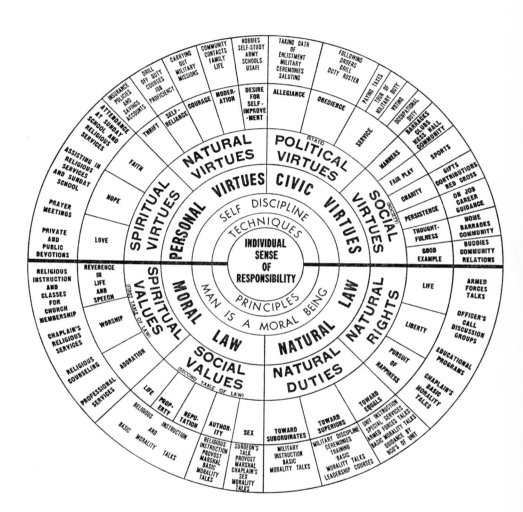

and the natural law. The former has to do with attitudes toward God and fellowmen, and gives rise to spiritual values such as those specified in the first four Commandments, and to social values, such as those specified in the last six Commandments. The latter has to do with the tenets underlying natural rights and duties, and gives rise to natural duties toward equals, subordinates and superiors, as well as natural rights such as life, liberty and

the pursuit of happiness. The application of moral law to life will produce spiritual virtues such as faith, hope, and love, and natural virtues such as thrift, courage and moderation. The application of natural law to life will produce political virtues defined by the state and social virtues defined by society.

Implementation

Now, the development of character requires the implementation of principles, and implementation requires discipline, and thus the military life affords innumerable opportunities for the development of character. Natural duties are supported by the clear distinctions of rank and

echelons and authority in the military organization. Natural rights are supported by the military concepts of responsibility and accountability throughout the structure. Political virtues are developed by participating responsibly in the chain of command and functioning as a citizen in a civilian army. Social virtues are developed by participation in company life and off-duty sports and social life. Spiritual values and social values are supported by the military's provision of a chaplain to give religious instruction and offer personal spiritual counseling. Natural virtues may be developed in maintaining personal, family, and community life. Spiritual virtues may be developed by participation in the worship, religious education, prayer meetings, and other activities of the chapel program.

The chaplain is provided by the military establishment as a clergyman in uniform, responsible to God and his fellowmen. His primary job is to minister to the spiritual needs of the persons to whom he is assigned. Participation in the chapel program is not coerced, and the chaplain must win and lead his congregation much as he would in a civilian parish. He is a remarkably free person in the carrying out of his spiritual responsibilities as defined for him by his church and faith. In addition, however, the Character Guidance Program integrates him into the training program required of all soldiers. His primary responsibility there is to give lectures in the field of basic morality. He is required not to preach or teach his special religion, but to become an expert in "natural theology." His job is "to help produce the rainfall needed to keep the soil of our social order from becoming a moral desert." He is trained for this task in special courses at the Chaplain School and through regular publications helping him in his preparation for teaching. His function is as a lecturer, taking examples from the Old Testament and "from the flesh and blood of our history." His responsibility is to inspire "with the urgency of the gigantic struggle of our day between liberty on the one hand and slavery on the other, a moral conflict involving the very foundations of civilization."

". . . the clergyman in uniform"

". . . the expert in natural theology"

Education into Christian Essentials

"A very considerable part of the task of education is to transmit tradition," says the English historian and educator Victor Murray. He is also a Methodist layman who became principal of Cheshunt, the Congregational theological college at Cambridge, and adds that Christianity is "history transmuted into character." Christian education is literally an impossibility, because the definitive transmutation takes place in the divine-human encounter, the two-party personal relationship between God and man into which no third party may intrude. However, education implies the function of just such a third party, the teacher. Yet, wherever there has been religion there has been education. Religion requires teaching. At the same time, the goal is beyond teaching, the act of personal commitment without which no further growth is possible. Murray frankly prefers to deal with Christian education as a dilemma rather than as a technical problem.

The Special Nature of Christian Education

Christian education is a special form of education because Christianity is a special form of religion. Love is the characteristic of the Christian religion. Loving is a human act and must express itself in personal relationships. The special fact about Christianity, however, is that these horizontal relationships of interhuman loving are defined and made possible for man by the gift of love to man by God in an act of grace. In the matter of personal relationships,

". . . a corroboration of the Gospel and also a preparation for the Gospel"

A. Victor Murray, *Education Into Religion* (New York: Harper, 1953). The other volumes are extensions of this basic one: *Personal Experience and the Historic Faith* (Harper) and *Teaching the Bible* (Cambridge University Press) both published in 1955.

it is always the divine first and the interhuman thereafter. "We come to the threshold and he pulls us through," says Murray. And further, the community created by loving acts is itself part of the Christian religion. Christian education is thus far more than instruction, although it may begin there.

The Special Center

"The centre of Christian education," says Murray, "is Christ." His life and death and continued influence provide the standards by which everything in Christianity is to be judged.

Murray calls Christ "the norm," a type rather than an average, the "true nature" of man revealed "in its highest development." This norm applies to individual human life, of course, and in this regard Christ's uniqueness appears as moral character. "He alone is the type to which all others only approximate." His completeness is a judgment upon all resentment and rejection of goodness. It is also an invitation and support for those who accept his completeness as a claim.

". . . the norm of humanity"

Murray also applies the norm of Christ to psychology. Much psychology has gone astray, Murray contends, for lack of a norm becoming preoccupied with the "abnormal" or "the lowest common measure of humanity." In the Christian view, psychology had better concentrate on "the creative activities of men which differentiate individuals from one another." It needs no more than one Christ, he concludes, to demonstrate our real intrinsic humanity.

Christ also provides the norm by which history is to be evaluated. Indeed, were it not for him there would be no biblical or church history. More specifically, he becomes the center in relation to which history is to be understood. "The character of Christ" is the test Murray applies to the

". . . the factor that links together all thought and existence"

reliability of the Gospel narratives and to the speculations of the theologians. It is the "organic" unifying theme of the Old Testament and becomes a tool for historical understanding of its parts. His "attitude to the universe around us"—treating the world "as His Father's house"— becomes for Murray the key to a Christian "science" viewing the world "as a vast system the purpose of which is to be found in Christ."

The fundamental aim of Christian education is therefore "to present Christ as the unifying factor in all this varied world of time and sense." Then Murray adds, not as an afterthought but as a basic principle: "And it can be done without appealing to dogma at all."

The Special Educational Principle

"... the personal demand"

Christian education is different from all other kinds of education in that it makes a personal demand on both the teacher and the pupil. "Of what does it profit," Murray summarizes by quoting Thomas à Kempis, "if thou art able to discourse learnedly concerning the Trinity and lack compassion and so art displeasing to the Trinity?" Christianity has doctrine, but it is not doctrine. When he quotes Thomas the second time, he adds: "as long as we have compassion and are apparently pleasing to the Trinity, need we bother about the Trinity at all?" It is the purpose of Christian education to carry instruction "into those regions in which God not only is a necessity for thought but is Himself a reality, and is found to be taking the initiative." The transmutation is accomplished by God. "At a certain stage of experience," Murray says in several different ways, "God is able to do things with us and for us that he is not able to do earlier."

"... the transmutation of religion into life"

The teacher is the key. His role is something like that in teaching art. He must be able to show pupils how to paint. He must also be able to show them what it means to him to paint. It is "worthwhileness" that he must communicate, "and he cannot do that," Murray insists, "by mere insistence." In the teaching of Christianity, this need for self-identification is not satisfied by pointing out morals, or by enforcing doctrine, or even by professing Christianity. It is the teacher's responsibility to discover the "inwardness" of the faith and its documents. A personal knowledge of the primary sources is required. So also is an understanding that this is a religion by which men have lived and died. It is only when the teacher is willing to expose his inwardness that it may move inward to the pupil.

. . . the communication of "inwardness"

The Special Method

The path to inwardness is along the pupil's own inner capacity and understanding. The subject matter must be graded according to the development of the pupil intended to receive it. "With the child," Murray says, "there is a time for learning by heart, a time for joining a cause, a time for quiet and reflection, a time for stimulus, a time for action, a time for doctrine, a time for taking up responsibilities." Murray proposes to take developmental psychology seriously. "To seek after the right thing at the wrong time turns it into the wrong thing." So much any education worthy of attention attempts to do, "and in the last two or three generations we have learned a great deal about the psychology of children, adolescents, and adults." This is, however, but half of the situation for Christian education. The subject matter itself has undergone development. Particularly in the biblical material, the theme moved from God in nature to God in man, from action to thought, from desert to town, sin to repentance, sorrow to joy. "The historical beginnings of faith," says Murray,

. . . grading subject matter according to the pupils

. . . and according to its own development

"are also the historical pattern of a continued experience." The special possibility in teaching this material is to correlate the developing capacity of the pupil with the developing God-consciousness of the material. This two-way correlation will make possible a relation to life, an examination of contexts, criticism, and evaluation, but most specifically and importantly, independent conviction.

The Special Goal

"Exeunt omnia in mysterium."

"So long as we think that the sole business of education is to make things clear," Murray says, "so long shall we delay our discovery of the meaning of life." It is the special goal of Christian education to lead pupils to the threshold of the unknown and the unseen. "Indeed," Murray says, "it has not properly done its work until that point is reached." God is, of course, acting all along. But human nature being what it is, it is precisely at the point where one has done all that he can do for himself that God comes in. Christian education leads the pupil, by invitation and challenge and by exhaustion if necessary, to the limits of his own selfhood. "It is the half-educated man," observes Murray, "who has not yet arrived at the place where God can take the initiative."

The Communication of Information

"To be a Christian involves knowing about Christ and about the Bible," writes Murray. "With no one to teach him," he continues, "he would know nothing about either." Murray is emphatic about this matter. Religious experience—or at least, religious education—begins with knowledge. That is largely because Christianity is a historical religion. It is also because knowledge *about* God ordinarily precedes knowledge *of* God in Murray's under-

Knowledge about God is first

standing, and knowledge about God comes as a result of study and instruction. "There is in religious education," he says, "a great deal that is factual, external and explicit and has to be learned."

Content

The distinctive factual and historical content of the Christian religion is contained in the Bible. The Bible, in turn, focuses on Christ. This book is, in short, the source of our basic religious knowledge, "the primary document of our religion." Now, teaching the Bible is not an easy thing to do. It requires a great deal more of the teacher than retelling the Bible stories in his own words. "It is entirely concerned," Murray says, "with the exposition of one authoritative book." No biology teacher would spend a year in weekly discussions chapter by chapter of Darwin's *Origin of the Specials*. But this is what the Christian educator is required to do with his book. Further, there is what Murray calls "a resistance in the material itself." It constitutes, after all, a judgment and claim upon the pupil. It requires a looking backward and a contemporary focus simultaneously, and this, too, is difficult to learn to do. Indeed, "Not one student in a hundred will ever appreciate it," Murray says, "but to afford an opportunity of appreciating it is nevertheless a fundamental aim of religious education."

"Knowledge of the Bible is our chief aim."

Method

The first stage with small children is to read the Bible to them. They will respond to it as to music; they will appreciate it for its narratives and for its people. But it must be well read, by experts in the art of reading aloud who themselves savor its sounds, especially at the highest level of their native language, which for Murray is contained

Hear the Bible

in the King James Version. "There is music in this language," he says, "and music for its expression requires a musician, somebody trained and experienced in the job."

As soon as the children possess the skills for reading well, they should begin to read the Bible for themselves. But "none of this reading round the class, a verse apiece!" he cautions. And not in versions "adapted for the young." What is needed at these early stages is an acquaintance with the material itself. It is good, when they appreciate it "for what it is," for children to learn passages by heart. "At a later stage, when it is well within their possession, they can learn its meaning." The music first, when the music of words is exciting; the relevance may come later when the situation demands and enables.

The Bible has what Murray calls "high correlation value." Educationally that means the linking up of one subject with another. The Bible correlates with the study of geography. One of the fundamental themes of historical geography is the contrast between the desert and the town: in the Bible the desert is the home of monotheism, the fertile farm towns the home of pluralistic fertility religions, and the contrast runs through the Old and New Testaments. The Bible correlates with the study of literature. The themes are what the author is trying to say, whether he has said it, and whether it was worth saying: the biblical material with its variety of literary forms should be asked the same questions. The Bible correlates with the study of history. There is the necessity to establish dates where possible: the biblical material should be studied as a record of historical development. The Bible is a religious book: it addresses itself to "the everlasting man" who is to be found "under all the veneers of rank and nationality and race." The Bible should be studied in relation to other subjects throughout the middle school years, but correlation means also that the parts

Read the Bible

Correlate the Bible

"add up" into a whole, "joining together what should never have been put sunder," showing the life of man and its meaning.

Understand the Bible historically

The historical method consists in placing the narrative back in the setting in which it originated. The Bible should be understood by the personal effort to step back into the situation of the people who originated it, whether they sang it, retold it, or copied it. It involves attempting to recover the historical background, the character and purpose of the originators, the meaning it had to them and to their first readers or listeners. To understand the Bible historically is to find out how men arrived at the belief that God is a God of love from what they seemed to know of him, not merely from their own ideas of love.

This sort of appreciative, correlative, and analytical education in the content of the biblical material "will bring home to every reader sooner or later," Murray is confident, "that it is not just a story of how man finds God, but also a record of what God has done for man."

The Information of Emotions

"The goal of every intellectual process is feeling."

Murray's educational strategy is to get at the emotions through the intellect. Of course, feeling is primitive and instinctual in man, and at this primary level emotion is inhibited by intellectual awareness. However, emotion is discoverable again as the cumulation of the intellectual process, and then "on a deeper, more appropriate and satisfying level." Thus "the purpose of education in religion is to inform the natural religious feeling."

The Natural Sense of God

The sources of Murray's concept are two philosophers who hold opposite opinions about "the natural," Aristotle and Rousseau. Rousseau held that the most primitive is the most natural and that education should be a process of returning to and reinforcing man's original unspoiled condition. Aristotle held that the most highly developed manifestation of anything is its natural form, and that education should be a process of developing man to the limit of the capacities suggested by the highest possible examples. Murray is with Aristotle and against Rousseau, asserting that what is natural lies at the end rather than at the beginning of the educational process. That is to say, man must learn what is most natural to him. Now, "the natural sense of God" is "what chimes in with man's nature." And if man's real nature is man at his highest, awareness of a Being whose nature is more perfected or higher than man's will be natural. For those who take the other, Rousseauean view, the Christian concept of the holy and righteous God would be precisely unnatural.

"The real nature of a thing is shown in its highest manifestation."

Human Relations

If Christian education is the process of bringing human nature to the acceptance and practice of its own highest manifestation, the nurture of a special constellation of feelings is implied.

"Ye are not your own."

The actual experience of love is a basic example. Everyone experiences and needs affection, and this means that no person is or can be complete in himself. "Mere individualism," Murray says, "is a state rather less than human." Everyone also experiences ambivalence in loving. "At one and the same time there is a keen sense of unity and also an enhanced sense of difference," says Murray. The test of the reality of personal relationships is whether the sense of difference is enhanced, whether both parties feel stronger or weaker as a result. "They cannot be perfect where one is strong at the other's expense or where both

Love enhances difference.

are weaker," Murray says. A certain austere aloofness is therefore necessary. Personal relationships are best when two people are drawn together by something outside them both, a cause or a third person. This positive austerity in personal relations nourishes emotions which Murray feels are basic to Christian experience. One is appreciation. To be continually concerned about one's own feelings is "to bid goodbye to all happiness," says Murray. A strong measure of objectivity is required. Being oneself depends on an appreciation of other people. Even originality depends on on appreciation of other people's work. Real appreciation of otherness leads to a sense of wholeness, and wholeness is of the essence of the Christian appreciation of the world and God's reality. It also leads to the emotion of humility, the birth of which is "a sign of the Christian faith," for Murray. Good manners are the outward sign of an inward grace. "The sense of the majesty of God and of his overruling providence" forms in the Christian what Murray calls "that willingness to serve others which is at the core of all good manners."

Appreciation is creative.

Humility is sacramental.

Worship

It is through the nurture of the emotions of personal relationships that one discovers the friend behind friendship. The fact that we are spiritual beings as well as bodies and minds means that we require satisfaction on the spiritual plane as well as in other ways. The love of one person for another Murray calls "an experience of the fourth dimension." The deeper the level the greater its spiritual content. "We are mortal beings experiencing something which, however momentary, is beyond mortality."

Worship is the affirmation of the presence of this sort of beyondness which has been discovered because of the

". . . the friend behind phenomena"

"... a
positive
affirmation
of the presence
of the divine."

prior discovery that human need cannot be satisfied by human relationships. The sense of unworthiness may cause profound distress, and often does among adolescents. It may result in a demand that things be done "decently and in order" which is often the case among children. In any case, worship is the result of carrying instruction beyond thought of God to the reality of God. As relationship to God is the culmination and completion of human relationships, so worship is the peak and end of the education of human emotions.

The Education of Decision

"Christianity involves a choice," Murray says. Christian education is essentially a challenge to express the characteristic love of the Christian religion in loving.

God is like Christ, rather than the other way around for education, and it is loyalty to his way of life that *. . . conscience* constitutes the ultimate challenge. Education of conscience, therefore, proceeds on the principle that it is not ideas or principles that people tend to follow, but persons. It exposes children to "an ever widening circle of loyalties." At the first the school takes the place of the family. Then loyalty is enlarged to the Christian community and its standards, which are as real as the world's. Personal loyalties are extended from local heroes to an attachment to persons of greater and greater universal significance. The goal is for this extended loyalty "to be fixed upon the person to whom the hero too is loyal, namely Christ himself."

"Short of work," says Murray, "there isn't anything most people wouldn't do to become a good Christian." *. . . discipline* Real education of the emotions consists of "prolonging the intellectual effort with greater thoroughness and greater faith." It must be disciplined enough to reach the breakthrough into emotion and vision. Men's minds are "a hotch-potch of ideas unorganized, impulses uncontrolled and ideals unfulfilled." The purpose of education is to make them useable. There is no credit for "bits and pieces" accomplished. Tasks must be carried through. The work must be done. That is the nature of following a leader. Christians have the best. Discipline, in short, is the art of being a disciple. "A religion which centers round the Cross of Christ," Murray says, "cannot but be disciplinary in its very essence."

The "raw material" of the Christian religion, says Murray, is "ordinary folks and their relation to the God who made them." This primary source of faith has, of course, been translated into words, propositions, and doctrines. Christian education must deal with doctrine. We are thinking beings, and we have a natural bent for precision and definition. However, it is the task of education to treat all things educationally, and in this instance that means treating doctrine "ecologically" as well as history. But doctrine is the attempt to express experience, and its truth lies in its ability to play back the God-experience of ordinary folk. The educational task is to establish the two-way relationship between experience and doctrine. The decision Christian education is interested in is less for or against the truth of Christian doctrine than the decision for or against the experience of God-with-man. *. . . doctrine*

"No real Christian instruction is possible," in Murray's judgment, "if the teaching given is not intimately linked up with an actually existing, living, worshipping Christian community." The Christian religion is concerned not with what man has done but with what God has done. Spiritual things are to be discerned in a spiritual setting, and the highest expression of fellowship is to be found where people relate to each other as in relation to God. The local church provides this setting. But the school may *. . . the church* in some ways preserve Christian values better than the local church. If the school is offering Christian education, it will be itself a kind of Christian community, "a field of experiment," in "embryo a Christian society."

Educational method is not a substitute for the gospel, Murray concludes. Its fundamental aim is "to lead people to the point where the Gospel takes hold upon them." At that point, "the Gospel itself will provide a further education of the mind."

ESSENTIALISM

Theology	Neo-orthodox
God	The Wholly Other
Jesus	God and Savior
Man	Sinner
Salvation	Forgiveness by grace
Knowledge of God	Special Revelation
Religious Experience	Encounter, confrontation
Bible	The Word
Philosophy	Realism
Epistemology	"Truth is Knowledge"
Education	Classical
Symbol	The Lecture-Room and the Library
Curriculum	Content-centered
Method of knowing	Communication, transmission
Teacher skill	Lecture, presentation
Method of learning	Absorption, reception
Goal of learning	Cultural heritage, the facts
Evaluation of learning	Examination of memory
Christian Education	Instruction in the Word
Content	Biblical, creedal
Purpose	Confrontation
Goal	Acceptance of restored relationship with God

It would certainly be difficult and perhaps it would be impossible to measure the influence of realistic education in the United States. The variety of its forms presents an initial difficulty that would probably be finally insurmountable: formal, traditional and classical, realist and essentialist. Estimates, however, would run high. Presentational, content-centered teaching is almost exclusively the method in most departments of American graduate schools, seminaries, and universities. Large classes and high student-teacher ratios necessitate the immediate efficiency to be achieved by formal lecturing, textbook assignments, and objective examinations. High schools, plagued with the same quantitative problems and required to prepare increasing numbers of students for university study, have tended to adopt formal methods of instruction. The Russian challenge to American honor in the space race produced a crash program for excellence in the lower schools which at first, at least, tended to concentrate on content mastery rather than skill development. High level studies indicated that American teachers as a whole needed more mastery of their content and more skills in communicating it. During the fifties, church schools were flooded with children, and under the influence of neo-orthodox theologians Christian educators revised the curriculum materials of most of their denominations to emphasize the distinctive Christian content—Old and New Testaments, church history, Christian faith and life. The reforms achieved by Experimentalism in the public schools and Personalism in the church schools were not lost, of course. American education would neither be able nor wish to return to its old-fashioned, nineteenth-century styles. The postwar mood in America was a modern Realism in general education and a new Essentialism in Christian education.

Ground

Realistic philosophy gives its adherents the feeling that they stand on solid ground. In the American educational scene, one of the real functions of that ground has been to provide a base from which to attack and purify the ebullience and eclecticism of the "progressives" in education. F. S. Breed lays out the philosophical and educational problems: change *versus* permanence, progress *versus* conservation, intellection *versus* habituation, incidentalism *versus* guidance, activity *versus* content, project *versus* subject, percept *versus* concept, freedom *versus* authority, interest *versus* effort, expression *versus* repression. "The educational conservative," he says, will be aligned with the second set of terms "with strong or exclusive emphasis all the way down the list"; "the radical will place similarly extreme emphasis" on the first terms. The realist stance— "in things as they are," "facing the facts humbly," and within "the great tradition"—gives him a special perspective on educational experiments and fads and a sense of security in pointing out their educational shortcomings. He wants more than the accidental and incidental precipitation of educational values. "The indispensable cultural values, commonly referred to as essentials . . . are so difficult of acquisition as to require more attention than can be allotted in a pure project program." The realist is clear that education requires a responsible point of view, a mature content, and "a wise guidance of the immature," and he tends to use these convictions on the classrooms of the "progressives" as well as in his own classrooms.

The pluralism of philosophical Realism, however, plagues the realist in education. Under his banner of responsibility to the great tradition gather a diversified group of traditionalists. They tend to be as unrestrained in their attacks on "progressive" education as the radicals once were on "traditional" education. One of them, writing in the late fifties, excoriates "the insufferable non-entities" and "vapid ditherings about humdrum affairs" that "clutter up the pages of our texts" in elementary schools. He attacks as "guff" the method-over-content emphasis of experimentalists as an approach in which the child learns "more togetherness, more forward-looking, on-going, self-actualizing" through "basket-weaving, cake-decorating and advanced locker-opening." It has, he says, produced "a generation of quasi-literates." "Poor old Subject Matter" has been undervalued and despised, "kicked into the gutter and left to shift for herself." "The cold, clear beauty of Euclid; the tingling patriotism which Longfellow wrote into the midnight ride of Paul Revere; King Lear out on the heath defying the fury of Fate and the roaring of the elements; the fascination of the star-dusted light years that stretch from green earth to far Centaurus—what were all those wonderful, magical things compared to 'educating the whole child,' 'meeting felt needs,' and—of course— 'bridging the gap'?" Returning to instruction, homework, memorization, drill and examinations, comprehensive knowledge, history, classics, and basic principles is education for survival, no less. "It is designed to preserve our birthright and give us the tools to protect it." If education does not attempt this task, "in another generation we shall not have a country to defend and some one else will be educating our children's children."

"You have done your best to produce a race of barely literate savages."

Max Rafferty, *Suffer, Little Children* (New York: Devin-Adair, 1962).

Awareness of the importance of essentials in Christian education has also appealed to religious conservatives as a solid ground from which to evaluate the progressive educational methods of liberal theology. Dewey has long been a favorite object of suspicion and attack for his anti-Christian bias. There was a resultant tendency to identify "naturalistic educational theories" with "liberalism" and "the Social Gospel" and to say that the result of both was "emasculation of the Bible" and "spiritually ineffective" Sunday schools. The critical question should not be "How many did you have in Sunday school today," but "Did Johnny relate himself to Jesus Christ through his study of the Bible?" In Sunday schools influenced by secular theories of education, "a student can go through Sunday School with perfect attendance for ten years and still not be able to use the Bible effectively for his daily life." Attractive new materials may be deceptive. The real test of the literature lies in the place and use of the Bible and whether students are required to use the Bible so as to become wise unto salvation. Audiovisual aids, phonographic narration, reproductions of biblical art, projection, movies, music, and drama may all be regarded as God-given teaching tools but must be utilized to tell Bible stories and deal with life problems. The Sunday school was organized for Bible study. Its purpose was "to get the Book into the boy." That must still be its chief concern.

"The Sunday School was organized for Bible study."

Attack on liberalism in philosophy and progressivism in education always creates a great deal of dust. It is important not to permit the skirmishes to obscure the battle grounds. Realism in philosophy has contributed to the discussion of education a needed emphasis on the importance of knowledge as a thing-in-itself, worth striving

Christianity Today, annual special editions on Christian education, e.g., III, August 31, 1959.

for as a standard of inherent value. It has been able to bring into religion a real sensitivity to the plural realities of human existence on earth, in terms of which a man may acknowledge without threat the ambivalences of life as challenge and opportunity. It has been able to introduce into thought and education the reality of that which is beyond man's sensory grasp and intellectual understanding. From the perspective of these insights, much that goes on in popular educational circles does seem to be somewhat less than important.

Limits

One of the most significant fringe benefits of Realism in philosophy is a sense of humility. In educational philosophy the result is an awareness that the educational approach itself contains principles that are dangerous. The tendency of Realism in philosophy is to become essentialism in education, and the tendency of essentialism is to become indoctrination, substituting words for knowledge, knowledge *about* for knowledge *of*, personal authority for individual learning. The responsibility for limiting the educational tendency of Realism to self-destruct lies with the teacher. A great burden is placed squarely on the teacher's shoulders, but it is the genius of Realism to face such realities without panic. "So be it," is the response. "The primary task and danger of education is getting the material across and into the pupil. Let us discipline ourselves to the production of realistic teachers who can do the job and know the risk."

The teacher is the key.

The teacher must know his subject. He must know as much about it as possible. One cannot teach the fundamental essentials to a beginning class, even elementary school children, without knowing infinitely more about it than the pupils will need to know at their present stage of

Knowledge prevents over-verbalization.

development. The facts must be reliable and authentic. The human mind is an extraordinarily capacious instrument, and one never knows how much information even the smallest child will want once the teacher has gained his interest. Incompetence is inexcusable in the classroom. Only a thorough knowledge of a subject will preclude one of the chief dangers of the content-centered approach, a tendency to verbalize everything, letting words substitute for reality.

The teacher must be fond of his subject. He must like it well enough to teach it again and again. He will enjoy it so much that every time he teaches it he discovers something new. It never becomes dull to him. He is so fond of it that he talks about it, studies it, and listens to other people on it. Indeed, he enjoys his subject so much that it seems that everything relates to it and that new information on his specialization intrudes itself upon him in daily events. He enjoys it so much that he deals with the primary sources more than with the interpretations and critiques. When he likes the subject he is teaching, the teacher does not need to whip up interest in it arbitrarily, a criticism often lodged against content-teaching: interest is contagious. But even more important, if the teacher is really fond of the material, the danger of authoritarianism is minimized because he points to the content itself rather than to his own knowledge of it. *Fondness for the subject prevents authoritarianism.*

The teacher must be fond of his pupils. A teacher who does not actually like students should find something other to do than lecture to them. He needs to like them well enough to recall his own youth. He should like them well enough to spend time with them outside of class. He needs to like them because they are young and immature and are trying to be wise and mature. He needs to like *Fondness for pupils prevents knowledge-about.*

Gilbert Highet, *The Art of Teaching* (New York: Vintage, 1950).

them well enough to be both determined and wise. A content-teacher once said, "The mind of a schoolboy is like a narrow-necked bottle; it takes in plenty of learning in little drops, but any large quantity you pour in spills over and is wasted." If the teacher is genuinely fond of his pupils, he will naturally avoid another great danger of content-centered education, the substitution of knowledge-about for knowledge-of.

Excellence prevents personal domination.

The teacher must enjoy teaching. That is to say, he is so fond of his subject and of his pupils that he gives a good performance. He will do everything he can to make his subject live. If his goal is transmission of knowledge, he will use every technique he knows, from good speaking to clear outlining to audiovisual presentations. The ever-present problem in effective presentation is, of course, personal influence. The realist tends to accept influence as a positive force in education. He also sugests that only the very best job of presentation will focus the interest of the pupils on the content rather than on the teacher.

The realist claims that, in the interests of educational excellence, the dangers built into his approach to education are worth risking, at least partly because he believes that humility bred of facts provides built-in limits.

Christian Education

There is an essentialist temper about Christianity. It claims, in one way or another, to possess a distinctive and true word of salvation: there is one God, reported in the Bible and revealed in the life and teachings of Jesus the Christ, who by his own death and resurrection demonstrated that God is on man's side in the struggle to establish love and justice as a way of life, first among his followers and then by them in the world at large. Those who have personally found this faith to be productive of meaning in their own experience tend to be so enthusiastic about their discovery that they want to share it. When they turn to education, they tend to concentrate on the content of the distinctive and true word of salvation and to be content only when the pupil gives evidence of having accepted and mastered it. Though Christian education need not become indoctrination, it tends to. Christian educators acknowledge this possibility, and many answer that objective realities themselves limit it. There is the very beyondness of God, who is what he is and moves as he wills and reveals himself to be what he is quite independently of man's doctrines and intentions, preventing the teacher from dominating the pupil by revealing and relating himself directly to the pupil. There is always a risk, therefore, in effective Christian education, but it is not the risk of teacher-authoritarianism so much as it is the risk of teacher-displacement.

In the nineteenth century, Horace Bushnell identified the key issues which came to characterize Christian education in the twentieth century: *historical change, religious experience and knowledge, the God-man relation, and personal growth.* Contemporary Christian theologians influenced by neo-orthodoxy and Christian educators influenced by classical education address themselves to these issues, but feel deeply that Bushnell and his direct successors have taken the wrong stance in regard to them. For them, the God-man relation is the primary issue and puts the others in perspective. God is vertically beyond—"above" man in every dimension but space—and the divine-human relation comes to man from God on God's initiative. Man is thus, in a definitive way, the recipient of revelation. The function of the self-disclosure of God is to change man's horizontal relationships, redeeming them and saving him. The kind of religious knowledge that counts is thus the result of personal relationship to God. Personal alertness may be nurtured by study of God's ways of revealing himself to other people in other times, especially biblical, but education ends when God makes himself known. Personal growth in faith and act comes about as the result of this divine-human encounter in experience. Historical change is wrought by God in his relation to man. In fact, nothing really changes in history because events are precipitated by the acts of God who is the same, yesterday, today, and forever. Therefore, those historical changes wrought by man alone are presumptuous and wrongheaded leading to sin and evil. Therefore, Christian education will tend to look to events in which God has been demonstrably active for paradigms. Because it takes time for the human results to validate the divine-human events, these are mostly in the past. Christian education will tend to be classical in that it finds most of its primary source material in a great tradition against which contemporary events are tested and measured. Christian education of this temper is a distinct alternative to educational thinking and forms created by both Personalism and Experimentalism.

Direction

Christian education frequently appears to be at a crossroad. Especially among scholars with relatively stable subject matters, the impression is that Christian education is forever seeking directions. To some this questing condition is occasion for friendly condescension. To others it seems merely an occupational characteristic. Christianity has been described by a Dutch missionary as a religion "en trek," by a German theologian as a movement with "a capacity for self-criticism," by an American social critic as "a faith with a self-righting tendency." Education itself is a discipline with a foot in individual processes of change and an eye on the future. The combination of Christianity and education often seems to double the quality of precariousness.

Along most main roads, however, a succession of intersections indicates movement.

For a long time, Christian education has offered several different lanes on the same westerly highway from the ancient to the modern worlds. During the last hundred years, the lanes seem to have been diverging and recent maps indicate that the traditional lanes have become alternate routes through modern mountains.

Pragmatism in education has become the route of Experimentalism in Christian education. Its distinctive principle is practical reconstruction. Its educational concept is that the immature gain maturity by solving problems of daily living, in the conviction that efficiency in problem-solving is evidence of maturity. It is said that because problem-solving is the highest achievement of man, it is God-like.

Personalism in Christian theology turned Idealism in education into a melding of psychology and theology for Christian education. Its distinctive principle is progressive revaluation. It urges cooperation between the immature and the mature in the conviction that, since cooperation is the way of maturity, by cooperating the immature will become mature. By the assertion that God intends persons to become mature, this education is defined as Christian.

Classical education and neoorthodox theology combined to produce an Education in Christian Essentials. Its principle is restoration. Its program is to expose the immature to the racial and cultural maturity of the great tradition in the conviction that the immature will be matured by the worthwhileness they have encountered there. Because God reveals himself in this encounter, the education is said to be Christian.

It may be observed that the destinations do not differ as much as the routes.

However, the changing terrain of history is a reminder that inquiry for directions is seldom irrelevant. In times past, it has been the custom of Christian educators to make their inquiries primarily of travelers in other vehicles and of local residents. There are signs now, though, that the time has come for Christian educators to become their own navigators. For a century they have been growing a history; they need to read its evidence. They have developed techniques of research into developmental and cognitive processes; they need to adapt and apply them independently to religious experience and knowledge. They have drawn from philosophy a set of analytical disciplines; they need to put them to work in their own way for the service of man. They have built from the theologies a special perspective; they need to invite its disclosure of God to man in a world of rapid change. There is the possibility that the time has come for Christian educators to weigh their situation, number their alternatives, and offer their own route into the future.

In the course of the last hundred years, Christian education has become one of the most active and widely extended strategies of the Christian movement. An analysis of the present situation in the light of that century of vigorous and varied development disclosed four principles for understanding Christian education.

During the nineteenth century, with its cross-currents of science and theology, Horace Bushnell initiated Christian education as a modern movement by opening basic theological questions about how man as a natural product of the physical world is related to God, its Creator. His concept of the growth of man from natural being to spiritual being through the personal nurture within the Christian community of an unfolding consciousness of relation to God laid the foundation for a new understanding of Christian education. Christian education as a distinct discipline is the result of dealing both theologically and educationally with the personal relationship between God and man in the natural world of God's creation and continuous action. It may now be guided in the right direction by seeking *to demonstrate, both theologically and educationally, that man is a spiritual being at home in a natural world.*

A century of scientific and artistic ferment has subjected almost every inherited concept and assumed value to scrutiny and challenge. Christian theology, fixed in the third, thirteenth, and sixteenth centuries, has not escaped. Biblical vocabulary and concepts seem archaic. Ancient theological concerns seem irrelevant. Faith is transferred from other-worldly to this-worldly objects. But the Christian movement did not dry up and blow away in the hot winds of criticism. New circumstances exposed new truths in the old gospel. At times the Christian point of view seems more alive and contemporary than it has been for a long time. Therein lies a clue. Christian education may be guided in the right direction by seeking *to demonstrate that the truth theology tells is relevant to man in his present circumstances because it is true in more than present circumstances.*

One of the most distinguishing characteristics of the last century is the increasing onward speed of historical events. In a technological age, each new scientific discovery releases a sequence of technical applications, all of which affect the lives of ordinary people. Increase of movement, however, often produces only uncertainty of direction, and the faster the speed the more significant the uncertainty. It is in this circumstance that education, both Christian and general, must carry out its work with young people whose adult lives may be lived in a cultural situation very different from that in which they learn to learn. Christian education may be guided in the right direction by learning how *to help learners live meaningfully now in an ambiguous situation and eventually in one that will probably be revolutionary.*

In a century, Christian education has grown from a haphazard off-shoot of Protestant churchmanship to one of its largest and most demanding projects. The tendency, under the pressure of too many children and too much to do educationally in an hour each week, has been for Christian educators to concentrate on practical methods of getting the immediate jobs done, and to pick them up where they are most readily available, that is, from the secular and general educators. The Christian goals for life, however, are special rather than general. Therein is the hint that Christian education, while not arrayed against secular education, is spiritual. Christian education may be guided in the right direction by seeking *to devote itself to the development of a total approach to the task of the Christian movement in the world based on a deepening understanding of the nature of spiritual communication and the radical nature of the Christian faith.*

If Christain education were to rediscover these emergent principles of a century and to apply them as clues to its task in the future, it might well find itself launched in a new direction and serving the Christian movement in new ways.

Context

Something enormous is happening to Western man. His outlook on life and the world is changing so radically that in the perspective of history the twentieth century is likely to rank—with the fourth century which witnessed the triumph of Christianity over paganism, and the seventeenth century, which signaled the dawn of modern science—as one of the very few that have started something genuinely new in human thought.

From the fourth century triumph of Christianity in the Roman Empire through the Middle Ages and the Reformation, the Western mind was, above all else, theistic. "God, God, God: nothing but God!" In the Middle Ages anyone could have said that, though it was a theologian who did. In such a world, life was transparently meaningful. "Can anyone understand the thunderings of God's pavilion?" Elihu asks Job. The Christian man of the medieval world answered quietly that he did not understand and that he did not need to because God was in his heaven and the way to happiness on this earth was in doing one's daily duties as the appointed representatives of God made them clear.

It was the assumption that man did not need to understand that the sixteenth and seventeenth centuries began to question. The new rage to know God's handiwork began to rival the medieval rage to know God himself. Newton's exclamation about the marvel of scientific method caught the excitement: "O God, I think thy thoughts after thee!" The universe was greater than he had supposed, but it was a coherent, law-keeping system, and it was intelligible. The rewards were quick in following: health was improved, hard work lessened, goods multiplied, leisure increased. God, it seemed clear, is to be known through nature, and human fulfillment consists in discovering nature's laws and utilizing them for the benefit of man.

In the twentieth century, science is telling its followers that they cannot even imagine with their ordered and space-limited minds how the universe is constructed or works. "The structure of nature may eventually be such that our processes of thought do not correspond to it sufficiently to permit us to think about it at all." If the scientists have become agnostics about nature, it is little wonder that the philosophers say that there is practically nothing of importance that they can say about man's life. Camus proclaims the absurd, Sartre talks about the "too much," and Beckett writes plays about "the void." Ethicists say that there are no fixed moral principles except possibly the exercise of power. Theologians toy with the idea that God is dead.

All this has been called "revolutionary." It is a big word. It stands for something genuinely reconstructive in history. It has, however, been applied to many specific programs. It was applied to the American labor movement in the 1880s, and in newly industrialized Germany to the strikes of the 1840s. It was applied to political reconstruction in France in 1795 and in the North American Colonies in 1776. It is a word large enough to have stood for the restoration of human rights to oppressed and deprived human beings, the American Colonists' right to self-government, the French peoples' rights to liberty, equality, and fraternity. It is sometimes a beautiful word, standing for passive resistance, freedom, and the righting of wrongs. It is sometimes an ugly word, standing for violence and mob-rule, bloodshed and hatred. It is currently applied to the Marxist revolution so exclusively as to imply that it is the only one there is.

When Albert Camus ran full tilt into the revolution while resisting the Nazis in the French underground movement during World War II, he developed a distinction between revolution and rebellion. He was attracted by the dreams and devotion of Communist individuals but repelled by the violence and ruthlessness of the Communist revolution. Both revolution and rebellion are dedicated to change, but social revolution is change institutionalized, self-perpetuating, and made an end in itself. The claims of revolution, Camus found, are total. Therefore, he says, it assumes that man may be molded to its own needs and becomes an ideology of contrived consent. "Every revolutionary," Camus concluded, "ends by becoming either an oppressor or a heretic." The rebel, however, is devoted to the morality of freedom and change, refusing to permit it to become stabilized. Camus found that he was forced to take sides against the Marxist revolution. "Instead of killing and dying in order to produce the being that we are not," he wrote, "we have to live in order to create what we are." The rebel protests against the human condition. He attacks a shattered world to make it whole. On the other hand, he is a free and creative agent. He confers unity and beauty upon the world because he loves his life in it.

The Christian movement, too, is devoted to something genuinely reconstructive in history, though in neither the revolutionary sense of the Marxists nor in the rebellious sense of Camus. Like Camus, Christians tend to be sensitive to the monstrous things man can do with devotion to government, with zeal for agreement, even with passion for right and freedom. They have seen it at work in their own institutions, becoming manipulative, oppressive, self-perpetuative. Unlike Camus, they do not rebell against the universe. They may find the world to be absurd, but it is no surprise, really, because they have learned to trust a God whose wisdom and logic do not seem to be limited to syllogisms. The change they are for is a New Creation. They have been known for changing things ever since that celebrated incident in the Greek city of Thessalonica when the local Jews called them "these men who have turned the world upside down." They might well have responded that the world was being turned right side up at last by the Creator himself. That sort of change seems to have been built into their faith by the man whose life and teachings a generation before had changed their own lives and whose death and resurrection convinced them that many of their theories needed to be changed, too. After all, it was Isaiah who had said that Yahweh himself was so unhappy with conditions in the infamous city of Tyre that he "turned the earth upside down." They are for changing things so that God's will is done. A scholar thought the medieval church to be autocratic and challenged it to use democratic processes. A preacher found Renaissance Florentine nobles so dissolute that he told them of the righteousness of God. When a modern German pastor was convinced that Hitler was demonic, he plotted to have him killed. Each of those paid with his life. Others have cared about prison conditions, the exploitation of working men, the continued slavery of an imported race. Because they cared, there have been prison reform, the labor movement, the black revolution.

However, the change in which Christianity specializes is not the same as the revolutions, the rebellions, and the movements. It is a concern for new direction that lies behind all of them, generating and criticising them because it is more radical and more original. It is defined by the conviction, however it may be phrased theologically, that God is actually at work in human history and that it is a Christian's personal destiny to be on God's side. It is characterized by the belief that faith in God and his judgment on the world must be loving enough to bring the world to an acceptance of God's revelation and reconciliation. It is not a material but a spiritual revolution. It is not intellectual so much as inner. It is not an insurrection but a resurrection. It is not a rebellion against absurdity but a rebellion against alienation. It finds its definition not in programs and reforms but in the conviction that the presence of God in human life is so potent and his will for human life so creative that if it were taken seriously the entire world would be refashioned.

Such a massive proposal implies a real engagement between Christianity and the world, grounded in a real investment in human life. And Christians must be the first to acknowledge that the church may lose some of its familiar and precious ways of thinking and acting, some of its pet forms and traditional shapes and favorite programs. A loving revolution implies that the revolutionary will be transformed while transforming. To do this, the Christian movement needs to be secure enough about its ground of faith to be able to change its doctrines and purge its errors, certain enough of its heritage to develop and project it. In successive encounters with the Roman Empire, the feudal society, and the scientific world, Christianity has been able, with no little struggle and pain but with a great and inspired creativity, to maintain this living balance between faith and risk.

Love is an interpersonal rather than an institutional affair. It creates institutions, guiding, criticising, and losing them. Its basic strategy is the chain reaction. Jesus won his followers one by one, in face-to-face encounter. Ever since, the direct impact of one who knows and cares upon one who does not has been the Christian program for change. The genuinely new thing that Christianity seeks is a New Being, a man creatively bound to freedom, who exposes other men to divine self-disclosure. Thus the revolution the Christian seeks will probably come slowly, like the growth of a plant from a seed, imperceptibly like the leavening of a loaf of bread by a bit of yeast. Its method will probably be the same as its goal: the quiet but radical changing of the loyalties and behavior of real human beings, one by one.

Perhaps the best way that Christian education can serve a society that appears to be learning to distrust change is to become the servant of the New Creation, establishing direction for itself by enabling the New Life in a world that exists only as a process.

In education, what is taught and learned gives its own special style to how the teaching and learning experience develops.

When content is regarded as objective—inert items of data to be transmitted from the teacher to the learner—education tends to become dull, mechanical, and routine. The teacher is active, the learner is expected to receive passively, and the content is transported. The time for that attitude toward content has, however, passed. The revolt that began among the public megauniversities during the 60s has made that clear, and it is now reaching down into the secondary schools.

When content is regarded as subjective—activities enlarging the learner's experience—education tends to become fun, lively, and thin. Factual content, together with the skills for amassing and handling it, tends to disappear. The time for that attitude toward content has also passed. The revolt that began among parents in the local elementary schools during the 50s has made that clear and now reaches upward into the secondary schools.

Dissatisfied with the exclusivism of both attitudes, educators are now talking about focusing on the interaction between teacher and learner and of the content as standing exposed in the intersection to the passing traffic of relations between teachers and learners. A dynamic relation is reciprocal, meaning that both parties to it are modified, not only by the other but by the relation as well. In the classroom the relation itself can be considered content for the educative process. What has been called subjective content has been altered by interactional understanding.

Meanwhile, the knowledge explosion may turn out to give direction to education in the 70s. In the present scientific world, research proceeds simultaneously on many fronts in an interlocking reinforcement that produces not only data but new combinations and possibilities more rapidly than any mind, or manageable team of minds, can comprehend and utilize. Instant worldwide communication has added to the sheer amount of information available. The only hope for coping with this vast input has been to develop an electronic technology for preserving information that can be itemized and for handling information that can be programmed. The mind is thus freed from data retention to turn to data application. Philosophers who take this situation seriously are turning the technological explosion into a conceptual revolution by discarding the traditional subject-object discriminations of epistemology in favor of transactional modes of thinking about knowledge. There is talk about the difference between "naming" and "knowing" and the tendency to substitute "acting" for "meaning." The whole process of naming-knowing-acting involves an interchange between persons and things in which not only the behavior of persons—the subjects of knowledge—but also of things—the objects of knowledge—though less obviously are as significantly altered. Knowledge, as thus understood, becomes a transactional event.

For educators this would suggest that the *known* (the content) also becomes a dynamic element in the reciprocal equation of *knower* (the learner), *knowor* (the teacher), and *knowing* (the educative process). In short, what has been traditionally called objective content and thought of as hard and inert is also shaped and activated by its transactional handling.

Christian education has been pushed and bruised by these changing modes, of course, but there is reason to suppose that, when true to its own sources, it has never been anything but personally interactional and epistemologically transactional. The word *dialogue* has sometimes been used to describe this dynamic. It has the advantage of being a personal word—a divine-human speech-act—thus reflecting the distinctive nature of the Christian gospel. The content of Christian education is God-wanting-to-be-known, taking the initiative in the action and supporting the knower in his knowing, an interaction which changes the knower and feeds back into the transaction affecting not only what is known but also the One-who-is-known. The result, of course, is far more than a manward stream of qualities and ideas to be named and catalogued and eventually placed alongside others in epistemological formulas and knowledge equations. Everything is changed; not only is there a New Being but also a New Creation—a new earth and a new heaven. The educator enters this dynamic process of revelation-grace-salvation as an enabler who is also altered by his enabling activity.

Tradition is an element in the Christian knowledge-event. There is no question whether the Bible and history are to be part of the content of Christian education. There is only the question how the knowledge-events of the past may become contributory to knowledge-events in the present. In this case, the teacher bears the responsibility for dealing accurately, selectively, and effectively with the past. He understands his limitations as an objective scholar but he is persistent in distinguishing between "hard" and "soft" facts and he deals with the primary sources at whatever level possible to him. It is his joy over the mastery of the material that communicates directly. He understands that every event of the sacred history he deals with is important, but he knows that it cannot all be encountered directly and chooses carefully what will be omitted and enthusiastically what will be shared. It is his willingness to stand by his choice that the learners understand. He understands that he cannot make the distant near, but he does everything in his power to show how it was real in the lives of persons and he labors to uncover the manward actions of God in it. It is his yearning that present existence may be illuminated by ancient events that makes immediate contact. Knowing occurs when divine disclosure is met by human discernment, and history becomes sacred when it alters the future Godward.

Community is an element of the Christian knowledge-event. The *koinonia* is more than the social context of Christian education. It is the mode in which the event occurs. When the community has been taken to be the content of Christian education, it has become both flat and fat—short on both the depth of history and the discipline of thought. The *koinonia*, whether it occurs in ecclesiastical institutions or not, is the relationship that cuts cleanly across the increasing tendency of modern men to huddle together in protection against the fragmentation of life to expose the heart of an authentic relationship which consists in belonging to each other because all care about being children of God. The dynamic of this interpersonal, transhuman reciprocity is the model for the teaching-learning-knowing transaction. It may also be the model for a three-termed logic of actor-act-reactor. In any case, it is part of the living content of God-man-world to be experienced in ever widening and more complex circles, but also to be concretely created in chosen circles.

Stance is an element of this Christian knowledge-content. Theology is every Christian's business. It is more than a set of suppositions and propositions woven into a coherent and consistent system with which one can do battle against those with whom one disagrees. It is the art of seeing things from the side of the One-who-wants-to-be-known. It means, in short, to know more than one understands. That involves a continuous quest—using whatever logical and intuitional tools one possesses—to guess responsibly and humbly how the world might look to God as history and community reveal him. It implies a constant attempt to clarify and purify one's insights by matching them against the evidence of facts, applying logical tests, comparing with the conclusions of the seekers and nonseekers one knows. Concurrently and conclusively, it means testing one's theology by actually standing on it in the hurricane of events.

Style is a product of the Christian knowledge-event. The Christian life-style is more than a descriptive catalogue of activities to be condemned or condoned. It is life lived toward wholeness. It is a spin-off of the dialogical process, formed by the effective interaction of giving and receiving tradition, joining and forming community, testing and taking the stance. It shows itself in activity on the behalf of others—serving, sharing, shaping. It shows itself in activity on behalf of God—confessing, creating, celebrating. The Christian life-style is not an educative strategy so much as a sign of an educative strategy at work.

Thus the Christian content, being the engagement between a Person who forms things and persons who do things, is both concreted and emergent, the result of an interpenetration of beyond and here. Use of the human experience of love as an analogy has been neither accidental nor temporary. In life, this Christian content is not dispensable. In Christian education, it forms the process.

John Dewey, George Albert Coe, and Maria Montessori were master teachers. Following their philosophical principles, many teachers have become more effective. Together they have changed schoolrooms from places of childhood oppression to adventurous places of light and growth.

Dewey, Coe, and Montessori were genuinely different people, however. No matter how widely he studied, Dewey gave the impression of having come straight from the Vermont hills, preserving the angularity and earthy sensibleness of New England. Though his roots were traditional, Coe reflected the restlessness of spirit characteristic of the far west which he loved. In spite of fame and travel, Montessori always reflected the personal trust in children for which Italian families are known. Dewey was unalterably set against the theologies of both Catholicism and Protestantism. Coe was determined to develop a theistic stance clearly alternative to both naturalism and orthodoxy. Montessori, without abandoning Catholic orthodoxy, built a philosophical concept of humanity on the biological processes of growth and maturation. Pragmatism, Idealism, and Realism are clearly separable philosophical trends. Three alternative educational philosophies extend these trends. In the textbooks, the philosophies of Dewey, Coe, and Montessori appear to be three poles apart, but in the classrooms all the philosophies produce good teachers.

In education, classroom teaching rather than academic philosophy is the payoff. One direction for Christian education to move is toward improvement of the actual teaching-learning process in the classroom.

The recent production of much-needed new curriculum materials by denominational staffs soon revealed a degree of truth in the ancient aphorism that no classroom is better than the teacher: the new materials were excellent enough, the classrooms were not improved enough. Teaching now needs attention. The current development of training programs for teachers in turn reveals that too many teachers handle the new materials in old ways, droning on in uninspired monologues taxing the interest and discipline of restless children beyond reasonable expectation. However, new resources are becoming available and others glitter on the horizon.

THE TEACHER OF CHRISTIANITY SEEKS

TO MINISTER TO	ACCORDING TO	IN THE LIGHT OF	BY MEANS OF
PERSONS individuals	**THEIR OWN NATURE** (developmental psychology) infant child youth adult old age	**GOD AND HIS PURPOSES** (theology) the world man sin destiny Jesus Christ	**THE INVITATION TO DISCIPLESHIP** (*kerygma*) personal ordered continuous
groups classes races labor and capital rich and poor churched and unchurched good and evil	**THEIR OWN SITUATION** (depth psychology) alienations anxieties defeats achievements wholeness	**AS REVEALED IN THE CHRISTIAN** (*didache*) TRADITION (given) STANCE (chosen) LIFE (growing)	**THE ART OF TEACHING** every class an experience in (dialogue) sensitivity encounter creativity worship
nations	**THEIR TOTAL SITUATION** (ecology) world home friendships public school livelihood values	and **HIS OWN FAITH** (witness) questions answers failures hopes	**THE SCIENCE OF EDUCATION** using the best possible (*educare*) teaching techniques buildings and equipment curricula leadership training

IN RELATIONSHIP TO GOD AND THE WORLD

New equipment promises new efficiency for teachers. The use of electronic hardware has introduced a new dimension of objectivity into laboratory methods of teacher training and supervision. Audio tape and now video tape devices make it possible to play back, repeatedly and selectively, the teacher's leadership in a contained laboratory situation. Under the guidance of an experienced master teacher, the learner teacher may review and analyze the dynamics of the rapidly moving, real-life relationships between teachers and learners. Through facing the objective revelation of his own strengths and weaknesses, he is led to a better performance. Even more exotic equipment, already being used in scientific laboratories, makes possible the extension of teacher effectiveness through programmed subject-matter, machine-teaching, computerized information banks. Public school people think of freeing overburdened classroom teachers from a kind of slave labor at routine and data-gathering responsibilities by turning many of these tasks over to computers programmed by subject-matter and process specialists; the teachers are then freed to devote more time to personal attention to individual pupils and their special learning problems. Some of these methods have already been extended to programmed instruction in values, the teaching of biblical subject matter, and computerized analysis of Old Testament language useage. Costs may be prohibitive to church schools for a long time to come, but there is already some talk, for instance among executives at the archdiocesan level of Roman Catholic school systems, of the practical possibilities of shifting on a massive scale to a style of teaching made possible by the use of mass media techniques.

New teaching practices promise new excitement for classrooms. Team teaching, a dream of public schools as a method for dealing with large classes, seems ideally suited to church schools. There, more teachers will not raise the expense of the school because all teachers are volunteers. Since the teachers are not specifically and professionally trained in subject matter, a division of labor makes that responsibility more manageable. The presence of other teachers in the classroom is sometimes a threat to professional teachers, but in the church school it helps meet one of the greatest problems of the volunteer church school teacher, sheer loneliness on the job. It is an almost universal report from church schools that feelings of frustration and lack of support debilitate the teacher's effectiveness in the classroom and often take him out of it in defeat before he has had a chance to learn to teach. The case study method of teaching was pioneered in professional schools of law and medicine, introduced into university education by colleges of sociology, filtered into high schools through history and civics departments, and is now being investigated as a method of biblical study for church schools. The presentation and analysis of cases can, however, be a highly analytical and sophisticated exercise. At lower levels of learner age and skill, it is often more meaningful for students to play out the roles of the case in live, if somewhat artificial, action. Only recently has role-playing as a method of content-learning come under serious study, though one is reminded of Dewey's children at the Experimental School role-playing knights and peasants as a method of learning history, and Montessori's children producing the materials for the Mass as a method of learning religion.

New learning tactics promise new enthusiasm for learners. Interest in ways of assisting learning is now moving beyond traditional verbalization as method and objective content as matter. Significant experiments with sensory awareness, bodily movement, and creative activities are being conducted at educational institutes interested in reaching feeling-levels in adults and at rescue projects devoted to behavior-change in drug addicts. Techniques borrowed from art education demonstrate that painting helps bring feelings to the surface and fix intellectual content as well. Teaching methods long used in the theater suggest that pantomime and dance are kinesthetic modes of learning effective in much wider areas than hitherto suspected. A great deal of work is being done in methods of sensitizing whole physical reactions to subject-object and subject-subject relationships. Work with culturally deprived children suggests that the enrichment of environmental stimuli is an effective teacher of customs and values, and the possibilities of applying these techniques to children of average advantages and to the learning of biblical culture and thought forms have only begun to come into view.

New educational research promises new effectiveness in the educational process. Christian education has suffered immeasurably from a kind of genial good-naturedness about teaching and learning. No real tests of what has been accomplished are even applied. Christian educators need information about the results of teaching and learning special subject-matter such as history, both biblical and postbiblical, and doctrine, both credal and personal. Cognition studies may produce new concepts of the meaning of historical data, and that could lead in turn to more effective practical methods of teaching. More elusive to quantification, but at the same time more essential to Christian education, is a better empirical understanding of the processes by which experience becomes religious—by which information is transformed by a learner into thought, thought into attitudes, attitudes into convictions, convictions into life-styles. New information and thinking is needed about the capacities for and processes of learning this special historical and doctrinal content at the various age levels. Understanding is still primitive regarding mass-media reacting, indirect communicating, subliminal believing, noneverbal thinking, multidirectonal reasoning.

New theoretical reflections promise new understanding of personality structure and development. Deterministic approaches which have long dominated the thinking of psychologists are now being supplemented by studies of how and why persons change, the influence of experience on cognition and even on intelligence, how thinking copes with the unknown, sensory avenues to conceptual ideas. The result for educators will someday be a more comprehensive approach to developmental phases and their sequence. No distinctively Christian view of religious growth has yet been offered. Not enough is known about the relation between the socialization of personality and the Christianization of personality, between concrete thought and religious thought, between physiological maturation and spiritual maturation. But there is promise that a view of human selfhood as defined by divine personhood and of religious growth as a process of coming to terms with mystery can be fitted to some secular theories without losing religiousness. By discovering how to enable the expansion of learning problems to spiritual dimensions and how to assist the extension of the reach of human awareness to spiritual realities, Christian education would be establishing new directions with its own disciplines. Today modern education may well be a pioneer without a frontier; tomorrow Christian education could supply it—a frontier lying beyond appearance and immediacy, bordering on the universal which is inward as well as outward.

With techniques and insights now becoming available, Christian education can begin to stake out and deal with its own special need to improve the effectiveness of the teaching and learning processes in regard to Christian subject matter and Christian goals. Movement should be made in the direction of developing a highly refined science of Christian education.

There is, however, the live possibility that the significance of scientific research may be minimized if the artfulness of teaching is lost. If education is refinement of common sense by science, teaching may be said to be created by the addition of wisdom to education and turned into the teaching of religion by the addition of love to teaching. Teachers of Christianity must remember that what they are after is the establishment of a working relationship, on the model of Jesus and his Heavenly Father, between man and God. Of course, the teacher must be orderly in his methods, knowledgeable about the learning processes, informed about his pupils, precise in dealing with his subject matter. Teaching, however, is metascientific. It includes the knack of turning learning into sheer delight. Teaching religion involves the art of turning discovery into transforming joy. It involves emotions which have not yet and perhaps can never be systematically appraised and employed, human values which still elude empirical quantification, convictions which are not entirely explicable by objective analysis, and the reality of God which remains a mystery. Teaching Christianity involves inducing the pupil to risk the acceptance of divine love. That is not like inducing a chemical reaction. It is more like painting a picture or making music or planting a garden or writing a letter. Like art, it requires considerable active doing, the exercise of skills, and the development of sensitivity. Christian education can best set its own directions by developing empirical data about the teaching and learning processes in its special subject matters and by learning how to make this data function creatively in a new and independent art of teaching.

The experiences of growing people	N 4　K 5	I 6　II 7	III 8　IV 9	V 10　VI 11
The experience of God	Presence	Father	Pal	Person
The sense of worship	Belonging-ness	Wonder	Awe	Adoration
The discovery of love	Simple Response	Acceptance	Sharing	Extension
The awareness of dialogue	Given Mutuality parent family	Developing Individuality' school play-groups	city area	nation frontier
Areas of Tension: People	Parent	People	Individuals	Heroes
Nature	Plants	Animals	World	Universe
Intellect	Security	Curiosity	Skepticism	Adventure
Problems of personality: Againstness	Obstinacy	Pugnacity	Selfishness	Fair play
Inversion	Shyness	Reluctance	Sensitiveness	Competition
Fear	Fears	Failure	Inferiority	Abandonment

Spiritual Development

VII 12	VIII 13	IX 14	X 15	XI 16	XII 17	The Religious Experience — Life situation	Universal themes
Enemy		Friend		Comrade		God-Beyond	
Commitment		Mysticism		Creativity		God-Within	} I. LOVE
Idealization		Identification		Participation		God-Among	} II. SEARCH-RESPONSE
Social questions		Chosen Mutuality — Personal questions		Doctrinal questions		Individualization-Socialization	} III. COMMUNITY
Heroism		Self-reliance		Fellowship		Problems	
Science		Philosophy		Faith		Anxiety / Challenge	} IV. TENSION
Idealism		Materialism		Empiricism		Growth / Adventure	
Independence		Conformity		Mass-mind		Failure	
Evasion		Loneliness		Rebellion		Pain / Tragedy	} V. ISOLATION
Ridicule		Social disparities		Despair		Grief / Evil	

One way to establish a direction for the philosophical development of Christian education is to choose one of the alternatives. If Experimentalism, Personalism, and Essentialism are actually the extension into education of three distinct philosophical temperaments, it is likely that each Christian educator will find himself more comfortable in one than in the other two. Each of the three philosophical alternatives has made its own special contributions to the development of education. Each position has been extensively and competently refined. Each provides a workable base on which to build a philosophy of Christian education. If one were to decide that this was the best manner in which to approach the philosophical question, the method would be to list the strengths and weaknesses of each position, and, after comparison, to choose the one in which the strengths seemed most clearly to outweigh the weaknesses. The exercise might work out as follows.

The strengths of Experimentalism are its rigorous monism, its critique of otherworldliness, its insistence on the centrality of experience as a philosophical principle, its concept of meaning as instrumental in nature, its focus on change as the primary ontological reality, and its conviction that education is the laboratory of philosophical thinking. Its weaknesses are its oversimplification of reality in its monism, its stubbornness about refusing to admit even the possibility of an overworld, the excessive individualism implied in its emphasis on experience, the fractioning of meaning by the insistence that meaning is exclusively operational in character, the question of whether scientific method is alone able to give man a place in a world that is said to be completely indeterminate, whether education is a sufficient guide for the production of the whole man. The Christian educator must decide whether Experimentalism provides a sufficient account of God and religion.

The strengths of Personalism are its insistence that reality is personal, that God is not over against man, that man is a responsible agent in a universe friendly to personal growth, that personality is a becoming rather than a given, that personality is social and man is formed in personal relationships rather than merely in response to environment. Its weaknesses are its subjectivism which seems to lead to a lack of realism in dealing with the objective world, its optimism which seems to come from the assumption that God is on man's side, its humanization of God which seems to lead to a lack of theological principle, its tendency to pantheism which seems to come from a lack of objective authority, and its groupmanship with the consequent tendency to overlook the values of tradition. The Christian educator must decide whether Personalism gives sufficient ground for living in times of cultural disintegration and personal danger.

The strengths of Essentialism are its realistic acknowledgment of the ambivalence of nature in regard to the existence of man, its insistence on the subject-object nature of knowledge and the importance of its possession, its readiness to accept certainty as a product of interaction rather than of thought or problem-solving, its conviction that many things do not change, its humility in the presence of the vertical dimension of human excellence and divine transcendence. Its weaknesses are a tendency to confuse knowledge about with knowledge of by treating knowledge as objective, the hazard of supposing that verbalization of ideas is the same as control of them, the temptation to become authoritarian especially in education, the problem of permitting personal influence to substitute for objective evaluation. The Christian educator must decide whether Essentialism permits God to be relevant to daily life and equips learners to deal with a rapidly changing world.

Using the method of choosing among alternatives, the philosopher of Christian education would evaluate the strengths and weaknesses of the live options, finally choosing the one in which the strengths seemed most clearly to outweigh the weaknesses. In this case he would do well to become a specialist in the primary works of Dewey, Coe, or Montessori, putting his mind to being as thorough and independent about it as possible. Christian education would almost certainly be improved by a clearheaded choice of philosophy and a hardheaded application of first-line, primary philosophical sources.

However, to many contemporary thinkers, the age of exclusive and airtight philosophical boxes seems to have passed away. To them the differences between systems seems less actual than theoretical. There are many insights in each system that seem immediately useful and promisory of further development. Opting for this approach, one would work through the materials gathering those ideas that appeal to him, arranging them in some useful order, and standing on the collection as his own philosophical platform. In this case, the best philosophical procedure is to be as thoroughly eclectic as possible. One could list all the strengths of the whole spectrum of educational philosophy, eliminate all those which are canceled by mutual exclusion, and take his stand on the remainder. Thus the Christian educator might settle for an ontological monism of personality and a creator God, an existential scene of duality between subject and object in which knowledge is gained by experimental method, change taking place in the area of subjective reality alone and leading to a development of personality in man but without change in the value structure of the objective universe. The result of this special set of propositions would be a kind of experimentalist education built on a realistic personalism. Christian education might well be improved by taking a firm philosophical stance in such a methodical syncretism of first principles.

To some, probably, neither of these ways of dealing with the alternatives will be altogether satisfactory. The first seems overly objective, the second seems overly subjective.

The first way was followed by Christian educators during the thirties and the forties. The result was a period of masters and protégés with competing schools of thought. The field of Christian education was separated into camps, the battles were real and sincere, and the leadership frequently brilliant.

At Teachers College on Morningside Heights, John Dewey vigorously rejected Idealism as an archaic remnant from a once-religious and obsolescent past. At New York University down in Washington Square, Herman Harrell Horne proclaimed Idealism as the only valid philosophical basis for educational theory and practice, religious or secular. Out in California, George Albert Coe grew steadily more radical in political philosophy as an implication of his steady religious faith. Theologians in conservative seminaries linked Coe and Dewey and inveighed against them both as dangerous and even as diabolical. Presbyterian curriculum writers moved decisively toward neo-orthodox theology. Methodist curriculum materials clearly reflected Personalism. Stories are still told of the encounters in the quadrangle at Union Seminary in New York when the paths of Harrison S. Elliott and Reinhold Niebuhr crossed. Elliott was strongly critical of neo-orthodoxy, regarding it as a theological betrayal of the progressivist faith of Coe. Niebuhr was an aggressive champion of revealed theology and human sinfulness. When these two articulate antagonists met in the public arena of the quad, the open air crackled with excitement and students even postponed study to witness the combat.

The second way was followed by Christian educators during the fifties and sixties. The result was a period of synthesizing among the schools of thought. Aided by the ecumenism of the fifties and abetted by the secularization of the sixties, there was considerable cooperation among denominational leaders, genuine development of curriculum materials, and a lively search among teachers and their students for a point of view that would add the attractions of the other schools to the strengths of their own.

It became comforting to remember that Dewey wrote the preface for one of Horne's books, and that Horne had once estimated that about half of the methods used in the classrooms of his students were the same as those used by Dewey's. It was recalled that William Bower, in many things an apostle of Dewey, had once said that there was very little essential difference between himself and Coe philosophically. In turn Coe was discovered to have written many sentences indicating heavy reliance on the experimentalism of the hard sciences in addition to those more familiar ones relying on the experientialism of psychology. It was emphasized that Whitehead had resisted the separation of the theoretical from the practical and insisted that knowing something well involves doing something well. Bruner, the scientist, talked about mystery. Sherrill, the teacher, related depth psychology and revealed theology. Murray, the classical scholar, placed heavy emphasis on the emotional life.

At the beginning of the seventies, however, there is a profound restlessness among Christian educators. Perhaps, if Christian education is to establish its own philosophical direction, a method rather more creative than either separation or synthesis is needed.

Students of contemporary philosophy will recognize that the dragon of logical method has herewith raised its head. During most of the eighteenth century (with ancient philosophical backing) it was thought that this dragon was a two-horned beastie called Dilemma. Dealing with it required Choice between the horns. During the nineteenth century, however, the dragon was renamed Contradiction, and the method of dealing with it was Dialectic. One horn was regarded as a positive pole, the other as negative, and the task of logic was to find the essential parts of each position and put them together in a synthesis. Later it seemed that the Contradictions that refused to yield to Dialectic were precisely the most significant ones. The method of dealing with unyielding Contradiction was Paradox. The opposite of Choice, Paradox required holding both horns of the beast, uniting them only by the affirmation of one's own existence. Thus held together by life, the logical contradiction says something true that neither pole could say alone.

So long as the method was Choice or Dialectic, logic could be said to be linear, Choice using a sort of arithmetic model ($2-1=1$), Dialectic a sort of geometric model (base $+$ intersecting lines $=$ triangle). Paradox, however, introduced a third dimension, one's own existence. The logical problem was to be settled (though not solved) in an extra-logical manner by a faith affirmation. The affirmation becomes a living thing holding together two logical opposites.

All three of these methods work on the assumption that in every situation the choices are two in number. Indeed, the derivation of the word *alternative* suggests that there is one position and its "alter"—other—form. In strict useage, it could not have a plural. But, in actuality, the world is not merely dual, and facts can seldom be reduced to a choice between two things to be settled by linear logic. Existence comes into play, as Paradox demonstrates, and three things exist, two logically self-consistent mutually exclusive positions and a nonlogical connection between them. The inference, which is more and more accepted as a reality, is that the only way to settle living issues is in a non-Euclidian, multilinear way. Poets and prophets seem to have more to say about that than laboratory scientists and classical philosophers. The models of the knowing process are now shifting significantly from the two-dimensional analogue of sight used by the classical philosophers to the multi-dimensional analogue of touch. A Chinese poet says that the poet takes up his position at the hub of reality, relating himself to all things. An American poet likens the search for poetic truth to the hunt for a lion— "stalking"—using tracks and traces and reports of hunters but without knowing exactly what a poem looks like until one has found it. A novelist speaks of the attempt to snare the really big ideas in a net "as large as the quarry." An American philosopher of science proposes "a three-termed epistemological relationship" challenging the linear two-termed subject-object concepts of knowledge. A British philosopher of religion suggests a logic derived from "the form of the personal," which is a three-poled model, the positive pole being action, which is given its form by the negative pole of reflection, which is composed of a dialectical interplay of withdrawal and return, which together are brought into personal existence by active relation to other personal beings: "I act, therefore we exist."

All this suggests that the intuitive impatience of the younger Christian educators with the logical separation of educational philosophers into categories and with the logical synthesis of all educational theories, may be right. Both the impatience and the more flexible forms of multilinear logic would suggest that the traditions are actually distinct and that they will contribute, with sufficient imagination and rigor, to a whole that will not only be more true and more useful, but genuinely new.

Martin Buber provided a clue when he adopted a wholistic view of education as the practical application of an existentialist philosophy. Conveying the impression that he hadn't really intended it, Buber's thinking about education breaks out of traditional limitations into matters of producing character and inducing meeting with reality. Education is, in short, a way of offering reality to the learner. It specializes in influencing a life through another's life. The fulfillment of life, for Buber, is becoming *Thou*. All phenomena in this world are either personal or nonpersonal, "thou" or "it," and all human experience is either *I-Thou* or *I-It*. It is the special capacity of human life to be able to relate directly to *Thous*. Thus, to relate to *Thous* impersonally deprives both the first person and the second person of personal existence. *Thous* ought never to be treated as *Its*. When *I* relate to a *Thou* personally, *I* become *Thou* in my own being. Because we live in a world of *Thous*, we are constantly being addressed in thought and speech and action. However, we seem to be predisposed to reject the address by treating *Thous* as if they could be ignored or manipulated. This predisposition must be broken through, the "spark of the soul" must be kindled. It happens in many ways, of course, much of the time without particular thought or preparation. The educator, however, makes the breakthrough his special business. He offers the pupil a selection of the world for the pupil's response. Further, he encourages the response by voluntarily leaving his own individuality to "cross over" to the student's side of life. The successful teacher is a specialist in experiencing the pupil's own experience of being educated. This action of enabling a personal response to the world by personally crossing over oneself is the teacher's specialty: in education what happens rarely elsewhere in life becomes a function and a law.

This is a concept of education which is multilinear and dynamic. It seems to be significantly different from the three categories discoverable in educational tradition. It is Judaic rather than Greek, European, or American, existential rather than idealist, realist, or pragmatist. It proposes that they be evaluated neither idealistically, realistically nor pragmatically, nor in terms of a dialectical or comparative method, but in terms of a principal not definitive for any of them. Rather than forcing the necessity of scrapping the other approaches, it offers a different concept of the nature of education as a principle for selecting related insights from the three discrete and competing educational philosophies. It offers a somewhat different approach to subject-object Realism, it adds a vertical dimension to subject-subject Personalism, it suggests a moral imperative for Experimentalism, and puts religion at the heart of education by defining it as the process of bringing the pupil "to his own unity," helping "to put him again face to face with God." The Christian educator must decide whether Buber offers a sufficient concept of the Christian essentials. A Christian education with such principles as these at its foundation might be a significantly new thing.

SOME ELEMENTS OF A NEW DIRECTION

Theology	Empirical Personalism
God	The personal "Other"
Jesus	Unconditional I-Thou
Man	The creative creature
Salvation	Co-creation of relationship
Knowledge of God	Search and Response
Religious Experience	Transforming meeting
Bible	Divine human inter-action
Philosophy	Existential Realism
Epistemology	"Truth is relation"
Education	Interrelational
Symbol	The cross-disciplinary seminar
Curriculum	Context-centered
Method of Knowing	Creative sensitivity
Teacher skill	Interpersonal communication
Method of learning	Encounter and Participation
Goal of Learning	The creative community
Evaluation of Learning	Evidence of productive involvement
Christian Education	Practice of the Presence
Content	Divine-human relationship
Purpose	The New Being
Goal	Experience and practice of *agape*-love

Theology is inevitable. Whenever anything of importance happens to anybody, he needs to share it, and the usual form is verbalization—formal, declarative statements of conviction about the meaning of life. The result of putting religious experience into words is theology. Three purposes are served: preservation, clarification, communication.

To many, especially to laymen and especially in an age of rapid change, it seems that the sole purpose of Christian theology is preservation. It is true that history, both ancient and modern, furnishes numerous examples of theology concentrating on this task. In this mood, the institutional church has on occasion resisted the advances of science, rejected programs of social betterment, eliminated dissenters, and even refused to recognize the validity of religious experience. Examples of theology working in this way are so well known that it is easy to forget that it has on some other occasions prevented the outright collapse of society by insisting on unchangeable truth, and much of the time has worked quietly and effectively for the conservation of a set of convictional propositions that have turned men to unaccountable greatness. It is one of the tasks of Christian theology to keep alive the reality of the God who made his will known in creation, who gave words of judgment and love to Jeremiah and Jonah, Hosea and Haggai and others and gave them the courage to speak them, who saves the world he has created and to which he reveals his will by a complete personal act in the life, death, and resurrection of Jesus Christ. Theology preserves, not by attempting to keep God alive, of course, but by doing its best to keep alive the meaning of his reality. Thus doctrines have been formulated differently in different ages, and have reflected the needs and nature of the times.

However, theology is always doomed to a certain degree of inepititude in this task. God is an unobjectifiable reality above and beyond man's experience and comprehension which enters human experience in a manner so native to man's concrete existence that it can be recognized as an ingression of reality which man needs but is unable to produce merely from within, and, further, is unable to express adequately even when it has been consciously experienced and recognized. The man who has known the reality of God usually employs language more like a poet than like a philosopher, often lapses into logical nonsequiturs, and sometimes into mind-boggling and unintelligible assertions. Therefore, one of the tasks of theology is clarification, in spite of the fact that the achievement of clarity would be misrepresentative and misleading. The experience of recent centuries has amply demonstrated that the simple logical and linguistic unambiguity of some forms of science and arithmetic is not the sort of clarity that is most helpful in theology. Theology arises out of a complex and dynamic situation in which God and a man in the world and among other men meet in an existential moment. The kind of theological assertions that will be most useful are those which reflect the dynamism and complexity of that situation. It is, perhaps, not accidental that some of the clearest theology in the Christian tradition has been the product of a dynamic and complex human situation. The Nicene Creed, which was neither logically nor linguistically unambiguous but has stood the tests of time as a clarification of Christian doctrine, was precipitated by a tumultuous situation. The theological dispute between Arius and Athanasius was public, bitter, and complex. The council called by Constantine to settle the matter was always spirited if not always spiritual. Reports indicate that the debate was logically toe-to-toe and personally chin-to-chin. All the emperor wanted was peace. What he got was more theological insight than political compromise: Jesus Christ is wholly man and wholly God! Showdown disputation in medieval universities has given way to controlled discussion in modern seminaries, but both are ways of clarifying theological statements which reflect the dynamic personal interpenetration induced by God's presence among men. Recent discussions of the nature of language reflect the same sort of direction. The demand of empirical philosophers for linguistic clarity from their theological colleagues has led at last to the acknowledgment that the only adequate use of language in theology is the sort that reflects not mathematical realities but personal realities. The language of theology is the language of person-in-relation. The language God used in addressing men is not contained in the symbols of human speech but in the personal incarnation of God. The language men use in speaking of that reality most effectively is probably language about personal acts and realities, the ordinary, everyday speech about personal affairs. It will probably be formed of words like "communion," "fellowship," "love," and of other words like "alienation," "isolation," "hate." Speaking it with precision and richness will require translation of classic theological language, with its implications of mathematical precision and linear equations, into terms that have reference to contemporary, personal life, with its implications of personal richness and multilinear dynamic.

Theology also attempts to communicate the meaning of the reality of God. For there to be communication, the language of religious experience must be spoken in a manner reflecting the nature of the experience. That means that it is to be spoken in acts of personal relation. And that means, in turn, that the communicator commits himself to the reality of God (staking his own existence as a person on the existence of God, a thing which may be more difficult to do honestly today than it has been for the last 1800 years), to the reality of the communicant (risking his own theological conviction on the faithfulness of the listener even as he does on the faithfulness of God), and to the reality of the relationship (for, since the listener is human, the risk may not be justified, ending in failure and pain). Christianity is thus learned *as* it is taught, in a three-way act of personal risk between God, teacher, and learner.

It would appear, then, that theology is more a working discipline than a theoretical discipline. It is concerned with the whole range of man's life, but especially with its fulfillment. The Christian affirmation is that through Jesus Christ a personal relationship is offered by God which makes all other relationships valid and vital and in which man may become the person he has a right to hope to be. That point of view relates theology to science with its concern for fact and to art with its concern for beauty. Put to work in life, it provides a distinctive experience, more of meaning than of fact or beauty. Applied to experience, it develops a distinctive form and content of knowledge. Utilized in philosophy, it becomes the basis for a dynamic and relational logic. Released between persons, it enables a form of communication creative of personhood in both parties. An educational enterprise, conceived and carried out in terms of an experience, knowledge, logic, and manner of communication made possible by a functional appreciation for the meaning of Jesus Christ to the God-man relationship in which personhood is defined and actualized, would be a Christian education. It would both resemble and differ from all other educational enterprises.

SOME SOURCES FOR A NEW DIRECTION

The Bible

Buber, Martin. *I and Thou*. New York: Harper, 1958.
Camus, Albert. *The Rebel*. New York: Knopf, 1954.
Dewey, John. *Art as Experience*. New York: Putnam, 1959.
MacMurray, John. *Persons in Relation*. New York: Harper, 1961.
MacMurray, John. *The Self as Agent*. London: Faber & Faber, 1957.
Northrop, F. S. C. *The Meeting of East and West*. New York: Macmillan, 1946.
Ramsey, Ian. *Religious Language*. Naperville, Ill.: Allenson, 1957.
de Unamuno, Miguel. *The Tragic Sense of Life*. Gloucester, Mass.: Peter Smith.

Berdyaev, Nicolai. *The Meaning of the Creative Act*. New York: Collier, 1967.
Bonhoeffer, Dietrich. *Life Together*. New York: Harper, 1954.
Brunner, Emil. *Truth as Encounter*. Philadelphia: Westminster, 1964.
Kierkegaard, Soren. *The Works of Love*. New York: Harper, 1962.
Kierkegaard, Soren. *Training in Christianity*. Princeton University Press, 1944.
Niebuhr, Reinhold. *The Self and the Dramas of History*. New York: Scribner's, 1955.
Tillich, Paul. *The New Being*. New York: Scribner's, 1955.
White, Hugh Vernon. *Truth and the Person in Christian Theology*. New York: Oxford, 1963.

Allport, Gordon. *Pattern and Growth in Personality*. New York: Holt, Rinehart & Winston, 1961.
Buber, Martin. *The Prophetic Faith*. Gloucester, Mass.: Peter Smith.
Erikson, Erik H. *Childhood and Society*. New York: Norton, 1950.
Johnson, Aubrey R. *The Vitality of the Individual in the Thought of Ancient Israel*. Cardiff: University of Wales, 1964.
Piaget, Jean. *The Moral Development of the Child*. London: K. Paul, 1932.
Sullivan, Harry Stack. *Conceptions of Modern Psychiatry*. New York: Norton, 1953.
Wolpe, Joseph. *The Conditioning Therapies*. New York: Holt, Rinehart & Winston, 1964.

Borton, Terry. *Reach, Touch and Teach*.
Bruner, Jerome. *On Knowing: Essays for the Left Hand*. Cambridge: Harvard, 1962.
Buber, Martin. *Between Man and Man*. Boston: Beacon Press, 1955.
Calahan, Raymond E. *Education and the Cult of Efficiency*.
Gordon, Ira J. *Studying the Child in the School*. New York: Wiley, 1966.
Highet, Gilbert. *The Art of Teaching*. New York: Vintage, 1954.
Hartootunian, Bruce and Joyce B. *The Structure of Teaching*. New York: SRA, 1967.
Kneller, George F. *Education and Existentialism*. New York: Wiley, 1964.
Leonard, George. *Education and Ecstasy*. New York: Delacorte Press, 1968.

Skinner, B. F. *The Technology of Teaching.* New York: Appleton-Century, 1968.
The Saturday Review, monthly education supplement, *passim.*

Cully, Kendig B. *The Search for a Christian Education Since 1940.* Philadelphia: Westminster, 1940.
Jackson, B. F., ed. *Communication-Learning for Churchmen.* Nashville: Abingdon Press, 1968.
Kraemer, Hendrik. *The Communication of the Christian Faith.* Philadelphia: Westminster, 1956.
Nida, Eugene. *Message and Mission.* New York: Harper, 1960.
Rood, Wayne R. *The Art of Teaching Christianity.* Nashville: Abingdon Press, 1968.
Snyder, Ross. *On Becoming Human.* Nashville: Abingdon Press, 1968.
Religious Education magazine, *passim.*

Christian education may be understood as the product of the creative interpenetration of a historical context, an active content, a personal process of growth, an educational science and art, and a working theology. It is practiced, however, as a discipline with its own life.

The essence of the educational process in Christianity seems to be the creative comradeship between persons which illustrates the definitive, redeeming encounter between God and persons concreted in human existence by Jesus Christ. Redemptive relationship with God in life's affairs is the special possibility which the Christian religion offers here and now. Its ultimate reality was verified once and its potentiality has been demonstrated again and again in history. Though a similarity between God and man is thus affirmed, equality is not. When man is aware of relatedness to God, it is always with a characteristic disturbance, a judgment on failure, a participation in suffering, an unanticipated hope and joy. It is a tension that transforms.

The transformation is creative. It turns men into rebels against the injustices and inequities of social arrangements and inclines them to the production of historical change. The result is sometimes called revolutionary because the changes are radical inasmuch as they are defined by the relationship between Creator and creature. The process is sometimes called evolutionary because, in the long-perspective view, the prophetic demands have been absorbed and secularized by culture.

The transformation is productive. It turns the experience of man alone into a dynamic relatedness which envelopes all human interaction and penetrates all human life with a dimension of significance. The result is sometimes called wisdom, because experience has been turned into knowledge and knowledge has been illuminated by the reality of God imbedded in existence.

The transformation is redemptive. It turns men into suffering servants of others for the spirit's sake and unites elements of personality structure into a genuinely new being. The result is sometimes called growth, because from man's point of view it has involved movement toward a quality of experience that is more productive and creative than the old.

Toward historical change, personal growth, and wisdom, God loves and yearns, man strives and hopes. God's action is creative, man's is frequently obstructive. Into that matrix of divine and human action, Christian education plunges, with both courage and humility. God is not man, teacher is not pupil, adult is not child. Yet God became man, the teacher learns, the adult is as a little child before God. Together they face the situations and problems of history. Each takes initiative and responsibility. Together they live, by mutual thrusting beyond creating and suffering, loving and wrathing, redeeming and judging, laying waste and building again, breathing, sweating, caring, forgiving—to bridge fragily the chasm between what is and what may be by altering the universe. Together they quest for the sources, impelled by incompleteness straining for fuller meaning.

Christian education is a concept of teacher and learner discovering how to act within existence, by encounter with divine flesh giving to human life a quality beyond survival, turned by persons into a process which is informed by knowledge, refined by science, practiced as an art, and actualized by love.

INDEX

Andover Theological Seminary, 14
Anselm, of Canterbury, 222
Aquinas, Thomas, 130, 284-85
Aristotle, 45, 111, 113, 130, 217, 280-81, 282-84, 345, 346
Art, 51-58, 136-38

Bacon, Francis, 108-10, 116
Barth, Karl, 64, 300-303
Bauer, Ferdinand Christian, 35
Berkeley, George, 211-12
Berdyaev, Nikolai, 62
Bible, 42, 64, 71, 72, 74, 167-68, 253, 300, 337, 342-45, 378
John, 207-8
Sermon on the Mount, 151
Boston University, 183, 200, 221
Bower, William Clayton, 139-45, 387
Bowne, Borden Parker, 183-84, 221-22, 223
Breed, F. S., 315-22, 353
Brightman, Edgar Sheffield, 223, 225
Bruner, Jerome S., 147-62, 387
Brunner, Emil, 64, 190, 258, 304-7
Buber, Martin, 389-90
Bushnell, Horace, 10-30, 83, 177, 182, 365
Buttrick, George, 174-75

Calvin, John, 13, 15, 24, 176, 241
Calvinism, 14, 16
Cambridge University, 315
Camus, Albert, 368-69
Change, 30, 66-70, 82, 84, 178, 263, 359, 365
Channing, William Ellery, 35

Character, 150-56, 323-32, 332-37
Chave, Ernest J., 145-49
Christ, 14, 21-23, 64, 36-37, 207, 234, 242, 296, 298, 305, 307, 339-40, 348-49
Church (and Christian Community), 15, 64, 242, 245, 253-54, 278-79, 320, 350, 374
Coe, George Albert, 256-57, 259, 261, 288, 376, 385, 386
Biography, 181-92
Creative God, 202-3
Creative Principle, 196
Educational Principle, 196-99
Personal God, 200-202
Personality Principle, 194-96
Revaluation of Values, 192-94
Columbia University, 96, 99, 100, 139, 145, 171, 181, 189
Comenius, John Amos, 162, 309-11, 314
Communism, 68, 323-32
Comte, Auguste, 106-7
Conant, James B., 66, 174
Content, 237-38, 331-32, 343, 372-75
Curriculum, 126-27, 144, 154-55, 376, 386-87

Darwin, Charles, 38, 109, 113, 183, 343
Democracy, 68, 139, 202, 332-37
Descartes, René, 116, 208-10
Dewey, John, 46, 106, 108, 110, 145, 157, 166, 171-73, 174, 201, 232-33, 256, 260, 376, 385, 386, 387
Biography, 93-101